Retrospections of Dorothea Herbert

1770–1806

Retrospections
of
DOROTHEA
HERBERT
1770–1806

Foreword by
Louis M Cullen

**TOWN
HOUSE**
DUBLIN

First published in 1929-30 by
Gerald Howe
London

Published in hardback by TownHouse, 1988

This edition published 2004 by
TownHouse Dublin
THCH Ltd
Trinity House
Charleston Road
Ranelagh
Dublin 6
Ireland
www.townhouse.ie

1 2 3 4 5 6 7 8 9 10

ISBN: 1-86059-220-1

Printed by Bookmarque Ltd, Croydon, Surrey

This note from Geoffrey Mandeville (GFM) appeared in the original 1929 edition of the book. A descendant of the Herberts, he transcribed Dorothea's original text.

Who Dorothea Herbert was, will sufficiently appear in the early chapters of her book, which has been awaiting publication for more than a hundred years. The following additional notes may prove of interest.

Dorothea and her sisters Fanny and Matty, it is believed, died unmarried, their possessions passing eventually to their youngest brother Nicholas, who for forty years or more was rector of Knockgrafton, the scene of Dolly Herbert's love story. He died at a great age, a bachelor, leaving everything, including the manuscript of these *Retrospections*, to his nephew, Nicholas Herbert Mandeville.

The manuscript has been in the Mandeville family since then. It consists of 260 pages, 12¾ x 7¾ inches, in a limp cover, and is written in a clear hand. The original text has been faithfully followed in this publication. Peculiarities of spelling and punctuation have been retained, except that the long s is not so printed, and that here and there, extra dashes have been inserted, and full stops used to close the paragraphs. The title pages which follow have been reconstructed in imitation of the originals. Of the numerous 'cuts' (actually watercolour sketches) only two are shewn: the authoress's portrait of herself, on the dust cover, and her view of Carrick as a frontispiece. A family tree has been added, and an index of names. The endpapers are reproductions of two pages of the manuscript, slightly reduced.

It is not known whether any of Dolly Herbert's other writings have survived. She mentions four volumes, viz Poems, Plays, Novels and these *Retrospections*. She also promises that she may continue the *Retrospections*, 'in the form of an Appendix, partly unconnected with this work'. It seems likely that the few notes, in diary form, for the year 1807, which are extant, are part of the rough material intended for this Appendix.

The present volume does not include these notes, nor, indeed, more than half the *Retrospections*, which are continued down to the end of 1806. Sufficient remains for another book, should there be a demand for it. So far as it goes, this one is complete in itself, for it ends at the moment when Dolly Herbert knows that her heart is lost for ever.

GFM
April 1929

CONTENTS

FOREWORD

Dorothea Herbert was a daughter of the rectory. So in England was Jane Austen. Indeed, a first reading of Dorothea Herbert's *Retrospections* might give the reader the impression that she had read Jane Austen, because faint but real echoes of the same language and social conventions abound. But Dorothea Herbert had put her retrospections in order in 1805–6, whereas Jane Austen's novels, almost ignored at first, began to appear only from 1811. The two women came from a similar background, that of a rectory, and described a society similar in many ways, even if the comfortable, prosperous, rustic world of south Tipperary is very different from the much richer and far more urbane society of Hampshire and Bath in which Jane Austen sharpened her powers of observation of English landed society. Dorothea Herbert's account is, of course, autobiographical, whereas Jane Austen's writing, sharp and realistic in the quality of its penetrating social commentary, is fictional.

The significance of a rectory background is that it, more than most milieux in the eighteenth century, was a cultivated one. Clergymen were very well educated by the standards of the day – a very high proportion of the students of Oxford and Cambridge and Trinity College Dublin were destined for the church – and, in proportion to their numbers, clergy far outnumbered any other category in society with a serious interest in the arts or learning. Churchmen, when not recruited from the ranks of existing church families, were younger sons of gentry. Dorothea Herbert's father, Nicholas, was the eighth of nine children of the Herberts of Muckross, the smaller of the two landowning families of Killarney in County Kerry. Still more to the point, he was the youngest of the three sons. That meant that the family's expectations for him were modest; he was destined for a career in medicine, a profession which involved a university education but which in the eighteenth century commanded neither great prestige nor great earnings. The army and the church were more typical and more illustrious careers for the younger sons of gentry. Dorothea's mother, Martha, was the youngest of seven surviving children of John Cuffe, first Lord Desart, of County Kilkenny. As one of the three daughters of a peer whose family was in financial trouble a little later, she was not in material terms an exceptional prospect. But neither was Nicholas, and hence the alliance was a classic one, dictated by the narrow horizons that a cadet position in a family imposed on a son, and a numerous family progeny on a daughter.

However, good family position in society conferred connections on its members and they stood to gain from them. The Herbert family were connected to the Blennerhassets in Kerry, and to the Hedge Eyres of Macroom and the latter link in turn connected them to the Eyres of Galway. More importantly, the English branch of the Herbert family was the rich and powerful house of Lord Powis in Wales. Moreover, it was the Herbert circle in Dublin, not his Tipperary clerical appointments, which eventually found Nicholas a wife. Nicholas's marriage to Martha Cuffe was one of several Herbert links with the Cuffe family, and it brought Nicholas further connections. One of his sisters had also married a Cuffe, and in 1780 the Cuffes' daughter married the only son of the rich Lord Farnham of Cavan and Wexford. Martha's own mother was a Beresford, a half-sister to the Earl of Tyrone; and her sister Lucinda married the first baronet Sir John Blunden of Kilkenny. For Nicholas, his Herbert connections were the crucial ones. The prospect of advancement in the church led him to abandon the dismal prospects of a career as a gentleman doctor for the church. Lord Powis secured his first living for him at Ludlow; his father later secured for him the united parishes of Carrick-on-Suir, Kilmurry and Kilsheelan and also Knockgrafton near Cashel (p 4). He counted on even further advancement, but his subsequent disappointment must have been re-echoed in the family, even in the hearing of his children. In 1776, according to Dorothea, 'my father went up to London to visit Lord Powis his former pupil, the later lord being dead. Lord Powis received him kindly but being in opposition he had no power to serve him in an application for a bishopric which was then in contemplation but which failed by the supineness of my father's friends' (p 30).

However, the connection which had got him his livings had served Nicholas quite well. The income from them was large and put him into a select category of high-income clergymen, distinct in their good fortune from the struggling rectors, who were by no means few, quite apart from the penniless curates. Even after one of the livings, Knockgrafton, had been surrendered in 1796 to create a living for the eldest son, Otway, on his ordination, the other three livings at the time of the father's death provided an income of £1800 a year. This was a gentry-style income, exceeding that of many of the lesser gentry families in the countryside in the 1790s.

The family was riding high in terms of income in the 1780s and early 1790s. This is interesting, because in 1774 Whiteboy opposition to the payment of tithes first emerged in Nicholas Herbert's parishes, and local resistance to their payment or lawsuits by Dorothea's father in the ecclesiastical courts to recover tithes became a constant source of passing comment in the *Retrospections*. The trouble was widespread in County Tipperary, and in 1791 so serious that the Cashel races were not held. But whatever shadow it cast over rectorial life, agrarian trouble seems to have reduced neither income nor expectations. In 1785 Nicholas bought some land in County Waterford (p 111), though that involved him in lawsuits, as it so frequently did in Ireland, before he entered into possession of it. Required by the archbishop to live part of the year in Knockgrafton (probably as a response to the tithe unrest and to criticism of clerical absenteeism), he erected a glebe house at Knockgrafton in 1788 (p 171) at an outlay of £1000. Indulging in the newly fashionable hobby of sea bathing, after an uncomfortable season in a wretched cabin at Bunmahon, they built the first seaside cottage there at the end of 1791, and in 1793–4, the house in Carrick-on-Suir, apparently erected in Restoration times, was itself extensively done up.

In understanding Dorothea, one of the most relevant features is her education, and the wide range of social activities that revolved around the house. According to the *Retrospections*, she first started to learn to write from Thomas Wimpe, the parish clerk, on 2 March 1772 (p 18). This suggests incidentally that the genealogy may be in error in giving 1770 as the year of her birth and that she was probably one or perhaps two years older. Wimpe's instruction took place before her serious education began and hence could conceivably have begun in her fourth or even third year. The two eldest boys had an old Latin master who came in the evening – both boys were intended for university and hence Latin was a must. The girls' education, colourfully described by Dorothea herself (p 41), also proceeded apace, and by 1782 the four girls in the family went as day pupils to Miss English's boarding school in Carrick. Miss English herself was the daughter of a clergyman schoolmaster (p 82). Reading parties in the evening and amateur theatricals either at Castletown-Cox or Carrick also enlivened the scene.

Though the Herberts were below the level of the country's gentry, their landed background and substantial income gave them a frequent entrée into grander society. Thus, through the link their Cuffe mother conferred on the family, they were fairly frequent visitors to Curraghmore, near Portlaw in County Waterford, the home of the Beresfords. The Beresfords, living only eight miles from Carrick-on-Suir, were by far the grandest and richest family in the region. Mr Herbert and sometimes the family were also entertained on occasion by the Butlers at Kilcash, Lord Cahir at Cahir, or more frequently by the Coxes at Castletown-Cox. The Coxes were an ecclesiastical family; an earlier member, an archbishop of Cashel, had built the house; and the ecclesiastical mantle of the family and the proximity of the house ensured that it was the great house most intimately connected with the Herbert circle.

There was little chance of reciprocating the hospitality of the grander families, nor was it expected. If it did arise, it was in the height of the rustic social season and for a handful of occasions in a lifetime. In 1793, when at Knockgrafton, the Herberts gave a grand dinner, but it was something of an innovation for them and reflected a social ambition whetted by the good economic fortunes of the family at the time. The following year with 'uncommonly crouded' races at Cashel, the Herberts cut a poor figure in the social scene (p 331). Their own grand connections might have little enough time for them. At the Clonmel Ball in 1789, their Blunden relations largely ignored them at the outset, and lavished time on the Herberts only towards the end of the evening (p 179). The Herberts had been encouraged to rise to the occasion in 1793 by their relationship to Crofton, who was colonel of the Roscommon militia. Two years later at Carrick, they had their greatest social triumph on the occasion of a visit from Kerry by two Muckross nephews: Lord John Beresford and Mr Maude, son to Lord de Montalt, both came over from Curraghmore (p 357).

The Herberts were among the guests at the *fête champêtre* at Annfield, given by the Osbornes in 1785, a grand affair held in marquees on the lawn to which 'everyone within twenty or thirty miles' around was invited. The guests included two local celebrities, the Kennedy sisters. They were daughters of a rich County Waterford Catholic farmer, and had been abducted in 1779: three men were subsequently executed in Kilkenny. In the south-east at the time, the whole story was a *cause célèbre*. Dorothea Herbert affords us an interesting glimpse of the two girls, made freshly notorious by their marriages, apparently in 1785 (p 112). The facts are not quite as Dorothea gives them. The executions had taken place in 1780 in Kilkenny city, not in 1785 in Waterford as her narrative suggests. But the two girls were from County Waterford, and if their marriages occurred in 1785, a girl of around seventeen years like Dorothea may easily have assumed from the excitement around her, provided by the Kennedy girls' presence, that the executions as well as the marriages had taken place in the immediate past, and that the place of sentence had been Waterford.

By describing in recollection the high points of the family's social life, the *Retrospections* tend to underplay the simple or even humdrum character of much of the year. When they first went to Knockgrafton in 1789, the range of food was quite lavish (p 197). But this was because the visit was a housewarming, and the family had invited their friends the Jephsons, a landed family from Carrick-on-Suir, who as far back as 1775 had an income of between £1000 and £2000. Apart from the short but sometimes hectic week-long season that revolved around the Cashel races, their social circle in Knockgrafton was normally very restricted: the family of the Rev Patrick Hare, who had established the academy at Cashel, at which the Herbert boys were educated, and who was also vicar-general of the archdiocese, the Clarkes, a schoolmaster at the school who was married to one of Hare's daughters (the school was her portion), and two neighbouring families of gentleman farmers, the Doghertys and the Roes.

Invitations to gentry occasions and some degree of familiarity with grand families like the Beresfords were vital for the social standing of a lesser family like the Herberts in a society every bit as obsessed as Jane Austen's England with connection and birth. Thus, the assemblies at the Cashel races in 1789 were disappointing: 'we went to one which was as stupid as possible, very few being at it and those that were not of the first class' (p 284). A dreadful fracas over a pew at Knockgrafton church illustrates the social pretensions that underlay this society. In their first year there, Mrs Herbert was allotted the head pew by the church warden, and enjoyed uninterrupted possession for some weeks until the Hon Mrs Robbins, daughter to Lord Massy, entering with a large company of gentlemen one Sunday, demanded the top pew. An unseemly scene, and a horsewhipping bout among the gentlemen, ensued. This led to more formal complaint. Miss Roe, the church warden's daughter, receiving it pronounced:

That my mother had an indubitable right to the

seat as rector's lady. Mrs Robbins alleged her being a peer's daughter. Miss Roe sneered at such a claim of privilege in church, but that no doubt should remain she showed her in Lodge's Peerage that Lord Desart was a much older peer than Lord Massy. (p 187)

Production of the *Peerage* in a childish fashion recalls Sir Walter Elliott in Jane Austen's *Persuasion*, 'a man who for his own amusement never took up any book but the Baronetage'. Dorothea Herbert's relative, the charming and eccentric Edward Eyre, had an answer to this in his way of dealing with his mother, herself a Muckross Herbert, by:

> taking up the *Almanack* and pointing out where his cousin the haberdasher and his relation the shoemaker lived in Dublin. She always stood up with her hands clenched telling the puppy he was the only blot in the family from the time they came over with William the Conqueror. (p 169)

A test of the social position of a family is the extent to which it travelled and in particular participated in the Dublin season. In this sense, the family's position on the fringe rather than at the centre of social life comes out very clearly. Rather surprisingly, the family featured little in the Kilkenny social life of their relatives, Lord Desart and the Blundens. In 1786 (and again in 1801) the family visited Muckross, and Dorothea has left informative pages on the visit. Through the Eyre connection, they were encouraged to visit Galway. In

1787, they were accompanied by Ned Eyre, 'proprietor of great part of the town' of Galway (p 161). The pages on the Galway visit are fascinating and all too brief. In 1776 Dorothea accompanied her family to England, making in the course of the visit an excursion to Bath 'to see the New Crescent Circus and everything worth remarking' (p 30). However, it is the fewness of the Dublin visits which is striking. The Herberts' Cuffe aunt had a Dublin house, in 7 Gloucester Street. They stayed there in late 1779, and this account of the celebrated Volunteer season of 1779, one of the most memorable in Dublin parliamentary life, even if seen through the eyes of a girl not more than eleven years old, is particularly interesting (pp 42–56). Apart from a short visit in 1785 for a Blennerhasset wedding, when they stayed in the same house (which was now in the hands of Lord Maxwell), their next visit was only in 1794. They dined once at Lord Maxwell's, and once at the new Custom House with John Beresford (p 327). They came to Dublin again in 1799, travelling for the final stage by canal, on board the boat from 4 am until 10 pm, 'cooped up in the cabbin as the snow lay thick upon the deck' (p 377). Lucinda and her husband Bradshaw were 'now settled in one of the handsomest houses in Mountjoy Square, which part of the town was then newly built.'

The rise in the family's social role and outlay in the 1790s cannot have been good for their finances. Mr Herbert, more than his wife, was careless in matters of money. According to Dorothea, 'my mother was a famous œconomist... but my father was far from being a careful providore' (p 5). For a clerical family much more than for a landed family, a high social life had its dangers, because their income dried up with the death of the head of the family. Mr Herbert died in 1803. Effectively, his sons had already been provided for by their education and careers. The landed property left to the sons was probably both modest and already mortgaged to provide for the womenfolk of the family. In his will, he left his wife and daughters £1000 apiece (with an extra £200 for Dorothea). If Lucinda had already been provided for at her marriage, this suggests an estate of around £5000. However, the investment income would amount to only £60 or so a head. In other words, the éclat of the family did not outlive the father. The eldest son died in 1800, and Nicholas survived as a mere curate in Carrick, apparently living with his mother and sisters, until he became rector of Knockgrafton in 1824. Thomas was a barrister, but made his way surely perhaps but modestly, as in 1806 he was seeking to turn his connections into an official employment 'to carry him better through life as the Bar affords but a fluctuating profit to a young lawyer' (p 406). Of the five daughters, only two married. Lucinda's marriage in 1793 to an attorney seemed a promising one, but the husband's drinking, debt, jail, and a bankruptcy settlement with creditors followed (p 414). Sophia married John Mandeville in 1804. It was neither a happy nor in economic terms a successful match, as the Mandevilles were going down in the world, and Dorothea has left some gently ironic lines on them. Poor Dorothea had a sole proposal from a curate, which her parents turned down (though without evidence of great regret on her part), and the later match she set her heart on never materialised. It is out of this disappointment that the *Retrospections* grew.

The story of her romantic grief goes back to the family's first summer at Knockgrafton. Mr Herbert built the rectory, called Parsonage, there at the end of the 1780s, and the family began their annual three-month peregrination in 1789. The Roes were large gentleman farmers in the parish, and Mr Roe was himself church warden (his first name, not provided by Dorothea, is Andrew). Since there were two sons, John and Andrew, and the Herberts had several eligible daughters, it was inevitable that the families would see much of each other. For whatever reason, the intimacy of 1789 was not repeated in subsequent years. The two families seem to have drawn apart, and John and Dorothea saw little of each other. All subsequent meetings, whether treasured moments of reciprocated joy or more searing experiences, are carefully chronicled in the *Retrospections*.

The Roes, of whom there were two branches, one near Thurles, the other at Knockgrafton, belonged to the category of Protestant head tenant whose favourable conditions of tenure had helped their gradual economic ascension in the eighteenth century. Their economic position would have been much the same as the Herberts, though their social standing would have been decidedly inferior. Along with the Doghertys, another Protestant gentleman farmer family, they seem to have been the only substantial families in the vicinity of Parsonage. The Roes' house was, in fact, only a mile from

Parsonage. Heads of both families were also magistrates.

Rockwell, the Roe house, is the site of the present Rockwell College. In the 1790s, the property had a lake, a long avenue, and handsome iron gates, though the house itself was 'quite in the stile of a head farmer's house, like most of the houses in that country' (p 202). The Roes feature little in the story of Tipperary. The house and demesne are shown on Taylor and Skinner's maps of 1778, one of 184 properties so marked. Details *c.*1850 give more information about the property. It had a demesne of 400 acres. Rebuilding of the house had been in prospect in the eighteenth century, but the freshly cut stones were laid aside when Mr Roe became estranged from his wife, and the project was not executed at least within the years covered by Dorothea's account. Rebuilding was completed by 1833 on a rather large scale which put it in terms of valuation among the top sixty-two houses in the county. The task must have been beyond the resources of the Roes: the estate was in chancery by 1850, meaning that it was insolvent. The actual occupant was no longer a Roe. John Roe's son, William, was murdered in 1847: thus, tragedy and financial problems speeded their departure. At the end of the 1780s, the lifestyle of the Roes at any rate was simple. According to Dorothea, 'they lived very secluded in genera' (p 181). Mr Roe himself seems to have been a plain man.

There is no evidence of serious romantic interest in Dorothea's preceding life, and she may have been bowled over by the eldest son, John. As to whether John Roe would have made a good spouse for Dorothea or indeed for any lady, we cannot be sure. There is no evidence of refined interests on his part, and the reference to old Mr Roe coming over on one occasion to Parsonage to dine, 'as the young men gave a great entertainment at Rockwell to their turf acquaintances, and Mr Roe was glad to get out of the way' (p 225), seems to hint at a horsy, hard-drinking set. The picture too of the Roes at home after the mêlée over the pew in the church 'in great glee about their late triumph' (p 188), does not present a reassuring picture either.

The Herbert world narrowed abruptly from the outset of the new century. Otway, next in line to Dorothea and the sibling to whom she was most attached, died from a fall while hunting in 1800. Her father's death followed in 1803. Her appreciation of his qualities is explicit – for instance she praises someone as having 'all the pleasing manners of my father except his meekness and patience' (p 169) – while this warmth is never implied in the references to her mother. In Dorothea's account the tale of illnesses and of her personal withdrawal from social occasions outside her home becomes something of a refrain from the 1790s onwards. On her telling, when she was treated by a doctor at her mother's behest in 1804, she noted that he 'gave me some learn'd advice but I thought it a folly to see doctors for disorders of mind and brain – however, I was passive under his investigation, (p 409). Thus a pattern of growing isolation was being built up before she heard in 1805 news of John Roe's marriage. When her mother was away in Dublin in the same year, Dorothea kept 'at work' in her room (p412). A disturbing pattern thus existed before she made the accusation in the year 1806 that the rest of the family both beat her and confined her in her room. How much truth is there in this? She was closer to Otway, Tom and Fanny than to the rest of the family. The ill treatment which is not specified for any year preceding 1806 is attributed to her mother, the two homebound daughters and Nick, the youngest son, motivated, she claims, by their urge to divide her fortune among them. She actually claims that the 'old lady' kept back a great part of her 'yearly' income. The Herberts' interest in the house was a life occupation. The father's death did not therefore entail a loss of the home. However, the yearly incomes of the house's occupants must have been very modest, and Nicholas too seems not to have kept a separate establishment. On balance it is a more plausible speculation on the facts to assume that the final pages of the account were written when Dorothea was somewhat deranged, as her interpretation of what appeared an unreasonable and forced imprisonment. As to whether John Roe – and we must remember that his role may be written into events through her derangement more than the affair really warrants – or the blows conferred by the deaths of her brother Otway, and her father, her two great anchors to reality, were the cause, we can never know.

The internal evidence suggests that the *Retrospections* were written in the final seclusion described at the end of the book, and indeed written as a whole in a relatively short period of time. She seems to have kept a journal or diary; the fact that she states emphatically that she wrote up some events in 1795 from 'a fragment of an old journal I burned' suggests as much (p 342). As well as the *Retrospections* she wrote three volumes of poems, plays and novels 'in my prison'. These seem to have been completed before the *Retrospections*, but it is not clear whether they were completely new compositions or a compendium, as in the case of her *Retrospections*, of both old and fresh material. her literary compositions were already well known in the 1790s in the family social circle.

Her powers of observation are considerable, the insight into character and situations quite powerful. There is never evidence of conscious exaggeration, apart from some forcing of events in the telling to make a funny incident still funnier. Suffice it to say that her historical accuracy is striking. Incidental historic detail, relationships and facts seem invariably to be accurate or in harmony with their context, and the errors in the retelling of the story of the Kennedy sisters are not inconsistent with these qualities.

The diary touches little on political events. Dorothea's concern was not with them. Neither, however, are they avoided, and where they impinge on the family they are referred to, as in the case of Whiteboy opposition to tithes, the murder of their proctor and his wife in Parsonage in 1798, or the aftermath of the rebellion. We cannot assume on the authority of the diary what was the attitude of the family to the events of the day. Some of their circle were certainly reactionary. The Beresfords were for instance; and when the Herberts visited Parsonage, they dined once a year at the house of the Judkins, who were relations of the Herberts' close Carrick friends, the Jephsons. Thomas Judkin Fitzgerald, the notorious high sheriff of Tipperary in 1798, by birth a Uniacke, was a member of the Judkin family through his mother, and assumed the name Judkin Fitzgerald simply to meet the terms of a bequest from a Judkin relative in his favour. However, Hare, the vicar-general of the archdiocese, the Herberts' friend in their annual visitations to Parsonage, had expressed the view that Fitzgerald was 'absolutely a madman'. Nicholas Herbert himself, perhaps surprisingly for a propertied rector, was not a magistrate. Moreover, the fact that the Butlers, with a liberal and partly Catholic background, were patrons of his ecclesiastical benefices, would also tend to ensure a moderate political line. Dorothea has left a sympathetic vignette of her brother, Tom, in disturbed times in 1796 while still a struggling barrister, defending 'poor wretches' at the assizes with no prospect of a fee (p 363).

Catholics are neither numerous or intimate in their circle, though propertied Catholics were in fact numerous around Carrick. Even the Mandevilles, who were mixed in religion, seem to have entered their milieu ultimately only in 1803–4. On one occasion when her father married a Catholic girl to a Protestant in a runaway match, Dorothea mentions that 'the Roman Catholics made a great sputter about it' (p 268). However, at Parsonage the parish priest, Father Becket, was a regular visitor. The use of the term Father before the priest's name, only at this time becoming a regular usage, and of the term Roman Catholic, rather than the still widely used and offensive word 'papist', reflects a sensitivity on the part of a Protestant. At Galway the family and Ned Eyre visited the nuns who had recently experienced the indignity of a night-time raid by soldiers on the pretence of searching for contraband goods.

On Dorothea's death in 1829, the *Retrospections* passed to her unmarried brother Nicholas, the clergyman, and from him to a Mandeville nephew. One of the Mandeville descendants had them published in 1929 and 1930 in two volumes. At that time, the other three volumes containing plays, poems and novels had disappeared.[1] The *Retrospections* manuscript also now appears to be unaccounted for. This is a pity since the foreword suggests that the published account contains somewhat less than half the entire material. It is possible that in some location one or all of Dorothea's original manuscripts may still survive, and one can only hope that they may yet come to light. They appear to have been edited in 1929–30 with care and sensitivity. The frequent contemporary practice of using a dash in place of a full

---

1. While the reference can be read as suggesting otherwise, the manuscript was in fact published in its entirety (the transcription was made by a naval officer descendant, GFM Mandeville, in the hours of long watches in the South China Sea in the late 1920s). Dorothea's journal for 31 July 1806 to 31 December 1807, also existing in its entirety, is the sole surviving evidence of the record keeping which was the basis for the *Retrospections*. The manuscripts are now in the Manuscripts Room, Trinity College Dublin Library.

point has been faithfully reproduced in the text. To modern taste, this gives an impression of a somewhat frenetic mood, which is of course false.

The *Retrospections* are interesting on many counts. Women were more sensitive diarists than men, more personal or intimate in their interests, and diaries such as Dorothea's or Mary Mathew's unpublished diary for 1772 provide a perspective on the eighteenth century which can be obtained from no other source and link together many strands of life around them. Dorothea's account, too, with its keen powers of observation, provides much evidence of living conditions and social life. Of course, we can get much of this information from travellers, whether the industrious Arthur Young in his *Tour of Ireland* (London, 1780) or the incomparable Coquebert de Montbret (summarised in articles by S Ní Chinnéide) who was as much interested in the Catholic middle classes as in the Protestant. However, Dorothea's *Retrospections*, more than accounts written at a point in time, have the advantage of viewing events over a long period from the perspective of a single family and a single district. Life was what it actually meant to families and it is only if we enter into the intimacy of a family in some continuous fashion through childhood, adolescence and womanhood that we can comprehend, however imperfectly, what life at the time really meant. Her diary is particularly invaluable because it documents the social conditions and relationships of the circle of gentleman farmers, that fascinating circle which occupied a position between the occupying farmers and the great landowners, and which frequently and very inaccurately is described as middlemen. Dorothea's family, as a rector's family, is perforce somewhat set apart from them in source of income and in function, but it was the Herberts' social milieu. No other known account brings us so clearly into the heart and soul of this little world so pervasive in Ireland in the closing decades of the eighteenth century.

It was of course a peculiar milieu, quite up to date in some ways and in other ways a generation or two behind society in England or France. The after-dinner behaviour in 1793 of the officers of the Roscommon militia, when they joined the ladies for tea at the Herberts, seems explicable only because the gentlemen had 'sat very late at the bottle'. The occasional bouts of horsewhipping hinted at in the *Retrospections*, though they would not have merited comment in England at an earlier age, would have been unthinkable by the end of the eighteenth century. Arthur Young saw the distinction in his tour, though both he and some of his very grand and sometimes very liberal Irish informants tended to exaggerate the unseemly characteristics of this gentlemanly class which they did not accept as equals. For a lower social level than that described in Mrs Delany's letters or Jane Austen's fiction, Dorothea Herbert's *Retrospections* people a lost world of the eighteenth century with a series of enduring images of daily life. Dorothea seems to have intended her *Retrospections* for publication. It was fitting then that they appeared in 1929–1930 at last. They are, in fact, too good to remain inaccessible and deserve to remain in print as a vivid introduction to the society of south Tipperary and as a still rarer guide to the mental world of an accomplished though ultimately anguished lady in rural Ireland.

Louis M Cullen
Trinity College Dublin
August 2004

The Works of
Dorothea Herbert
Consisting of
Plays, Poems, Novels
And Biography
In four Volumes
Adorned with Cuts
Volume the fourth
Manuscript

*Retrospections Of
An Outcast
Or the Life of
Dorothea Herbert
Authoress Of
The Orphan Plays
And Various Poems
And Novels
In Four Volumes
Written in Retirement
Volume the Fourth*

Adornd with Cuts

Vive Lamour *L A* *Belle Amour*

*Creative Love
Still bade Eternal Eden shine Around*

BOOK 1st

A Help to Memory
Or
Retrospections of an Outcast
By Dorothea Roe

CHAPTER THE FIRST

An Account of the Herbert family and Muckrus—
Description of the Lake of Killarney—Marriage of
Our Authors Parents—Desart Family

About the Year 1739, famous for being the
Year of the great Frost when Brandy froze before the fire, and a fair was held on the Ice of the
Thames—My Grandfather Edward Herbert
Esqr resided at Muckrus in the County Kerry,
Ireland, with a large family, of whom my father
was the Youngest but one—Mr Herbert when
Young, married the Daughter of Lord Kenmare, a Roman Catholic Lady, who exempli-
fied the force of Love by going off with him
privately, and Marrying him against her religious Prejudices, and Against the injunctions of her only Brother Lord Kenmare whom
otherwise she so dearly loved, that she lost
her senses at his Lordships Death some years
after, and never retrieved them to her own
Death.

This Worthy Couple had by their union, three

Sons and six Daughters as Mention'd in the
Margin (See Note*), Who whilst unmarried all
lived with their Parents at Muckrus, a famous
and beautiful Peninsula on the Lake of Killarney
—The Estate was bounded on the South by the
Lake all over the World renown'd for its romantic Beauties—A handsome Lawn Divided
the House from the Charming expanse of
Waters that rolld beneath, spotted with Rocky
Islands coverd with Arbutus, and every variety
of curious Shrubs, and bounded on the Opposite
Shore by the Mountains of Clena, and Toamis,
famous for their Woods and Cascade—Ross
and Innisfallen Islands rode sumptuously
amongst the Smaller Craft of Rocks and Isles
they seem'd to Convoy, and presented a scene
of Indescribable beauty on the smooth Glittering Lake.

The Most beautiful Island of the Lake belonged to my Grandfather—It is called Dinish

Note * 1st Thomas Herbert the Eldest Son, Married Miss Martin
an English Lady and afterwd Miss Bland—

2dly John married Miss Cuffe eldest Daughter to Lord Desart
Co Kilkenny—

3 Nicholas (My father) Married Miss Martha Cuffe his youngest Daughter—

1st Margaret Mr Herberts Eldest Daughter Married to Macarty
More Esq Co Kerry

2d Helena—Married to Richard Eyre Esqr Macroom Co Cork—

3d Frances Married to Edward Blennerhasset Esqr Co Kerry

4th Thomasine married Thomas Cuffe Esqr

5th Bella a beautiful girl died on the Eve of being Married to
Sir Thos Bell

6th Cathaline Married to the Revd Robert Herbert
They had all numerous progenies many of whom appear in
the following pages

2

and stands near the Straight that divides the Upper and lower Lakes, and is reckond one of the most romantic Spots in the Universe—But what strikes most is the Luxuriance of the various Heaths along the half natural, half cultivated Walks and Vistas which intersect its delightful Groves and velvet Lawns spread over its high Rocky Surface—whilst projecting Pinnacles of Rock continually vary the Scene and form a Grotesque and beautiful Contrast—A Charming Village bounded Muckrus on the West, and led to the town of Killarney, and the famous seat of Lord Kenmare, between the town and Muckrus.

In this celebrated Retreat my Father was born —The family were universally beloved for their conciliating Manners—My Grandmother was the Lady Bountiful of the Neighbourhood, especially in the Year of the great frost, when she saved numberless poor wretches who were perishing in the Wilds of Muckrus, half famishd and frozen to Death—The frost was so intense that the Woodcocks, and other Wild Birds flew into the House for Shelter—My Uncles and Aunts all married whilst my Father was yet a Boy—He was then very Wild, and full of Spirits, and his boyish Tricks render'd him famous amongst his Jovial Neighbours and Playmates, who still talk them over—One time he spoiled his Sister Eyre's Wedding Cake, and whilst Bradley the Cook was shaking in the Currants he interlayd it with

Sand crying "I'm Bradley—"I'm Bradley—
Another time he went to Sea in a Losset,
whilst Crowds stood on the Shore expecting
every Moment to see him sink; he however was
providentially drifted safe to Land—in short he
was noted throughout the County for his Boyish Archness and went by the Name of Wild
Nick—When he grew up he studied Physick
for a time—but his Relation Lord Powis offering him the living of Ludlow, he got into
Orders, and lived Many Years at Ludlow a
Batchelor very much beloved, and a great
favourite at Powis Castle—Those he deem'd
amongst the happiest Days of his Life—but a
better Preferment being offer'd to my Grandfather for him, he brought his Son over
to Ireland to take possession of the united
livings of Carrick, Kilmurry and Kilsheelan;
and also of the Parish of Knockgrafton under
the Patronage of the Butlar Family, now Lord
Ormond.
In Dublin he met my Mother, and married her
with the universal approbation of both their
families—A Whimsical Circumstance preceded
their first Meeting—His Sister Thomasine
and my Mother went to a fortune teller who
told My Mother she would soon be married to
a Man who was then pulling the Ropes at Sea
—My Aunts laugh'd, and said they were sure
it was their Brother, long Nosed Nick—The
Next Morning he landed, and at his first Interview with my Mother the Joke was renewd by

4

her friends, but it Ended in Serious Matrimony some Months after.

My Mother was a famous Œconomist, as she was factotum to my Grandmother Lady Desart (since dead) but my father was far from being a careful Providore—however when she arrived at Carrick, she found her New Abode most conveniently furnished—but in a Week, or fortnight, one Neighbour sent for his Chairs, another for his Tables, and so forth, till nothing remaind but the bare Walls—My Father and his friends laughd at her Embarassment, and furnishing the House anew, with other Expences, kept them under Water for a long time, but her Cleverness overcame all Obstacles, and they were at length comfortably settled in their beautiful little villa near Carrick on Suir—I shall Close this Chapter with the following Heraldry, that the ensuing Anecdotes may be the Clearer, as many of the Characters must necessarily appear in the Course of these Memoirs—

My maternal Grandfather Lord Desart resided at Desart in the County Kilkenny, a very fine old family Seat—He was a remarkably handsome, and good man, and Married Dorothea the Daughter of General Gorge, by whom he got ten thousand pounds worth of Plate, taken by her father at the Siege of Quebec —She was half Sister to the Earl of Tyrone, ancestor to the present Marquis of Waterford— His family consisted of four Sons, and four Daughters as follows—

John who succeeded him Married Mrs Thornhill, had three Daughters Mrs Cooke, Mrs Weldon, and Lady Burton—he died of an infectious Fever—

Otway who succeeded on his Brothers Death, married Lady Anne Browne had one Son and two Daughters, Lord Castle Cuffe, Ladies Elizabeth and Dorothea—

Revd Hamilton Cuffe married Miss Williams an Heiress had one Son 3 Daughters—

Major William Cuffe 17th Dragoons died a Batchelor in the Year——

Sophia Married Counsellor John Herbert had one Son Edward & many Daughters—

Lucinda Married Sir John Blunden Bart of Castle Blunden Co Kilkenny had 3 sons six Daughters

Martha my Mother married the Revd Nicholas Herbert had four Sons five Daughters—

Honble Margaret Cuffe died Young

| Herbert Family | (CHAPTER 2D) | and Neighbourhood of Carrick |

I shall here anticipate the Due Order of our Births, and mention that the Sum total of our spreading branches was as follows—My father and mother had nine of us in all viz—Namely Dorothea, Myself the loving but illused Wife of John Roe Esqr of Rockwell Co Tipperary,

who after seducing My young heart from
its Mansion of Peace most fraudulently
and unjustly married another—Edward my
Next Brother died an Infant — John Otway
— Thomas — Frances — Lucinda — Martha —
Sophia—Nicholas—These formd the rising
generation of our Family whose history will
hereafter appear—After My Father and
Mothers union, a Relation of the latter came to
live with her, Miss Cuffe, Daughter to the
Reverend Daniel Cuffe—She was an only
Child, reckoned very handsome, and every
way Much Admired—She was soon afterwards
Married to James Wall Esqr of Coolnamuck
near Carrick—The next Inmate my Mother
had was her Brother William Cuffe whose
Regiment was opportunely quarter'd in Carrick
—He was then a very Young Man—Head-
strong and hot—In a large Company here He
and Mr Butlar Lowe Brother to our Next Door
Neighbour, had a Dispute after Dinner about
a Horse—The Lie was given, the Company
engaged at either Side, and the whole party of
Gentlemen adjourned to Challenge, leaving the
Ladies their Tea Room unmolested—At length
my Father returned home all bloody from
wresting a Pistol, and Mr Laurence Smyth
explained to my Mother that Mr Butlar refused
to fight such a Boy as my Uncle, on which Sir
Charles Burton my uncle's Captain offerd to
fight in his Stead and the next Day was fix'd
for the Combat—My Mother being then big

with Child of Me, fainted away at the Intelligence—At twelve O Clock a file of Soldiers
entered and put my Uncle under an Arrest—
the next Day the other gentlemen went out to
fight, but the Magistrates interfered, and bound
them over—Lord Desart was sent for, and
found his Brother stark Mad at being confined
—all his endeavours to pacify him only drew
on himself a Torrent of Abuse—At length Mr
Butlar Lowe consented to appologize, which
ended the whole affair—Peace being once more
restored, the Neighbourhood met in harmony
as heretofore—As I am fond of ransacking the
Annals of the Days of Yore, I shall give an
Account of the Vicinage as it stood at My
Birth, and some Years after, which I reserve
for a Seperate Chapter—

" *While many a Pastime circled in the Shade* "
" *The Young contending as the Old survey'd* "

| Great people, low people | (CHAPTER THE 3D) | and little Folks of Yore. |

No More the Farmers News, the Barbers Tale
No More the Woodmans Ballad shall prevail

Mr and Mrs Jephson lived in a Handsome
rural Residence I may say next Door to ours,
as the two places were only divided by a small
Lawn at our Side, and a Bridge at theirs which
crossd a Rivulet running under their Windows

8

—Their Marriage was much of the same Date
as My Fathers and Mothers, and being both
young, gay, and handsome and just entered on
a large Property all things smiled around the
two Abodes—Their family consisted of Mr and
Mrs Jephson—Captain Jephson his Uncle,
and Miss Butlar her sister—they had afterwards eight or nine Children, most of whom
died Young—

At Curraghmore about 5 miles from our House
lived Lord and Lady Tyrone—His Lordship
was nearly related to my Mother—His Place,
improved by him and his Successor, is em-
bosomed amongst the Wilds of the Co Waterford Mountains and allowed to be one of the
finest places in the three Kingdoms—

3dly Castletown the fine Seat of the then Archbishop of Cashel and his son and Daughter in
law Mr and Mrs Cox with her Mother Mrs
Burton—This couple also newly married—

4thly Besborough the Noble Seat of the Earl of
Besborough an Absentee in England—

5thly Coolnamuck a beautiful place near a
romantic Glen within view of our Walks in the
Area of Wooded Mountains that charmingly
ornament the Vicinage of Carrick—This place
occupied by Mr and Mrs Wall who had been
lately Married at our House (See page 7)

6th Lodge a pretty place near Coolnamuck
the residence of Mr and Mrs Wolfe and
Daughter

Wilmar a Charming little place near a small

Glen where lived Mr and Mrs Nicholson—
Cregg, Sir Walter Esmonds since Mr and Mrs
Lalors—Mayfield Sir James Mays—Dovehill
Mr Newcomens—Tinvane, Bleachfield, Gar-
narhea all Briscoes—
In the Town lived Mr Coughlan a Clergyman
in an outlet Called Pill—Mr Anderson and Mr
Young both Clergymen—Doctor Carshore—
Mrs Dobbyn—three families of Smyths—
Hallidays—Ryans—&c Besides the Barrack
Gentry—The Castle of Carrack was inhabited
by old Mr and Mrs Galwey.
These as they encreased formd an uncommon
well stockd Neighbourhood and were already
a large and Gay Circle being mostly all newly
Married—An Incident that happened at that
time furnishd much Laughter—a conceited
Young Officer quarterd in Carrick had a trick
of loitering behind his Companions that he
might enter the Room alone and shew off his
graceful person—At a large Dinner party he as
usual loungd behind to wipe his Shoes—but on
being announced he forgot the House was an
old fashiond one and tumbled down headlong
a flight of Steps into the Parlour to the no small
Entertainment of the Company—This was
followed by another Curious Affair at a Club
of Gentlemen—One Rejean a french Clergyman who was a great Epicure observing a fine
Dish of dress'd Lobster resolved to have it all
to himself and taking out his Snuff Box he very
leisurely spiced the Lobster with Snuff—on

Which my Father in the name of the Company pulld him round the Table by the Nose for the daring insult on the Club.

The Houses Now began to fill with Children and as some of them will figure away in these Memoirs I shall introduce the tiny race in a Short Catalogue—

Curraghmore Lord Tyrone had three Sons and four Daughters—Mr Cox six Sons two Daughters—Mrs Wolfe one Daughter an Heiress—Mr Nicholson Wilmar, one Son one Daughter—Mr Lalor Cregg one Son two Daughters—Mr Halliday one Son four Daughters—Mr Carshore 3 Sons 2 Daughters—Ryans Smyths and Briscoes innumerable—

Mrs Jephson had 3 Sons four Daughters all of whom died young but Lory Salisbury and Fanny who lived to be married but Fanny died two years after—The Others still survive.

I have before given a list of our names (pages 6 and 7) and shall only repeat that we were eight Survivors in Number all bouncing Boys and Girls.

Old Standards of Carrick on Suir

Mr Galwey Wine Merchant
Mrs Ryan Miliner
Doctor Carshore Apothecary
Doctor Colton Man Midwife
Mr Wimpe Clerk of Parish

Old Bell Sexton
Old Deal Schoolmaster
John Cosgrave Constable
Old Leary Tailor
Old St John Staymaker
Old Hervey Butcher
Tom Phillips Shoemaker

"Time was like thee they Life possessd"
"And Time shall be that thou shalt rest"

Deaths—Estab-lishments	CHAPTER 4TH	And first Debut of Our Author

Besides losing her Eldest Son Edward my
Mother had now to lament the Death of her
eldest Brother John Cuffe Lord Desart—a Man
universally beloved and deplored he died of a
violent Fever caught by sitting for his Picture,
and what is more remarkable two Dogs and a
fine Horse that were drawn in the Picture
caught the Disorder—the Dogs died—the
Horse was never any good after and the painter
lost his sight—supposed from some poisonous
paint—Lord Desarts funeral Procession occupied the space of three Miles so much was he
beloved.

In the Year 1771 My Mother went to Dublin
to attend the Deathbed of Lady Dowager Desart
her Mother—She died at her House in Henry
Street and was the last of My Father and
Mothers Parents who departed this Life.

A pecuniary Demand for a large Sum now em-
barass'd them—In this Emergency they applied
to Sir John Blunden who had Married My
Mothers sister Lucinda who though very close
lent them eight hundred pounds and generously
refused to take more than common Interest—
Thus rescued the patriarchs lived for Some

Years with the greatest Œconomy till freed from
Debt.

I shall close this part of our history with some
Account of our Domestic Establishment—Par-
son Harwood was then my fathers Officiating
Curate at Knockgrafton—John Wharton an
Englishman who lived with him Many Years
before he married was his proctor and Steward
he was a very genteel and indeed Elegant Man
very Clever but totally given to drink which
Ended in his own Ruin and a great Defalcation
to my Father—Mrs Ann Wharton his Wife
lived with my Mother many Years before She
Married—She was a Wonderfully clever
Housekeeper, Confectioner, Lady's Maid and
Nursetender—and doubly valuable as being
Strongly Attach'd to My Mother—John Wharton and she married for Love here—They were
both of respectable Families and far above the
common Run of Servants in their Manners
Education and Deportment.

Besides them we had first a bad Nurse 2dly a
Mad Nurse, and 3rdly a sickly Nurse for my
little Ladyship (Its a Wonder Poor Miss Dolly
ever got over such an Ordeal) and Nurses apiece
for all the rest—Not forgetting old Mary Neal
who drynursed us all and lived with us upwards
of forty Years without ever stirring from the
Nursery Window, where she sat crying about us
or damning us unmercifully for our boldness
whilst she sat mending our Stockings and Rock-
ing the Cradles, Yet at Eighty Years of Age she

was upright as a palm tree in Carriage and was
indeed a rare Instance of fidelity and honest Attachment—Next Old Tim the Coachman drunk
every Night turned off every Morning and as
often retaken on promises of Amendment which
he never fulfill'd—Bob Fleming Pantry Boy,
turnd off same Way once a Month for Impertin-
ence, but pardoned on making proper Conces-
sions or at Miss Dolly's Intercession—George
Williams an Apprentice Boy constantly Running away, search'd for at great Cost, condemnd
to a flogging each time but forgiven on the
Screams of Miss Dolly—till at last the Ingrate
fled to England and never was heard of After—
Peggy Carew Dairy Maid and Susy Light
Housemaid two good Girls but a little Glib at
the Tongue lived with us Many Years—Old
Judith the Cook faithful and honest but a most
unbearable Scold lived a number of Years with
us—Richard Dalton the Gardener lived with us
till he died—Besides these were Tenants and
old followers innumerable, amongst whom I
must particularize Old Bridget Sweeny who ran
Crazy and fancied She had the Devil in her
Belly—At her Death she left Miss Dolly
Guardian to three Strapping Sons Brogue
Makers and one Daughter four of the biggest
and roughest people in brogue Makers Lane
Carrick—Miss Dolly their Guardian was then
about the Size of a Small Monkey but grave and
oracular as an Ancient Sybil.

Youthful
Pranks

(CHAPTER THE FIFTH)

And Occupa-
tions—A
Pilgrimage
(Birth of an
Heir)

"In Days of Prattling Infancy"
"Led by young wondering Extacy"

At this time My Greatest Solace was to be
Asked by John Wharton to drink Tea with his
Consort and Sup with him on Bread and Cheese
—After which he usually regaled us with Psalm
Singing or Old Opera Airs for he had a very fine
Voice—Or if Mrs Wharton gave me a few Baby
Cloaths—a Tart—or the Skimmings of the
Rasberry Jam I was the happiest of living Crea-
tures—However the Baby Cloaths had like to
cause me dear for stooping one Day over a Tub
of Water to wash them—I fell in and was nearly
in a State of Suffocation when found—My Next
perilous attempt was to wash a Mop in an old
Ha Ha but Miss Cuffe (since Mrs Wall of Coolnamuck) Saved me on the brink of Destruction
though the fright nearly cost her her Life.
But these were nothing to the Hair breath
Escapes I had when my Young Companions
grew up about me—There were six or seven of
us almost always in Mischief—Tom invented
Pop Guns that often blinded us—Fanny The
Art of Dyeing by which we compleatly spoiled
a set of new scarlet Stuff Gowns we had just

Got—We then washd them, and when that was
of no avail we threw them out to Bleach—peppering for fear my Mother or Mary Neal should
know any thing of It—Otway and I were great
Gardeners, And having Got Old Mahony the
Gardeners helper one Day to Ourselves, the
whole Set bullied him into digging up a fine
Plantation of Young Laurels, which we planted
in the Waste Garret having previously carried up
large heaps of Earth in our bibs and an old
Backgammon Box—The Old fool did nothing
but cry about his Laurels every ten Minutes exclaiming Ha na mon Diel (that is My Soul to the
De'el) but You're playing the Red Devil with
the Place—As we tore up the Garret flooring
for it the whole Lobby Cieling afterwards came
down.

When the Boys first returnd from School it gave
a new turn to Affairs—They spouted to us and
we stood gaping round till we were all Book
Mad—Dido and Æneas—Hector and Paris
fired our Brains, a Sixpenny Voyage of Lord
Anson, and Old Robinson Cruesoes Tale compleated our Mania—One time we fancied ourselves thrown on a Desart Island till a fight who
should be Crusoe and who Fryday ended our
play—Another time we were a set of Sailors
thrown on the Delightful Island of Juan Fer-
nandez—We spent whole weeks in an old blue
Bed under cure for the Sea Scurvy and eat such
quantities of Cabbage Stumps, Celery, and
Other Antiscorbutic Thrash that we really got

scorbutic Disorder with worms and a Variety of
Complaint that obliged us to submit to Continual Doses of Physick which old Mary ad-
ministerd with tear swoln Eyes to half a Dozen
of us at Once.

Thus passd our Hours of Relaxation from School
Studies which were emulatively pursued in the
forenoon—Mr Wimpe made us spell for Slaps
—but Tom having one Day egregiously cut up
Fanny She very deliberately went and hang'd
herself in the Garret—She was however cut
down by her more fortunate Competitor and
with Proper Care recover'd—It were endless
to recount all our prowess—Many noble and
Valiant atchievements will appear in this History.
An Event Now happend that caused General
Felicity in our Circle—In the year 1772 Mrs
Wharton put forth a Son after many Years
vainly wishing for One—however he died soon
after to the great Grief of the Whole family and
she never after had a Child.

Another Event this year caused great grief
amongst the Children and Nurses—Old Mary
Neal fancied herself Obligated to go on a Pilgrimage for the Good of her Soul—To Saint
Johns Well then she went walking bare foot to
Kilkenny over a sharp pavement, and doing
many Other Acts of Popish Penance—She returned after a long absence with a Bottle of
Sanctified Water, two pair of New Padreens (or
Beads) a holy Cross—A Dispensation—and the
priests Blessing—

N.B.—As I and 2 or 3 More of us were born in the Tower of Kilkenny Mary and Our Nurses took Care to plunge us in St Johns Well so that we were as sanctified as young heretics could be —thanks to good St Peter.

1772   *Further Occurrences of less Note*

March 2*d* I began to learn writing from Mr Thomas Wimpe Parish Clerk—*July* 19*th* I stood Godmother for Mr Valentine Smyth, Got a fine Babyhouse on the Occasion from his Mother Mrs Larry Smyth of Carrickonsuir— My Sister Lucy born this Year—Went with My father and Mother on a trip to Killarney, had a Narrow Escape at a frightful Causeway Where the Carriage had but a Hairsbreath to run over a dreadful Precipice on a Road newly turnd up —Saved by the Dexterity of Tim the Driver who drove over it full gallop—This Event was caused by my Fathers Absence of Mind in rid- ing on before without thinking of the Carriage which follow'd his Lead so that we lost the right Road—First Introduction to my Uncle Toms Wife and family nine in Number at Muckrus— Delightful Excursions about the Lake—Visit Mount Hedges near Macroom—Disagreement between My Aunt Eyre and her Husband who soon after parted—Her Eldest Son Ned Eyre and Mrs Maunsel went with her to Cork Mrs White her Eldest Daughter and Captain Hedges staid with their Father at Macroom.

N.B. Otway Tom and Fanny were Inoculated
this Year, Nurse Rourke here.

Carrickon-suir and its	(CHAPTER THE SIXTH)	Environs— The Vicars Villa

Seats of My Youth when every Sport could Please

It is Now time to give a short Account of Our
Residence and the Country about Carrickonsuir—The Town is Situated in a Delightful
Valley by the Banks of the Suir—It has a good
large Church, a Chapel, a fine old Castle, and
the remains of a Curious Ancient Abbey—No
other Buildings but Mercantile Ones of any
Public Note—It was then famous for the Rat-
teen Trade and sent over Some of its fine Manu-
factures for the Kings peculiar Use his Majesty
expressing himself Much Pleased with it—but
this has dwindled of late though it is still a great
place for Woollen Manufacture—The Country
on each side from Clonmell to Waterford is delightfully Chequerd with hanging Woods verdant hills Old Castles and Gentlemens Seats—
It is one continued narrow winding vale for
about forty Miles along the Meanderings of
the River Suir, and has been always called the
Golden Vale of Ireland on account of its romantic
Beauties and rich Soil and Pasturage—The Suir
is Navigable for large Boats from Clonmell to
Waterford and Carrick being the Central Town

is a Place of great Business—The Air is very
Wholesome and pleasant.

Our Villa in the Outlets consisted of three Delightful Meadow lands on a Slope which commanded a full View of the town, The River and
Sailing Boats and the beautiful hanging Woods
and Glen of Coolnamuck on the Right—To the
left we saw the Windings of the Suir and the
rich Country towards Waterford as far as Fid-
down a place six Miles off—Our House stood
in the Centre of four beautiful large Gardens, a
Lawn Shrubbery and Courtyard which parted it
from the High Road—In this little Spot we had
a very pretty Wilderness and a beautiful broad
Gravel Walk Shaded half way with Yews and
Elms which formed a Vista to the perspective of
Coolnamuck Hills and Castle—Our Pleasure
Garden was a Wilderness of Sweets and the
Whole Place bloomd like Eden with Woodbine,
Jessamine and the fragrant Rose.

The House itself was a Venerable old Building
with two Wings and a Centre quadrangular
fashion—It had once been two Houses and had
been built one hundred Years—King William
slept in it after the Battle of the Boyne—It had
three large Parlours 2 large Halls and 3 other
large Rooms below Stairs besides Kitchen,
Larder, Housekeeper Room, and Offices innumerable of every Sort—Above Stairs were 7
large Bedchambers 2 Closets and a front Lobby
with another long Winding One between the
two Staircases where many a Stranger lost their

way—Above there was a great low Garret a perfect Wilderness of Antique construction that
made the blood run Chill with Horror—My
Father was forced to take down the whole Roof
and rebuilding it cost no small Sum—Indeed
the whole Place underwent a New Modelling
and was Modernized into a Commodious and
handsome Dwelling Which kept my Mother at
her Wits End many years to supply the Exigen-
cies of a falling House and growing family.

Muckrus Family	(CHAPTER THE SEVENTH)	Their Names and Marriages

August 1773 Mr Tom Herbert my Fathers
Eldest Brother brought his family to Spend the
Autumn here on their Way to England—He
was Married to a Miss Martin Sister to an old
English Member of Parliament Mr James
Martin—His family were a fine Set of Young
People see their Names at Note‖ Mrs Herbert

Note ‖ Their Names were Henry Eldest Son afterwards Married to
Miss Sackville Daughter of Lord Sackville otherwise the famous
Lord George Germain.
Emily—Married her Cousin Richard Townsend Herbert Esqr of
Cahernane died soon after.
Anne Married a Major Kearney and Settled in Hallifax.
Catherine Married the Reverend Mr Dawson—Frances the
Reverend Mr Kenny—Mary married the Reverend Arthur Her-
bert—Edward to Miss Herbert of Brewsterfield—
Peggy a beautiful Girl died unmarried of fright in the late Rebel-
lion 1799

did not long outlive this visit and as she was the
best of Wives and Mothers her family had a Deplorable Loss in her—Mr Herbert married a
Second Wife Miss Bland by whom he had two
Sons—but his first set of Children were scatterd
by it amongst their Mothers English relations.

1774 White Boys	(CHAPTER THE 8TH)	Our Proctor beaten 1774

This Year great troubles broke out in My
Fathers Parish Knockgrafton about twenty
Miles from Carrick—John Wharton was sent
with a Posse of Tenants to Draw Tythe and
fight them with Processes—The White Boys
attack'd them at Night, Cut and hackled the
Whole Party and handled Wharton so desperately that his shirt seemd dipt in Blood—They
left him supposing him dead—but our Carmen
brought him home with a most dreadful Cut
Along the Head and his body so bruised and
Mangled that he never was the same person
after it and from thence fell into Drink—Luckily
he had sent home the Money collected the Night
before—His Landlord one McEncrow was
afterwards transported—but the Ringleaders
not being properly ascertaind could only be
punish'd in the Bishops Court at great Cost and
trouble.
Sometime after this Event we went to Desart,
Lord Desarts fine old family Seat in the Co. Kil-

kenny remarkable for its fine Woods and large
Oaks—The House is a very Grand One much
like Besborough but its chief Beauty is its two
Superb Staircases and Noble Gallery—It is altogether a very grand and venerable place and I
felt a pleasure in hearing My Mother recount
the Many Happy Hours she spent in the large
Hall where in my Grandfathers time the family
met and dined round a blazing Wood fire after
the Manner of Old Times—There is at Desart
a famous Suit of Tapestry representing the rising Sun—My Grandmother spent twenty Years
working it—Also a famous Service of Gold and
Silver Plate taken by General Gorges at the
Siege of Quebec value 12000L and given as a
portion to my Grandmother—At Desart is the
Large fatal Picture that cost John Lord Desart
his Life (see page 12) and many Valuable family
Pictures done by Italian Masters—Otway Lord
Desart resided there when we went Augst 30th
1774—He was a good Man an Affectionate
Brother and Afterwards a kind Husband but he
lived forty years a Batchelor and let the place go
to wreck whilst he resided mostly in England.
At Desart we met my Aunt Herbert and My
Uncle Hamilton Cuffe—They were both remarkably Sensible and Agreeable, but neither being
very Œconomical, Their Extravagance greatly
injured their families whilst Lord Desart and
the Other Branches lectured them in Vain.
From Desart we visitted Castle Blunden Sir
John Blundens Place and Danesfort belonging

to Major Weymes his Son in law—And were
cordially received by them all—In this Excursion We figured away in a New Coach and four
Just come from Dublin.

Same Year an Event happen'd which caused
universal Concern—This was the Death of Mr
Jephson our Neighbour who died of a Billious
Fever—As their family and Ours were I may
say One the Death of their Amiable Head made
a great chasm—The two families dined together
continually—And Mr Jephson was never himself when he could Not Play an Evening Game
of Backgammon with the Doctor and his Lady
—In his Capacity of Magistrate he renderd
them many valuable Services and they felt quite
desolate without him—My Father and Mother
attended him to his last moments—Mrs Jephson was now left a Young Widow with one Surviving Son and four Daughters—Her Son Laurence Hickey Jephson now married to Miss
Prettie—Ann Salisbury Married George Rothe
Esqr Co Kilkenny—Eliza died Young—Fanny
Married Edward Lee Esqr died shortly after—
Dora died at the Age of fifteen unmarried—
They were all a very beautiful Family of whom
only Lory and Salisbury now Survive.

The Chincough now raged everywhere—The
Children of both Houses caught the Infection
but all recovered Except Eliza Jephson who
died of it—this renewd her Mothers grief and
she remain a long time a Prey to it—Though
Young and handsome she remained a Widow.

This Year My Mother lay in of her Youngest
Daughter Sophia and being Subject to Nervous
Fevers she was forced to take a french Governess
for us—we did not much relish this but with
the help of the Young Jephsons we kept her in
Proper Subjection—They also had a french
Governess and the two Mademoiselles soon
found Conciliating Manners more efficacious
than Rough Work—Their Names were Charles
and Delacour—We had also a Dancing Master
Mr Tassoni whom we plagued heartily.

CHAPTER 10TH

After My Mother lay in she had a dreadful
Fever which was near Ending her Existence—
Never shall I forget one Day that she seemd just
gone in a high Delirium with the fever and burning Blisters—After the Doctors and Attendants
had left her She supplicated me in the most piteous Manner to get her a little Mutton Suet to
cool her Back—Her Face was like a Coal of
Fire with Agony and her frantic Vehemence and
Screams made Me run down for her own
Remedy contrary to Orders—Mr Carshore however who attended her interrupted My Surgical
Operations, and said her Life depended on the
torment of the Blisters—I must here introduce

Mr Carshore and his Family—He was a very
Eminent Man in his Profession—He was bred
a Surgeon in the Navy—had every Opportunity
of Improvement And being Agreeable and
tenderhearted as well as clever in his business,
his settling here was justly look'd on as a most
fortunate Circumstance and he was long a valuable Treasure in the Medical line here where
there was no regular Physician—His wife was
a Valuable Woman and She and her Eldest
Daughter came up almost every Night, Wet or
dry—The friendship between My Mother and
her subsisted, till a very violent Putrid Fever
carried her Off and left us all in the deepest
Woe—Miss Carshore was a pretty Girl with all
her Fathers Cleverness and her Mothers Jocu-
larity—She, the Jephsons, and We, were all one
Party of Playmates, Messmates and Marauders
—and Woe to the Governess or Servant Who
opposed us—On Mrs Carshores Death her
Family came up to us, My Mother had attended
her to her last Moments, and to her She con-
fided the Care of her 2 Daughters—They afterwards married Mr Curtis and Mr Barker—
Their Mothers Death threw a general Gloom
over us.

1776   CHAPTER THE 11TH

In the beginning of this Year My Mother lay
in of her youngest Son Nicholas—during her

Confinement My Father received an Account
that his Eldest Brother, Mr Herbert of Muck-
rus was going to be married a second time to
Miss Bland a Young Obscure Girl without for-
tune and Younger than his Daughter—In the
Midst of Frost and Snow My Father Set off for
Killarney but it was too late for the Business was
Concluded and my Father had only the Poor
Satisfaction of Giving his Brother a Blow on the
Occasion—After two Years however Mr Her-
bert and his Young Wife died, leaving two
Orphan Boys in Addition to his Numerous
family.

This Year Mrs Cuffe My Uncle Hammy
Cuffe's Wife and her two Daughters Dolly and
Sophy lived with us for some time, as She and
her Husband did not agree—Domestic Chag-
grins made her illtemperd and She, Mrs Jephson and My Mother had perpetual Squabbles—
She at length went home on being reconciled to
her Husband—My Mothers Constitution was
now quite weakened from the Cares of the
World, and Perpetual Sickness, and the Doctors
sent her over to Drink the Bristol Waters, in an
almost hopeless State of health and spirits—
Never was there a more dismal Parting—Our
Neighbours and the Poor Children wept about
us, sure that she never would return alive—On
My Side I thought to leave House and home,
and cross the Seas was an Affair that never could
be got over by Any of us—The Night before
our Departure, I walked about like a Ghost cry-

27

ing over everything, kissing every thing, and bidding each dear Haunt a last good bye—Old Mary stalk'd after me, half dead with grief, as every Moment one or other of the Children threw me into Crying fits—My Mother sat in the Parlour supported by Pillows, fainting every moment and Grieving away the little Spirits that remain'd—My Father sat by her distracted whilst their little Ones wept instinctively Around them.

Our Turret rebuilt this Year.

| Journey to Bristol | CHAPTER THE 12TH | Acquaintances |

Sun June 11th 1776 My Father and Mother, Mr and Mrs Wharton and I sailed for Milford on our way to Bristol after bidding a heartbreaking adieu to our Sorrowing Friends—Our Route through the South of Wales was | Hubbertston | Havreford West | St Clare | Clanstephan | Carmarthen | Llandillo | Llandovery | Brecknock | Abbergaveny | Usk Ferry | Old Passage | Hotwells Bristol || At Clanstephan we took Shipping again, but had like to be lost passing over the Bar—and were forced to put back—living for a week at a wretched Hovel—We then went by Caermarthen where we equip'd ourselves decently, for not caring to open our trunks we were quite filthy from our delay at Clanstephan —At Brecknock we paid but four shillings for a

dinner to 5 People—We had two Courses of
Seven Dishes, Tarts, Pies, Sweetmeats, Ham,
Honey, Bread and Cheese, Cyder, all for four
shillings with wine proportionately Cheap—
What a Regale was this after a Weeks Starvation—for at Clanstephan we were litterally
famishd and paid almost as much for an old
tough Turkey one Sunday as our Whole Breck-
nock Dinner Cost.

When we arrived at Bristol Hotwells (June . 76.)
we immediately took Lodgings on the Mall—
We had two or three very agreeable Families in
the House—Colonel Burleigh, his Sister, and
Niece—Two Miss Shepherds of Lancashire,
and many Others—Miss Burleigh came every
Day to teach me to make French Flowers, and
the Miss Shepherds could Not live without Us
—My Mother and I were out every Hour in
one Carriage or Another but we went to no
Publick Parties except one Ball and one Breakfast—Our Acquaintance at the Pump Room
was universal we knew every Body and every
Body knew us, and the little Girl as I was called
was as Public a Character, as the Woman in the
Pump Room.

My Mothers Bills were drawn on a Mr Meyer-
hoff a Dutch Merchant who lived in Bristol and
asked us to Dinner—We dined off a curious
Service of China, Part of his Wifes fortune—It
was reckond of immense Value and was as thin
as an Eggshell—My Mother was peppering for
fear we should break our Plates—Mr Meyer-

hoff had no Child and was very rich—He every
Sunday paid us a Visit, and pressd my Mother
to leave me behind with him Offering to provide for me as if I was his Own Child and that
she should never pay a Farthing for my education or Maintenance—His Wife however was a
Cross Brutal looking Woman and My Mother
rejected the tempting offer.

Mr and Miss Jackson of Sney'd-Park were particularly kind to us—They were related to my
Aunt Herbert of Muckrus—We spent a delightful Day at Sney'd Park which was one
of the Most beautiful Seats about Bristol—
Amongst other Company we met Mr John
Martin My Aunts Brother.

Sunday June 23rd My Father went up to London to visit Lord Powis his former Pupil—The
late Lord being dead—Lord Powis received
him kindly but being in Opposition he had No
Power to serve him in an application for a
Bishoprick which was then in Contemplation
but which failed by the Supiness of My Fathers
Friends—He returnd to our great Joy (July 1st)
For we were perfectly Miserable in his Absence.

We then made an Excursion to Bath to see the
New Crescent Circus and everything worth remarking—After spending three Months very
pleasantly My Mother being quite recovered
we set out for Lamplighters Hall having engaged
one Captain Clevelands Vessel a Trader for return by long Sea—After waiting there three

Days, He got other Passengers, and put to Sea
unknown to us in a Violent Storm—Vex'd to
Death at this disappointment We hired a Boat
and follow'd him three long leagues—The
Tempest encreasing every Moment, and the
Sea mountainous high—We had a Madwoman
with us who roared in Our Ears Blow Blow ye
Winds Blow—Our Oars broke, and the Boat-
men gave us up for lost—However as My
Mothers White Handkerchief floated astern—
The brutal Captain Cleveland tacked his Ship
about and picked us up from the Waves half
dead with Terror and fatigue.

His Ship the two Brothers was a dirty dark
Vessel laden with Rotten Eggs for the Sugar
House—had a quantity of stinking Meat on
board—and a dead Corpse to make it more
delectable—This last Article was hid under our
bed for neither the Sailors or we would have
relishd such a Shipmate the former being alway
superstitious on such Occasions—The Stenches
became so intolerable altogether that we kept
our Beds from Nausea and only found relief in
Embrocations of Vinegar—I was seized with a
Vomitting of Blood which was near ending My
Existence—From thence I grew quite heavy and
Stupid—The honest Tars however forced My
Mother much against her Will to pour down
my Throat a Whole Bowl of their Brown Pottage which stopd the Vomitting and cured Me
—This brought the Pottage into high vogue
amongst the Quality and was a most Seasonable

discovery as all our Hamper Provisions grew Putrid—To this Day I remember it was the most grateful healing Mess I ever tasted.

We now got Sight of the Irish Coast but the Captain would not put in without a Pilot—The Winds were fierce and changeable the Shore uncertain and dangerous, and the whole Ship Short of Provisions—after a horrid Bandying about amongst the Billows we got into Passage— from thence to Waterford—And on Thursday the Eleventh of June we arrived at Dear dear Carrickonsuir—The Joy at meeting was as great as the Grief at parting our friends—Every thing now promised felicity—My Mother quite recoverd—the Children all in rude health and spirits—All our Friends quite happy to see us, and proud of the Various little Presents we brought over.

Trifling Occurences The Spring of this Year was noted by a great Camp at two Mile Bridge— John Wharton escorted all the little Masters and Misses there we dined at an ale house on Beefstakes and returnd home happy as Kings and Queens in the old family Coach.

This Year George Williams our apprentice and old Play Mate absconded to England his Native Country—And left us all to break our poor little Hearts after him—My Mother took him begging and naked at the Door.

This Year Miss Matty was Inoculated and had like to die under the Operation.

This Year we began to take in the Leinster Journal.

| Juvenile Amusements | CHAPTER 11TH | Learned Ecclesiasticks |

Anno Domine 1777
"*And still they gazed, and still the Wonder grew*
"*That one small Head could carry All he knew*—

We had now another Addition to the Family which afforded the Young folks much amusement—This was a large Alabaster Doll I brought over—We christen'd her Miss Watts after one of the beautiful Miss Watts's of Pill —Mrs Jephson sold us a curious little Horse calld Roebuck no bigger than a large Dog and between Roebuck and Miss Watts the Jephsons, Miss Carshore, and we passd our time most Enchantingly—Sometimes indeed we had bloody Battles about them—which brought on a general flogging bout from our respective Mothers.

At this time Parson Young came to live with us —He had quarreld with his Wife who besides being mad Jealous, had too equal a Portion of learning to Obey her learn'd Husband—He was an amazingly tall Man with hardly an Ounce of flesh on him and as Yellow as Gold—But he was wonderfully agreeable, Witty, and Sensible and so learnd that his friends call'd him the Walking Dictionary—He was always walking

about from Neighbour to Neighbour, with a
Cane in his hand—a very old fashion'd three
Cockd Hat—a pair of very shining Shoes square-
toed with enormous plated Buckles—an Odd
cut blue Coat and small Wig—He was very
Satyrical, had a wonderful fund of Wit, wrote
and published very Clever Essays, and was on
every Occasion consulted as Lawyer, Physician
and Clergyman—so versatile his Genius—He
was besides fraught with Anecdote, Repartee,
and all the Brilliancy of Wit and humour—He
paid us so much a Month and lived here very
well Satisfied till his Wife and he were reconciled
—The Mornings he spent in visitting his
friends, or kissing and romping with the pretty
Girls—The Evenings he devoted to Study—
At Vacation his only Son Heck Young came
from School—He was a most Eccentrick Being
with all the ingenious Qualities of his father, and
a double Portion of his Satire—He wrote a Book
for us wherein he made Master Otway, Master
Thomas, Miss Dolly and Miss Fanny the principle Personages of his Epic Labours—Which
consequently made us all very fond of him—He
died a Student in the Temple where he was
esteemd so clever that he was buried near
Goldsmith in the Poets Corner Westminster
Abbey.
Besides Doctor Hercules Young we had Doctor
Daniel Cuffe and Doctor Thomas Rankin both
Justly esteemd for their learnd and agreeable
Qualities—Mr Cuffe was Father to Mrs Wall

of Coolnamuck and lived half the Year with us
being related to my Mother—Mr Rankin was
a North Country Man and dined with us almost
every Day—Those three Gentlemen though
elderly were remarkably facetious among the
fair Sex and particularly devoted to our fair
Neighbour Mrs Jephson and her fair Daughters
—Parson Young at this time made me a Present
of 8 volumes of the Spectator bound in red
leather, Gilt—A Valuable Edition not to be had
in Print—Mr Cuffe gave me Lord Lyttleton's
History of England and many other small Books
—Mr Rankin gave me Rasselas Prince of Abys-
sinia—Mrs English a set of pocket Voyages and
Travels and Mrs Larry Smyth The Death of
Abel—With this little Library and my Bible and
french Books I laid the foundation of my future
Erudition.

Town Belles   CHAPTER 12TH   Anecdotes

" *Beauty thou pretty Plaything, dear Deceit*
" *That steals so softly oer the Stripplings Heart*
" *And gives it a New Pulse, unknown before*

We had now a Visit from my Aunt Herbert of
Dublin my Mother's Eldest Sister, her Daughters and the two Miss Cuffes her Nieces and
Eléves—We met the whole party at Desart—
from whence they came here, and made a great
Racket—The Miss Cuffes being Co heiresses of
the late Lord Desart and Catharine the Young-

est was one of the most celebrated Beauties of
her time, but very delicate and subject to continual fainting fits—She afterwards married Sir
Charles Burton Bart—Lucy now Mrs Weldon
was too embonpoint to be a Beauty—She was
however so Enjoué that her Friendship was universally solicited—My Cousin Lucy was decidedly my favourite as she gave me a New Cap
and suit of Linen trimmed with Lace and french
flowers that cost five guineas.

One Day at Desart Mr Hamilton Cuffe who
was teazingly Nice, dressd the Parsons Nose of
a Duck for himself and she knowing his foible
laid her finger on it—A fit of romping took
place, which ended in a serious Quarrel and
violent Hystericks on her Part—This was no
sooner over than my Uncles affronted me by
recommending Mrs Jephson as a Step Mother
if any thing happend My Mother—This threw
Mamma and her Daughter into Hystericks and
all the Servants in the House were dispatchd for
remedies before our Sobs could be abated—
Many freaks passd at Desart that time which I
now forget—When they came to Carrick we had
nothing but Dinners, Balls, and Suppers, for the
beautiful Miss Cuffe—Miss Watts of Pill a
Clergymans Daughter rivald her in beauty and
many of the Carrick Ladies were famous Belles
and irradiated the assemblies with their Charms
—My Uncle William Cuffe was then also here
and by his fine flow of Spirits enliven'd every
party he Enterd.

36

" The veriest Gluttons do not always cram

Our Guests were not long gone, when my Aunt
Cuffe of Dublin my Fathers Sister and her only
Child Grace Cuffe arrived with Mrs Fleming a
poor relation of ours—Grace Cuffe was a most
accomplishd little Creature and knew it to her
comfort—They perswaded my Mother to let
me go to them for a twelve month, for the
Benefit of Masters in the Metropolis—At this
time we were at home as happy as Uncultivated
Nature could be—dressing out as Shepherds
and Shepherdesses with flower wrought vest-
ments, and Parasoles of Sycamore Leaves
studded with Daisies and Buttercups—Here
was a groupe of lovely Shepherdesses basking on
a Sunny Hillock with two or three pet Kids
browzing beside them—There a groupe of
Shepherds with their Dogs and Crooks—regaling on a frugal Meal of stolen Cold Meat with
a Wretched Sallad—" Their Drink the Chrystal
Well "—Except at the Season the Whiskey
Currants were thrown out when we were all as
fuddled as Couple Beggars—Nay one time the
Pigs, Servants, and Children were reeling about
the Yard where the heaps were thrown—Having once got a relish for the delightful Haut gout
we often found a pretence to stay at home from
Church, when the Jephsons and we used to say

37

family Prayers—dress'd out in our Mothers fine
flowerd Damasks with sticks across for large
Hoops—We first tossd up a Marmalade of
orange peels and Stolen Honey—then we got
to the Cellar and made a delightful warm jug of
Punch in the fine hot Summers Mornings—
After that we made Pews with the Chairs and
then most devoutly fell to Prayers never missing
one Amen—At length our revelry was ended by
my Mothers catching us one Sunday Morning
in such a State of Intoxication that not one of us
could stir from our Chairs or utter a Mono-
syllable—This stopd all our future Piety and
feasting—Our tastes were indeed rather Eccentric—We would eat nothing but pig Potatoes,
Pap or Stirabout for our breakfast and we ended
the Day with a Desert of raw Turneps, Cabbage
Stumps, or Celery Tops—In this wild state my
Aunt Cuffe and her accomplish'd Grace found
us—they were much Shocked at first but we
soon brought Grace over and conferr'd on her
the honour of being head Cook and Confectioner having just Politeness enough to shew our
Guest this Mark of Distinction.
Nothing now was heard of but hot Mutton Pies
and so forth with all the Varieties of Creams and
Candies that the Dairy and Garden could allow
—some were contriving small Ovens that we
might do without the cross Cook—others Stills,
baking Dishes, and Pudding Cloths, till my
Aunt Cuffe one Day found our Confectioner
regaling under a Tree of green Gooseberries—

on which she was confined, and put in Coventry
by her Mother and never after allowed to come
down till Dinner time—This was a terrible
Blow to poor Grace, who almost forgot her
Town Education amongst her Country Cousins.

Boys go to School	CHAPTER THE 14TH	The Authoress to Dublin— Odd Characters

" *Well had the boding tremblers learnd to trace*
" *The Days Disasters in his Morning Face*

The time now came when Otway and Tom
were to be sent to School and my Father chose
the Revd Patrick Hares school, Cashel, for
them—Mr Hare was an old friend and school
fellow of my Fathers—talkd over with pleasure
all their juvenile tricks and seem'd much attach'd
to my Father—He was a very handsome Comely
looking Man—amazingly clever and sensible
but very severe and satyrical where he took a
Dislike—Many were his oddities—and his Bon
mots, and Eccentricities were every Day repeated—He came here to fix the School terms
with my Father and dined at Castletown with
Old ArchBishop Cox—It happend that there
was a fine Turkey for Dinner dress'd with remarkable Selery Sauce for his Graces own Eating he being a great Epicure—Mr Hare calld
for some of the turkey—Pooh! Pooh! Man!

39

(said the Abp:) Eat Beef, Eat Beef Sir—Mr
Hare freely told him he could get Beef and
Mutton enough at home amongst his Boys, but
when he dined with his Grace he preferrd
Turkey and high Sauce—The ArchBishop was
himself an odd Character—He was very Close
and often blew out the Wax lights before half
his Company dispersed—The Clergy trembled
at his Nod and few of them escaped a severe
stricture at his Visitations—He was excessively
fond of Cards but so cross at them that few
would venture to be his Partner, for Mrs Cox
and my Mother only could Play so as to keep
him in tolerable temper—He had a Trick where-
ever he dined of slipping out to see dinner
Served—being one Day asked to meet Lord
Townsend (then Lord Lieutenant) He as usual
slip'd into the eating Room where Lord Townsend knowing his Oddity had hid himself behind
a large Skreen—The ArchBishop went round to
every dish with a Please God I'll Eat a bit of you,
repeating the same Grace at every Delicacy, What
was his Confusion when Lord Townsend pop'd
out laughing and asked his Grace what he would
leave for the rest of the Company.

To return to Mr Hare he was a blunt Man and
said whatever came uppermost—Smart at repartee and clever in his Opinions he made his
Own way amongst the Great, and got the Vicar-
generalship of Cashel when Charles Agar became ArchBishop there besides other good
Windfalls—Mrs Hare in gratitude sent frequent

presents of fine Butter to the Palace—The Arch-
Bishop one Day expressing his thanks to Mr
Hare the latter told him it was all fair that as he
got his Bread by the ArchBishop his Wife should
furnish his Grace with Butter in Exchange—To
this Gentlemans School the Boys were to be
sent—They had then an old Latin Master one
Jackson who attended them every Evening, and
whenever my Mother asked, Well Mr Jackson
how do you like the Boys, the regular answer
was b-a-d enough—b-a-d enough shaking his
head—Nor could any Assiduousness draw from
him a more good humourd Reply—The first
Rudiments of my Education and the Girls were
also laid under Mrs Charles an Anglo french
Governess — Seignor Tassoni an intinerant
Dancing Master, and Monsieur Dabeard a
blind drunken french Music Master—I had an
old Spinnet with about half a dozen tuneful Keys
—and thus prepared we had we thought nothing
to do but receive the last Polish to our Educa-
tions—Desart was the place fix'd for our Rendezvous where we were to seperate and set out for
our different Destinations.

| A Parting Scene at Desart | (CHAPTER 15TH) | A Dublin Reception |

" *Good Heaven what Sorrows gloom'd that parting*
    Day
" *That call'd them from their Native walks away*

To Desart then we all went screeching and roaring all the Way at the thoughts of Parting—
My Mother was as bad as any of us, and my
Father forgot he was a man and whimperd like
a Child—I had always formed a dreadful Idea
of School Vassalage, and to part with my two
darling little Brothers on such an Occasion filld
me with Agony—I thought I already saw them
bleeding under the rigid Usher or batterd to
Pieces by the big Boys of the School—Mr Hare
himself had a grand commanding look that
frightend Me—And the poor Boys themselves
dreaded School Discipline—Besides, I did not
much like my own Prospects—My Aunt Cuffe
and Mrs Fleming when with us were always
finding fault with Something or other in my
Conduct or Dress—My Aunt in her gentle way
reproved Me—Mrs Fleming severely fogh'd
at my Actions—Thus situated we pass'd the
Night at Desart in Tears, sighs and Groans and
could hardly be torn from each other at Bed time

" *Nothing but groans and Sighs were heard around*
" *And Echo multiplied the Mournful Sound.*

The Next Morning found us all in Convulsive
Woe and when the Carriages drove to the Door
the Scene beggard all Description—I step'd into
a Hack Chaize with my Cousin Edward Herbert who was going to a Dublin School and Mrs
Matthews his Sisters Governess—The Darling
little Companions of my Childhood were
wheeled off at the same Instant to the dreaded

School of Cashel—My Cousin Edward and
Mrs Matthews endeavour'd to amuse me on the
Road by playing Travelling beggar My Neighbour—The Person who counted most travellers
at their Side won the game and the Middle one
betted—A White Horse counted ten and was as
eagerly lookd out for by the three Observing
Travellers as St Peters Spire could be in a
Journey to Rome.

This Ninnyism however only afforded me a
temporary Quietus—And when I arrived at my
Aunts House (No 7 Gloucester Street) I was as
bad as when I first set out for which I was reprimanded by good Mrs Fleming who declared I
was a Mere rustic and transgressd all the Rules
of good breeding—The first thing Mrs Fleming did was to give me a compleat scrubbing
from top to toe as a Quarentine from the Land
of Potatoes—My Trunk was then search'd and
every Article criticized—Messages were sent
about by my Cousin Grace & Mrs Fleming to
the Stay Maker—the Mantuamaker and the
Hairdresser to attend at the toilette of Miss—
And I underwent a general admeasurement
and Inspection from those Gentlefolks—My
Mothers fine home made Linen was deem'd too
coarse, my Rich flower'd Cottons chosen by the
Crony Amateurs of Carrick were deemd vulgar
and unwearable—My new St John * Stays a
horrible bore, and my Philippian ** Pumps

* St. John the Staymakers name.
** from her Shoemakers name Phillip.

43

Abominable—Inshort I experienced the greatest
Mortification whilst they dissected my Carrick
finery of which I was not a little proud—Mrs
Fleming immediately bought me two or three
Morning Gowns—I was then deem'd decent to
appear before my Dancing Master my drawing
Master and my Music Master—Here I underwent fresh Mortification as they declared I was
quite spoiled by my Country Teachers, and
Must quite unlearn all that I had learn'd from
the Carrick Brogueneers as proud Mr Barnes
the Musician call'd them.

To add to my Vexation Mrs Ann Sullivan my
Aunts Housekeeper (an old Killarney follower)
came in to welcome me and asked me if it
was not better to be here than Bog trotting in
the Country? where, she was sure, I could *larn*
neither Ed*i*cation or Good Manners—I could
never like old Mrs Ann after and the next day
when desired to call her I obeyed with reluctance—But here I committed an egregious Faux
Pas for instead of Calling Mrs Ann I call'd out
Nanny—This brought Mrs Ann up in a violent
Passion, and exclaiming all the Way, Marry
come up my Country Cousin and Na re slane
the County Runaway—My Aunt also gravely
reprimanded me saying that none but herself
was privileged to call her Nanny, and Even her
Gracey calld her Mrs Ann.

After a time my Friends and my Masters grew
more good humourd with me having themselves
as they term'd it " The making of Me " and

even the Stately Mr Barnes and the Elegant Mr
Kelly declared I was making some Progress
amongst the Quavers and Graces—Mr Brooke
my Drawing Master had always been civil as I
was never under any other hand but his Own—
We spent some Months in rigid Seclusion and
Monastic Discipline—Every Moment devoted
to some Employment and a never failing Sermon
every Sunday Evening—I slept with Mrs Fleming who soon grew very fond of me and having
ventured privately to declare I never went to
Bed at home without a Bit of Meat for my
Supper, She as privately confessed that she never
could sleep herself without eating Something
and immediately produced from her Trunk the
Leg of a Goose which she had stolen from
Nanny Sullivan—This we eat in Bed with
Mutual Confidence—From that time out we
were never without a Tit bit in Bed, And when
our Argus Nanny was too Watchfull we club'd
for Bread and Cheese—Mrs Fleming then con-
fided to me all the Grievances she suffer'd from
Mrs Ann and my Aunt—That they prevented
her Marrying a rich Widower, and that she
sufferd continual Persecution about the Yellow-
ness of her Skin—Her wearing flannel at Night,
her taking Snuff, and other Lamentable Grievances.

" *Ah! Can you bear Contempt? The venomd*
     Tongue
" *Of those whom Ruin pleases? The keen Sneer,*
" *The lewd Reproaches of the Rascal Herd!*

The Season now arrived when my Aunt resolved
to treat her two Girls to an Evening at the
Rotunda—Great Preparations were made for
our Debut, And My Cousin Grace was all on
the Alert making up her own and my finery—
She was indeed a Charming well disposed good
natured Pet with only a few little foibles arising
from an affectation Natural to her Age and
Situation being an Heiress of large fortune.
To the Rotunda then we went dress'd out at all
Points—having previously engaged old Mrs
Bonham, her Son Dickey, and her Daughter
Betsy to be of our Party—Dicky and Betty
Bonham were both Oddities—He in particular,
being lame, sickly, and as great a Pet with his
Mother as Grace Cuffe was with hers—With
two such Jewels We all went in fear and trembling lest any thing should happen them—By
Miss Betsy's clever Management, we bustled
through the former Part of the night without
any material Mishap except a few Affronts put
upon Dicky and his Sister, which the latter
viragoed out—But when the Carriages were
call'd for and we got out amongst the Croud the

46

Scene changed—It turned out a dreadful Wet Night, Dark as Pitch and in the Confusion Dicky and Gracy were not to be found—My Aunt Cuffe had a trick of giving her Daughter a variety of Pet Nick-names and on Missing her she forgot herself, and ran about quite frantic crying out—" Oh wheres my Goosey! my Gracey! Oh Sir! Did you see my Gracey my Goosey! to every Chairman—Who the Devil is her Goosy Gracey said One—What the Devil is her greasy Goose said Another—Oh Sir My Cuffy wheres my Cuffy?—By G— she has lost both her Cuffs* said a third—At that Moment Mrs Bonham came up roaring out Oh My Dicky! My Dickey! Did you see My Dicky?— Egad and Here's an Old Lady has lost her Dickey ** too said a fourth Chairman—Inshort the Chairmen bandied them about without Mercy, till some friend came up and assured them, both Gracey and Dicky were safe lodged in Mrs Bonhams Coach—It happen'd that Dickey had taken it into his head to be more polite that Night than usual, and had requested the honour of leading Miss Cuffe to the Carriage, which offer She as politely accepted—So on they marched hand in hand to the Coach with all the formal Gallantry of their buckram Progenitors leaving their Mammas in the most terrible Consternation.

No other Event of importance Marked our

* Cuff—a short sleeve ornament worn then—
** Dickey—a flannel petticoat odly calld.

47

debut in Public except an awkward Mistake of my Aunt Herberts who joined us there She mistaking Kitty Cut-a-Dash the famous Thais of the times for her Daughter Fanny (they being dress'd alike in White Lutestring) made several Promenades leaning on her Arm and Conversing with another Thais her Companion whilst Kitty and her friend acted their Parts to a Miracle—After the late Accident we kept close House for a Long time but at length my Aunt ventured to treat us to a Play—And Announced her Intentions accordingly.

| A Play, Coteries, | (CHAPTER 17TH) | Balls and Suppers |

Young Ladies ought to be seen and Not heard

The Play was the Beggars Opera—And it being the first thing of the kind I had ever seen, I did nothing but laugh and cry during the whole representation for which I was rated by Mrs Fleming who declared it was quite against the Rules of Polite Decorum and betrayed a Vulgar Rusticity to laugh or Cry at a Play House—Nor was my Cousin without a Lecture from my Aunt for talking too loud in the Green Room to a Pretty Gentleman who paid her some Compliments—We had some pleasant Neighbours in Glocester Streets particular the Crawfords, and the Cramers who lived vis a vis where were two Daughters and Nine Sons—It was the greatest

48

treat we could get to drink Tea with Kitty
Cramer who had always five or six of her
Brothers to flirt and play small plays with us and
who was herself a smart droll little Piece—But
we lost this Indulgence by Graces one Night
dressing herself out in White and putting a Ring
on her finger as Mrs Coghill Cramer for my
Aunt Robert Herberts Children told the Parlour
Ladies what passd and my Aunt Cuffe ran up
and stripp'd her Daughter of her Bridal Attire
Scolding her most unmercifully—After which
our Intercourse with the Cramers was much
curtail'd and watchfully Inspected—My Aunt
R Herbert lived in Mecklenburg street—She
was my Fathers Youngest Sister a Widow with
three Daughters then Children and bold ones
enough—On the Other side lived my Aunt
Herbert of Cumberland Street my Mothers
sister with their Son Edward and three unmarried Daughters—This family Junto was encreased by the Arrival of my Aunt Eyre and her
Son Edward, who took a House next Door to
my Aunt R Herbert Mecklenburg Street—And
five of the Muckrus Herberts came to board
with my Aunt Robert Herbert—In this Neighbourhood we experienced a great Encrease of
Happiness for Ned Eyre Who was the greatest
Oddity and Spenthrift in the World kept open
House for all his Cousins—the whole set met
every Night at his House where there was a
Pope Joan Party—and a Sideboard laid out with
Olives Sweetmeats and every Luxury—Another

fund of Amusement to us was my Aunt R
Herberts Garden which was a large handsome
one for a Dublin One—Whenever my two
Aunts were out we clubd and had a feast in the
Summer House—there we read, wrote Novels,
and romantickized with the Muckrus Girls who
were as fantastic as Romance and the Wilds of
Muckrus could make them.

We had now Childrens Balls breakfasts Suppers
&c where Mr Kelly the famous dancing Master
presided, And No drawing Room or Levee ever
displayd half the State, form, dress, and fuss
that were seen in those Parties—Our Chief
Heroines were Lady Catherine Nugent—Miss
Glascott—and Grace Cuffe—such visitting,
such formality and such huffishness was not to
be met any where—Lady Catherine Nugent
was an only Daughter very handsome, very Conceited, and very Accomplished—her Spirit however was very turbulent and No Party ever passd
without a fracas between her and her Governess
—She was a most graceful little Creature about
the Age of Grace Cuffe and between those two
Belles there was a terrible Rivalry—and Endless quarelling—but where her Ladyship had no
Rival she was all Affability and Condescention
—We had besides concerts and other Parties
but it all ended in Lady Catherines picking up
such a flirtation that her Governess tore her one
Night from the Ball room and her father thought
it full time to keep her more within bounds at
home.

We were not without our more domestic feuds for in a party of nineteen or twenty Cousin Germans in the three Neighbouring Streets we had continual disputes, and Competitions— however we were all very fond of each Other— and spent our time most happily.

| An Orphan Heiress | (CHAPTER 18TH) | Domestic Feuds |

Inviduous Grave! how dost thou rend in Sunder Whom Love has knit, and Sympathy made one

Fanny Blennerhasset now arrived at my Aunt Cuffes for the Winter—She was Niece to my Father, an Orphan, an heiress, and lived about amongst her Relations the general Pet of Every one who knew her—When her Father and Mother died she and her two Brothers were left Orphans—Consequently she was their doating piece—They both grew up to be young men and both died in one Year leaving Her the disconsolate Heiress of a very large Property—This and the Unworthy derilection of an Early Lover threw a Shade of Sorrow over a Disposition Naturally Chearful—She had traveld much —had seen much of the World—And always lived in the highest Circles—She was very religious and had every Accomplishment Money could procure—besides great talents delightful Manners and a pleasing Person—Thus gifted her Society was much Courted and in Dublin

her Life was a continued Scene of Dress and
Dissipation—Mrs Fleming was her purse
bearer, and always employd in setting her off for
Company—I miss'd my old Chum a good deal
but was soon invited to the toilette and gave my
humble opinion on her daily Decorations—As
she always consulted my taste in Conjunction
with Mrs Fleming and Monsieur Le —— The
celebrated Frisseurs.

I soon received from the Miliner at her Expence
a beautiful pink Sattin Slip, pink Satin Shoes,
and a Suit of pink Satin Ribbon—A beautiful
Cap and flowers—A full Suit of rich Gawze
trimmd with blond Lace and plenty of Mare-
chale Powder and Rose Pomatum—Thus
equipp'd—I figured away at the Childrens
Balls, the finest Young Lady in the room—Add
to this that I had always the lone of six or seven
Pearl Pins, as She mostly wore a fine Set of
Diamonds and insisted on my wearing her
Pearls—My Aunt Cuffe too had a very fine Set
of Garnets which she lent me occasionally for
a Change, indeed She, and the two amiable
Heiresses shewd me every kindness whilst I
lived amongst them—And my friend Mrs
Fleming's Care and Attention I can never forget—My Aunt however was of a jealous disposition and accused Mrs Fleming of engrossing my Affections too Much, till the quarrel
rose so high that Mrs Fleming left the House—
She was our Relation and the poor Womans in-
digent Circumstances left her and her Children

wholly dependant on my Aunts Bounty—I cried
so bitterly at being the Cause of this fracas that
my Aunt took me out to Tea in hopes of amusing me, As Mrs Fleming had incensed her too
much to think of sending after her—At night I
went to my Solitary Room quite disconsolate—
I miss'd my Bed fellow, and miss'd my Supper
—I had been the Cause of her dismissal from
her only home, And I was far, very far from my
own dear home and friends—My Lamentations
and Sobs brought up Fanny Hasset who wanted
to sleep with me, but this I would not permit as
my Bed was in the Garret—She reason'd all she
could with me, but finding my tears encrease
she left me, promising to use all her Interest
next Day in Promoting a Reconciliation—Next
Morning she said so much to my Aunt that
Mrs Fleming was sent for, appeased, and fully
reinstated before Evening—Fanny Blennerhasset was indeed always Pacificator and Arbi-
tress in all the family Quarrels of the three
Streets as her Superiour Judgement and Excel-
lence were acknowledged by All.
Mrs Wall of Coolnamuck Now came over from
England and often invited me to her House in
Dublin—She also took me out to Dalkeith on a
Visit to my old friend Mr Dan Cuffe who lived
there as Parish Minister—This was a real treat
as he had a very pretty Place there and was himself always one of my most respected friends
from my earliest Infancy.

" —*Oh then the longest Summers Day*
" *Seem'd too much in haste*—

I had also another Solace in the regular Sundays
Visit of Susy Light who lived many Years with
us when I was a Child and was now Servant to
Mrs Wall—She always brought her pocket full
of Cakes or Barley Sugar, and the poor Girl
being as great a Stranger in Dublin as myself
often wept with Joy to see Me.

There were this Year grand Masquerades in
Dublin—We saw Masks—Fanny Hasset and
some of the Herberts went to them but my
Aunt thought her Grace and I too Young to
frequent such Places.

It was a very Gay Winter—The Parliament met,
and the Town as full as Possible—The Fran-
chises that Year were remarkably beautiful—
The Dublin Volunteers newly dress'd and
accoutred continually paraded the Streets, Inshort Dublin never appeard to greater Advantage—But—Still I sigh'd for dear Home! And
a Walk on the Circular Road gave me more
pleasure than all those gaieties as it reminded
me of the Country and my Native Air—At
length the long Winter pass'd away—And the
numerous Flower Girls announced the returning Spring—The first Bunch of flowers I got
threw me into strong Hysterick of grief and

54

Joy—The Well known smell of the Sweet Briar
and the Hyacinths sweet Perfume brought our
Gravel Walk and my Mothers little Garden so
fully to my recollection that I wept and sobbd
over them—An Acute Sensibility was ever my
foible, my Bane, and my Solace; and I cannot
express what I felt whilst weeping over these
sweet Remembrancers of Spring, and my
Natural Soil—My Mothers long sheets of
Coarse Paper scribbled all over with hers or the
family's hand writing always threw me into
Extacies of Joy, but especially after she had
heard from the dear Boys, who I had the pleasure
to hear were going on swimmingly with their
learning and were great favourites with Mr
Hare and his family, and with all their School-
fellows—But great and excessive indeed was my
delight, when a Letter from my Mother announced her Intention of being in Dublin on
such a Day and mentioning that she, my Father,
Mrs Jephson, Salisbury and Fanny Jephson
were all to come up in our Coach, and after
spending a fortnight in Dublin would take me
down with them to Carrick where I should meet
the Boys, Whose Vacation was near at hand.
I was for some Days in a perfect Delirium of
Joy—Never before had I left my Father and
Mother—Never been parted for so long a time
from my Brothers and Sisters—We had great
Parties for them when they arrived at which the
Jephsons were much admired—in return they
got us invited to Mrs Hughes their Hostess on

a Masquerade Night and her House was so
crouded that we saw all that [was] worth Seeing
at the Masquerades—My Aunt Cuffe and Grace
as the time approached for our leaving them
were piqued that I did not shew more Concern
on the Occasion, but the Pleasing Prospects
before me outweigh'd every Consideration—
My Mother paid off my Masters who express'd
their Approbation of my Assiduity and Improvement under them, And once more I found
Myself seated in the Old Coach, and destined
for Carrick on Suir.

The Concern manifested by my Dublin friends
and the regret I felt at Parting them kept me
decently Sober for some time—but every Mile-
stone we pass'd encreased the Exultation and
Joy of my Heart, at the thoughts of reaching
home once more—My Aunt and the Whole
Party in Glocester Street promised to spend the
ensuing Summer with us—After resting some
Days in Carrick and laying my whole Budget of
Dublin Anecdote before my little Sisters we
took a most Pleasurable Jaunt to Cashel for Our
two dear Boys and Shocked all the Genteels of
that City by our Vulgar Joy at meeting them—
Once more we assembled altogether at our Dear
Carrick Dwelling—All the Education we had
received had not worn away our rusticity and
fondness for Play—and we resumed our follies
with encreased Avidity.

A Review—
   Odd   (CHAPTER 20TH)   And
Characters   Ludicrous
                                         Incidents

" *Laugh where we must, be candid where we can* "

An Event in the county Kilkenny, Now caused
great Commotion and filld all the Newspapers
in England and Ireland—Sir John Blunden and
the New raised Volunteers fell out—they burned
him in Effegy, and he in contempt warmd himself at the fire—A fierce Newspaper War ensued
which was Publishd in both Kingdoms—Sir
John was the greatest Oddity of his time—He
kept my Aunt Blunden whom he calld his Joany
entirely at home—He would let none of his
Sons go to a public school, and kept his Daughters a set of beautiful Girls shut up in a Nursery
making Lace under an old Governess and their
Mammy Nurse till they were 15 or 16—It was
ridiculous to see a Set of fine tall young Women
so completely under Pupilage—He had a very
curious Cabinet which he took over to London
with him and throwing it over his Shoulders he
hawked it about till he was offerd thirteen
hundred Guineas for it—this Sum he accepted,
and immediately expended it in Jewels for his
Joany as he called his Wife.
After his Fracas with the Volunteers he signi-
fied his Intention of treating his Joany to a Sight
of the Review near Carrick—They put up at our
house—A most curious figure he cut, dress'd in

an old greasy Suit of blue Cloth, an old Shabby
Hat And a Wig twenty Years old—He made
great fun of his old friends the Volunteers, and
swore he would get out of the Carriage and inspect them—Accordingly he threw off his Hat
and Wig, put an old Newspaper about his head
to remind them of the Paper War—over this he
wore his rusty Hat, and march'd on commanding his Joany to follow him—In vain she remonstrated, he persisted, and she knew he must
be obey'd so she trudged after him in a plain
flower'd Cotton—The first Party we ken'd was
Lord Tyrone's and family with Lady Ely, the
Lady Gores Mr Uniacke and Many Others—
Sir John vowed he must have one kiss from the
beautiful Lady Elizabeth Gore, and marching
up to the party with his Newspaper spread over
his Neck and Shoulders he saluted her Ladyship most kindly—She was all astonishment Not
knowing who he was whilst Lord Tyrone and
his Company were in fits of Laughter at his
strange appearance and the Consternation of her
Ladyship—He then march'd up towards the
Kilkenny Regiment, And after making much
fun for himself in jibing with them he walk'd off
—When we quitted the field he took a Snack at
our house and went home very well pleased with
himself and us—The Next Day we had another
Relation Sir Richard Wheeler Cuffe quarterd on
us from Kilkenny—He was a very hard drinker
and there was nothing but tippling whilst he
staid—In the Evening we went to an Assembly,

where I danced with Mr Wheeler his Brother
Lord Dunsany, and some of the smartest Beaux
in the Room of which I was not a little proud
and it was a bon bouche to my Vanity for many
Months after—The Volunteers were invited to
a Grand Dinner at Curraghmore given on purpose for them, Many were the laughable Stories
told of them—One eat Salt with his Grapes and
Sugar with his Wallnuts, Another offer'd Lady
Tyrone a well aired Chair, which he (A very fat
man) had sat on—Inshort the Wits had their
own fun—However we spent a delightful Week
of it, and were quite dejected when it was over—
We now got a very fine Harpsichord over from
England and Nothing but Music was heard all
over the House—As my Brothers had Set us all
Book mad, I set all music Mad—My Father
was eternally at his flute and we had Jocanes,
Jews-harps, and an old wretched guitar going
from Morning till Night.

A Lunatic Wanderer	(CHAPTER 21ST)	Charitable Benefactors

" *Demoniac Phrenzy, Moping Melancholy,*
" *And moonstruck Madness—*

About this time a Young Person appeard here
dressd in Mens Cloaths who gave out that he
was a Woman—He calld himself Miss Gore—
Said he had escaped from a Mad house where
his Relations put him on Account of an Attach-

ment they disapproved of—He said he was of a
Genteel family but would not tell their Names—
And what between his flightiness and reserve
we could Never arrive at any Certainty either
as to his Sex or Situation—He really had all
the appearance of being long Confined—His
shoulders seem'd to have been tied back his legs
were crampd, and he shriek'd at the Name of a
Straight Waistcoat—His face was very handsome with the finest pair of black Eyes long
Dark Eyelashes and arched Eyebrows possible
—When dressd in Male Attire he appeard like
a Woman—but in Womens Cloaths lookd
Coarse and Masculine—He told such piteous
Tales and sang such Melancholy Songs, that he
quite soften'd all the Ladies hearts, so that they
were always bestowing some charitable dona-
tion on him but he would Never take Money—
Nice Cloaths he delighted in, and was soon
equip'd from head to foot—My Mother kept
him in her house out of Pity, And he made himself so interesting that he often spent weeks at
Castletown and the different places about the
Neighbourhood, In his lunatic fits he often
absconded but was pursued and brought back—
The Gentlemen laugh'd at the Ladies about him,
but he was too great a favourite to be relinquish'd on their raillery—At length he found
Means to Escape and we never heard more of
him—Mrs Carshore was then alive and bestowd much care and Attention on him though
Mr Carshore often scolded her for encouraging

so mysterious a Person—He sometimes made use of very illiterate Expressions but in general his Conversation was interesting, his Language high flown and his Manners extremely insinuating.

My Mother had Now some returns of her old Nervous Complaints but by degrees they wore off—Mrs Charles our Governess had left us so I was become housekeeper of the Money and keys—In My Mothers Illness My Uncle William who was here, out of tricks stole thirty Guineas I had for the use of the House—but my trepidation was so great, that my father perswaded him after two days to return it—From this Period My Mothers Constitution took a favourable turn and She soon shook off all her Complaints.

END OF BOOK THE FIRST

—" *Sing heavenly Muse*——
" *Things unattempted yet in Prose or Rhyme*—

We had now a new Visiter Miss Hare of Cashel
—I had seen her once before when we went to
bring the Boys home from School, And then
thought her one of the prettiest growing Girls I
had ever beheld—I was all astonishment to see
her in a few Months quite a large Woman—In
fact she was more grown in a few Months than
is common in so many Years—She quite put
me out of conceit with Myself, and I began to
fear I should never grow taller—Indeed I never
did encrease to any responsible Size.

Miss Hare was armed cap a pie for Conquest—
She came dress'd in a white Muslin with a
Colourd Border of her own Embroidery—She
was now a fine Woman but not the pretty florid
little Girl she was when I first saw her—We
were at first all on our good behaviour, and
heartily sick of each others Company—but by
degrees we relaxed from our formality and never

63

sure was any one better prepared for our Harum Scarums than Eliza Hare—Mad with spirits she was a Veteran Chief in every Mischief—We had an Old Milch Ass here for my Mother, and on this Animal she used to Straddle dressd out at all points with a remarkable large Bell Hoop and a pair of lace Lappets flying in the Air—She was then but fourteen but her size forced her to dress quite Womanly—She led us into a new Species of Culinary Preparations—Namely making up washes and beautifying Lotions—We had two or three of the Tenants every day hunting the Country for different sorts of Herbs, and such Plaisters and Milk Washes as We made up would be enough to ruin all the fair Skins in the Circassian Marts—Every Night we were wrapd up like Pomatum Sticks in greasy brown Paper, and I'm sure if any Stranger had seen us at Night they would have taken She, Fanny and I for three Egyptian Mummies ready Embalmd—Our Hands, Faces, and Chests were compleatly cover'd with Tallow and Brown Paper, made into various sorts of Ointments—Our Arms were Suspended in the Air by strong Ropes fastend to the Tester of the Bed—Our feet tied to the Valance to stretch our Legs and Make us grow tall, or to prevent our kicking and plunging in the Night by which we might have rubbd off the Precious Ointments that coverd us—To divert our Agonies, which never let us sleep till near Morning, we got into a Way of telling Stories in Bed,

And the laughter they excited, was the only thing that saved us from sinking under Excruciating Torments as real Martyrs to Beauty!

The fruit Season threw us into a great Dilemma —To spoil Complexions after all the pains we had taken and all the Sacrifices we had made to Beauty, was dreadful—but to stay from the fruit trees was impossible—We therefore set about making a Set of Masks—which we wore for some Days, but finding they Attracted the Sun beams we provided ourselves with thick Linen Veils and our Aprons—This was near proving fatal to Betty Hare, for crossing the Lawn one Day with her Apron over her, she step'd into the Pond, with a fine Pair of new Pink Slippers and was hauld out half suffocated with Mud and more grievously lamenting her new Pink Shoes—We had many Violent Battles, but Nothing produced such furious Ones as our Patriotism—She was a violent Stickler for Cashel, and we were as bigotted for Carrick— Nothing we shewd her here pleased after Cashel —Curraghmore was a Hovel to Thomastown— Besborough inferior to Dundrum—and Castletown not to be compared to the Palace in Cashel —This brazen Assertion provoked us beyond Measure, and many a boxing Bout the Boys and She had about it—I cannot recollect half the Wonderful Incidents her Visit produced, but if she was here, her tongue and Memory would furnish a Volume, as ludicrous as ever was written.

" *Beauty has been the Delight and Torment of the
World, ever since it began!*
Vide the Spectator No. 144

Some time before Miss Hare came we received
at a Castletown Ball an Account of Sir John
Blundens Death—My Mother had now to Pay
a Visit of Condolence to her Sister which was a
Meeting Purposely delay'd and Much dreaded
by both—We could not well leave Miss Hare
behind so it was agreed she should Accompany
Us—As neither of us knew much of the late
Sir John personally, We thought only of the
Variety our Journey Promised, And spent the
whole preceding Week in redoubling our Cos-
metic Labours, In dyeing clearstarching and
Gaufreying our old fripperies for the Occasion
—After Many Disappointments from the Tythe
business and Bad Weather we set out on our
Journey—and after breaking down five or six
times on the Road we arrived at Castle
Blunden.

The first Mortification we experienced was to
find that the Blundens had what we so earnestly
sought and Miss'd, viz the Whitest Hands,
Noses, and Teeth in the World—The More we
scrubb'd the more desperately Red did our
Skins grow—Every Day after Dinner we retired
to our Room with Shame and Dismay at the red-

66

ness of our Hands and Noses—which was encreased by the Blunden mischievously laughing
at it, And many a Weeping Bout did it cost us
—Before we left Carrick we thought ourselves
amazing fine having Notably Transmogrified
every Wearable we could beg buy or Borrow—
But here again we faild—for the Blundens just
become Mistresses of large fortunes entirely
eclipsed us—They were always dressd with
most exact Nicety in the finest Laces and most
costly Trinkets—We had neither Lace nor
Trinkets, and if we had would have scarce ven-
turd to Wear them as Diamond Rings or fine
Bracelets would have renderd our Capital Defect
more glaring—We however ventured to display
our flaming bobb'd Earings for Which we
underwent the painful Operation of boring in
Carrick—Indeed with all our Œconomical Arts
our Wardrobes were so defective that we wished
ourselves back a thousand times, and were continually weeping at one Mortification or another
—To add to it Old Doctor B came out with his
young beautiful Wife who was as superlatively
fine as Opulence could make her—When the
Doctor got fluster'd after Dinner he made such
game of the Cashel Girls that my friend Eliza
Hare openly burst out crying—Indeed he was
remarkably rude to her for which we complained him to my Aunt—and all present engaged in the Quarrel, some shocked at it, others
enjoying it—However in our own Room we
comforted ourselves by reflecting that he was a

very Old fellow and that his Lady who was a
Stay makers Daughter would soon flirt him to
the grave.

Our Room was a small Closet in the upper
Story—with a Window looking out on a Dark
Lobby which parted it from the large Barrack
Room where all the Gentlemen dress'd and lay
—We had only poor Mammy Shortal the family
dry Nurse on the same floor to protect us from
their Waggeries, And many a time their boister-
ous Mirth brought the poor old Soul to our Assistance—She was just the Counterpart of our
Old Mary—One Day in a Hurry we found ourselves without Pomatum and had a great battle
for the Scrapings of the Pomatum Pot and the
use of the Powder Puff—When we were startled
by a loud Tittering at the Lobby Window—We
found to our great Confusion that we forgot to
draw the Window Curtain and the Whole Set
of Gentlemen were stationed giggling at the
Casement where they had heard our fracas and
seen our Tears besides catching us En Chemise
or hard by—With the Assistance of Mammy
Shortal we routed them back to their Barrack
but no sooner was this Victory gained than
another Disaster completely undid us—We in
our Confusion overturned the Pot-de-Chambre
and the two Doors being opposite the Whole
Contents meander'd across the Lobby into their
Barrack—Immediately the House rang with
their laughter and left us au Desespoir.

{ 1780 }

Various
frolicks
CHAPTER 24TH
Family
pedigrees

" *And still as each repeated Pleasure tired*
" *Succeeding Sport the Mirthful Band inspired*

The Gauntlet we ran at Dinner on this Occasion
was terrible, Nothing could stop the general
Titter that ran against us—As we had six or
seven Neighbours in the Barrack room As bold
Boys as My Aunt used to say with a God bless
them as any in the Kingdom—Our Proximity
to them above stairs left us exposed to many In-
conveniences, but they amply recompensed us
by serenading us every Night at the Lobby
Window from as Many fiddles as there were
Gentlemen.

My Aunt and Mother wept over the late Sir
John's Death in Secret for the Young People
would never let his name be mention'd for fear
of hurting their Mother, and she out of Gratitude for their good Intentions indulged them in
the Prohibition—The present Sir John was very
handsome—with a delightful flow of Spirits and
had no fault but an overlove for the Fair Sex and
the Bottle—His three Eldest Sisters were then
married, Mrs Weymes, Mrs Baker, and Mrs
Bolton—His two Brothers William and Ovrington and his two unmarried Sisters Charlotte and
Araminta lived with him and My Aunt at Castle
Blunden—They were all uncommonly handsome Men and Women—And having nothing

to trouble them were full of Life and Spirits—
Mrs Weymes and Mrs Baker were often at
Castle Blunden as their places were within an
hours drive of it—Mrs Bolton came there once
or twice a Year from her Residence in the Co
Wexford—Each of those Ladies had large
families so that at Castle Blunden there was always a full and a Merry House—They were
then indeed a most pleasant family—We had
charming Boating there as a large Lake ran just
under the Windows and we could step from
them into the pleasure Boat whilst six or seven
fiddles serenaded us on the Water—The gardens
and immense Range of Hot Houses were fill'd
with fruit—The latter were remarkably fine as
the late Sir John piqued himself on their eclipsing the finest Hot Houses in the Kingdom—
Our Mornings were spent Nutting about the
Woods, and the Evenings in boating, Card playing, Music, Dancing; or Romping and playing
small Plays—Each Night we adjourned an hour
to the Nursery, to visit or plague old Mammy
Shortal, and her Pet Nurseling William Blunden whom we always found posted at her fire
with a Book in his hand for they gave him No
Peace below in his studies.

We soon got quite free with the Girls and their
affable good humour reconciled us to their
Eclipsing us in Complexion and Finery—Every
Hour was frolic and Pleasure, Every Scene Delight, When it was Suddenly Interupted by the
following Incident—We received a Letter from

My Aunt Cuffe, informing us that She, Grace, Fanny Blennerhasset and Mrs Fleming would all be with us at Carrick in a few Days according to the promise they made us in Dublin.

We wept most bitterly at this Interruption to our Carreer of Pleasure—Betty Hare in particular was quite Mad at it—She had but just got over the Mortification of a high Spirit Eclipsed in Beauty, and was so deeply engaged in flirtation amongst the Gentlemen that She flatter'd herself her Wit amply Made up for her inferiority in personal Delicacy—She damn'd My Aunt Cuffe most heartily in her jesting Way— And in Serious Earnest we both cried ourselves heartsick at quitting the Mirthful Haunts of Castle Blunden.

Generous Friends	(CHAPTER 25TH)	A projected Marriage

" *Union the Bond of all things and of Man*

My Goodnatured Aunt Cuffe and her Affectionate family were quite delighted to see us— Grace Cuffe and Fanny Blennerhasset came loaded with Presents for Me—My Aunt Brought Me a New white Cloth Habit, a gold lace Hat and Feather, A Fine side saddle, Bridle, etcetera—Grace Cuffe a Chip Hat and Suit of gawze full Trimmed with quantities of Lilac and Straw Colour Ribbon—Fanny Hasset a Straw Colourd Lutestring gown — Thus

71

Equipd I promised to go to all the Parties we were invited to for knowing My Penchant for home they made that a Condition—Betty Hare condoled with me for not having had my New finery at Castle Blunden, Though for her own Sake she was Glad of it—She now expected to come in for a Share of the expected Gaiety here, but two or three Days after my Aunts arrival Mr Hare came for her, and against all our earnest Entreaties said she must return with him on urgent business—After Dinner she and I retired to our Room, And with many Sobs and Tears she told Me she was going home to be married—I expressd my Astonishment as she had never before hinted the Affair to me—She then Mentiond that her Father had provided Mr Clarke his Head Usher as her Husband—He was a Clergyman but had no fortune but the place of Usher, and some farms he rented—Mr Hare however thought him so clever and sensible that he doubted not but that he would soon make a Rapid Fortune, if he got any kind of Preferment—The Next Day my Friend Eliza Hare was wheel'd away, leaving us all in deep Woe after her.

A few Posts after brought us an Account of her Wedding—Every One was astonish'd that Mr Hare would dispose of his Daughter at fifteen Years of Age without any settled Property—but it soon proved that he had rightly foreseen Mr Clarkes propitious Destiny, for he has since been extremely fortunate both in the Church and in

Lay Matters—After Betty Hares, (I shall henceforth call her Mrs Clarkes) Departure, we had
Nothing but Dinners and Parties of all sorts
throughout the Neighbourhood for my Aunt
Cuffe and her Girls—Grace Cuffe had been
taught to ride at the riding school—She had a
Beautiful little black Horse and I had a beautiful
strawberry one the same Size which I was taught
to manage every Day by the Barrack Riding
Master—Thus caparison'd we spent the Mornings in Horsemanship and riding about the
Country—Our first Dinner Debut was at Curraghmore where I exhibited my new straw
colour gown and Gawze Suit and Lilac Ribbons,
and made my Aunt and Cousins laugh heartily
all the Way at my Panicks and Nervous
Rusticity.

We were Next asked to a Grand Fête Champêtre given by Mrs English on which Occasion
Grace Cuffe cut up a piece of Buff Sarsnet between us—We got them made into Shepherdesses a picturesque sort of Short Jacket then
worn—hers was Mitred with Lilac persian,
Mine with blue—The Mitring quill'd with
white Love Ribbon—We wore Small white
Chip Chapeaus at one side of our Heads
with bunches of Natural Flowers—Whilst
every one admired the Elegance of our Fancy
Dresses.

Mrs Honoria English our Entertainer was a gay
old Widow Lady who had settled in Carrick on
the Death of her Husband to spend amongst her

73

friends and Relations a Jointure of 800 a Year
she having No Child or particular Heir—
Thirty Years of her Life she had lived immured
in a lonesome Wild of the County Waterford—
Her Husbands Death left her full Mistress of
herself and Fortune which she resolved to lavish
in pleasing her own Social Disposition—Immediately on her Settling here she open'd up her
House and Coffers, entertained every One, and
sent valuable Presents to all her Neighbours—
She sent Lady Tyrone and her Daughters
dresses of the finest Japan India Muslin with a
profusion of rich Lace Trimming—She gave
My Mother a rich India Shawl and I got a suit
of Muslin trimmed all over with the finest Edg-
ing besides Books Trinkets and other Presents
—Every Year she gave half a Dozen Balls and
as many publick Breakfasts in the rural Stile—
She had a general Levée every Sunday of All
Sorts and Sizes and her house was the general
Resort of Young and Old, Grave and Gay—In
her Retirement she had read much and Philo-
sophized More—She was always the Life of
every Company but preferred the Gentlemens
Society to the Ladies—She did not hesitate at
a Double Entendre if it served her purpose
and was often very keen and Satyrical on her
Acquaintance.
After the first round of Dinners and Parties
were over We had full leisure for our Rides and
were continually on Horseback the rest of the
Season.

" *Ferments arise, Imprison'd Factions roar*

In Autumn a dreadful Rebellion broke out in
our Parishes which lasted for three Years, And
my poor Aunt was frighten'd out of her Wits
thinking as we had Stacks of Corn up to our very
Windows that we should all be burned alive
some Night or Other by the Right Boys who
were then Marauding every where—At this
period John Wharton died of a violent fever
which carried him off in a few Days—The Fever
in the House added to my Aunts Terrors so that
she had but an uneasy Time of it—Lord Waterford Lent us twelve Horses and Cars—Lord
Desart came over to offer his Assistance—We
had all Mr Coxes and Mr Blundens Men and
Horses and odd ones from every family round
us—Fifty or Sixty Notices were sent for one
Day, to give them an opportunity of Stealing
and subtracting the Tythes—Feeding and providing for such a Number of Men and Horses
was a dreadful Expence and trouble—Every
Soul in the House was out from four in the
Morning till 12 or one at Night, Counting the
Sheaves to get the Property ensured on the
County—My Father stood out each Night
patrolling to see that all was Safe and My
Mother sat out in the gravel Walk with a Candle

and her Account Book till break of Day, Whilst
every Individual amongst us had a Station to
guard—Our Carmen never came home till
Morning and we were obliged to send fresh
posses to relieve them, besides spies scatter'd
throughout the Parishes to watch that None was
subtracted by Night—We had not a Servant in
the House the Whole time, and were in continual Peril of Our Lives.

After the Drawing we had Numberless Lawsuits in the Bishops Court with Many of the
Head Parishioners who joined in the Combination which continued three successive Years.

My Aunt Cuffe and family remained with us
that Year till all our troubles were over—And
before she left us imparted the important Secret
that Mr Maxwell only Son of Lord Farnham
had proposed for Grace Cuffe and she now engaged My fathers Approbation of their union
which if every thing turned out as expected, was
to take place on their Return to Dublin—My
Father and Mother of Course wished them all
happiness but nothing was to be mentioned
before Grace who was somewhat pettish on the
Occasion—They left us before the Winter set
in hard and in due time we heard of the Young
Couples Marriage—Lord Farnham soon after
got an Earldom, so that Grace became Lady
Maxwell almost on her Marriage—The first
Year they spent in wandering from place to
place—They then Settled at Adamstown Lord
Maxwells Estate—After 4 or 5 Years Lord

Farnham died, and they then came in for the
Title and an immense Property but never had a
Child to inherit it—She continued to write to
me for two or three Years and I have often Met
her since always the same friendly affectionate
Creature—Thus two of My Young Friends were
off the Carpet at the age of fifteen or sixteen—
My Cronies wished Me the same Luck but alas!

" *Clouds interpose, waves roar, and Winds Arise.*"

| A Play | (CHAPTER 27TH) | A Winter fireside |

" *Alike all Ages, Dames of Ancient Days*
" *Have led their Children through the mirthful
     Maze*

All our Travels and Growth did not prevent the
Jephsons and us from still acting the part of
fools and Children—To amuse our leisure
Winter Hours, We proposed acting a Play in
Mrs Jephson large Parlour—It was the Pad-
lock we performd and we made a real farce of it
—We had only Some old Bed Curtains for
scenery and every thing else suitable to them—
However we had no one to criticize but our
friend Mr Billy Galwey and Mr Roukee our
drawing Master—God knows we had more fuss
rehearsing and preparing than a Head Theatre
—Mr Galwey, Roukee, Revd Thomas Rankin,
Captain Dennis an Officer and Major Rivers an

77

old wandering Madman were the only Beaux
we had this Winter to keep us alive.

The Jephsons however knew how to strike fun
out of every thing and we could not have a Set
of Swains more adapted to us—Roukee taught
both families to draw, And I learn'd more from
him than I did in Dublin—He was a Waterford
Master and a Capital good one especially in taking most inimitable likenesses—I copied The
Bishop of Waterford picture and as his Lordship dined here every Visitation he knew it
immediately.

Our Chief amusement now was gathering round
the Parlour fire in a large Circle, where the
Jephsons and we used to laugh ourselves Sick,
for they were Mad with Spirits—We had always a plate of remarkable Winter Pears and
Apples and sometimes we broke open the Apple
Room Where we eat and romped away with
Light Hearts and few things to vex us Whilst
our Mothers sat in social chat in the Parlour.

A Disconsolate Widow	(CHAPTER 28TH)	Droll Incidents

" *Nothing but Groans and Sighs were heard
      Around*
" *And Echo Multiplied each dismal Sound*

When My Aunt Cuffe was leaving us she recommended to My Mother to take Mrs Cooke her

Niece as Lodger—She was Daughter to Lord
Desart my Mothers eldest Brother deceased—
She Married for Love and her Husband dying
soon, left her a Young handsome Widow with
two Daughters—Her grief at losing him was
most Excessive, but though Melancholy in itself it produced Many ludicrous Circumstances
—She shut herself up in her house at Clontarf
and for Weeks together kept her Room, Nor
would she admit either friend or Servant to
soften the Rigours of her Seclusion—She resolved to put her whole House in Mourning,
but kept it a Profound Secret lest her friends
should remonstrate against it—She privately
sent for a Dublin Upholsterer and paid a Carriage for bringing him out—He was shewn at
Midday into a large dark Room where the fair
Widow sat (with a Taper burning) in the deepest Woe and dress'd in her Sables—She arose
at his Entrance, received him graciously but
Silently, and after sitting sometime weeping she
told the poor wonder stricken Upholsterer that
she had a Job for him which she expected he
would perform with all Privacy and fidelity—
She then shewd him every hole and corner of
the house—bespoke hangings of black Paper
for every Room—Black Beds, black chair-
covers, black Window Curtains—The affrighted
Man listend with horror—In the Midst of her
harangue she discoverd a Carriage driving down
the Avenue and fearing the Upholsterer would
be seen She calld to her maid, " Oh Betty lock

79

him up lock him up—Betty dressd in deep black
ran to execute her Mistresses orders but the dis-
mayd Upholsterer gave one Spring from the
Top of the Stairs to the Bottom And though he
made her pay Coach hire for carrying him out,
He was glad to escape with his Life on foot to
Dublin.

She had already got all the Woodwork of her
house painted black even to the Stable Doors
and Mangers—this gave rise to another droll
Incident—An Old Gentleman who call'd there
on Money Matters had his Horse put up in the
Stable—It happen'd to be a White one, and
having well rubbed its snowy hide It was led out
to its Master an elegant Pye ball—The Old
Gentleman not knowing his Rozenante kicked
up a Riot for his own Horse with the Stable Boy
who desiring no better Sport humourd the Joke
and laughingly bore a caning for his imperten-
ence, till Mrs Cooke was forced to go out herself and pacify the Old Gentleman's wrath by
explaining that her Stables were newly painted
—She indeed carried her Mourning so far as to
paint even the flowerpots black that adorned her
Windows.

At our House she arrived with all the trappings
of Woe that Mourning could display—Her
poor Children were perfect dumb Statues with
Confinement and Melancholy, but my Mother
bullied her out of Many Whims, and got her to
put on second Mourning—She rode out every
Day and all the Gentlemen round this were

dying for Love of her—She had two or three
Sir Roger de Coverlys in her Suite who I am
convinced pined in Secret, And were never the
Same Men after it but contrary to the general
Opinion she never chose a second Husband.
When she was somewhat cured of her Melan-
cholies, we had nothing but innocent Mirth and
Conviviality in the Neighbourhood—we breakfasted dined and Supp'd out under the Shade—
Her Admirers gave us constant Fete Cham-
petres, and these were follow'd by Cold Dinners
at Curraghmore, Kilcash, Besborough &c—In
short every deserted or fine place in the Neighbourhood was enlivened by the Gay Throng—
We had Always dancing in the Evening on the
green Turf and regular Assemblies once a Week
in Carrick—The Widows certainly then kept up
the credit of the Vicinage—Mrs Cooke, Mrs
Jephson, Mrs English, Mrs Dobbyn, all rich
all captivating though not all Young—Captains
Curtis and Percival of the 12th Dragoons were
in All our Parties—Captain Curtis was an
humble Adorer of Miss Carshore—and afterwards married her—Percival attach'd himself
entirely to Mrs Cooke and escorted the fair
Widow in all her Excursions—Writing of
Officers I shall recite a Carrick anecdote I forgot to Mention which happend the preceding
Year whilst I was in Dublin—There was a
beautiful Creature a Miss Grace lived in Carrick with her Mother Mrs Grace, and her
Grandmother old Mrs Glasse a Clergymans

Widow—The two latter were hated in Carrick
and Mrs Carshore got my Mother to Matronize
the beautiful Anna Grace to all the Assemblies
—There was a Mr Pemberton an Officer
quarterd here who fell desperately in love with
her, but being ordered off to the Camp at Two
Mile Bridge near Clonmell he perswaded her to
Elope with him—My Father and Mother pursued them in their Carriage to the Camp and
found they had been married by one of those
itinerant Gentry called Couple Beggars—With
the Assistance of the Officers they forced them
to Clonmell and my Father married them again
by Licence Much against the Will of Mr Pemberton who afterwards took her out to the East
Indies and there forsook her—It was said indeed that she did not behave with due decorum
there.

| Boarding-school Traits | (Chapter 29th) | Reading Parties &c |

" *All Fools have still an Itching to deride*
" *And fain would be upon the laughing side*

At this time our four Girls went every Day to
Miss Englishes Boarding School in Carrick—
She was the Daughter of a Clergyman School-
master—And was in every Sense a compleat
Learned Lady—We had then a kind of Chaize
Marine which my Father christen'd Lady
Franceses Carriage in honour of my Sister

Fanny—It was shaped like a Waggon, but no
bigger than a common Chair—It had a Door
like a Bathing Box which compleatly shut it up
—Every Wet Day Lady Frances and her three
Companions went to School in this Vehicle like
Turkeys going to Market and afforded the
Town Wits the greatest amusement—Every
Evening Miss English used to come up to Tea
and a Reading Party consisting of Mr Rankin
the Carshores and Mrs Cooke who was a great
Amateur and Transcriber of Poetry—Miss English being a remarkable Reader was chief
Lecturer—At last however the young Ladies
affronted her by some Witticisms on her Latin
Learning Made by them and her pupil Miss
Carshore—She came up here one Night in a
furious Passion And declared she would never
give them further Instruction—from which
time they left her School—Miss Carshore now
Supplied her place as Lecturer aided by the
Reverend Thomas Rankin, who being highly
enamoured of the fair Widow Cooke was with
us every Evening—Whilst my Mother and
Mrs Carshore wished their Belle Lettres at the
Devil as it interupted all Vulgar Chat and Social
Converse.
On Saturday the 2d of June 1782 an old French
Woman came begging to us cover'd with Rags
and Sores—My Mother took her in out of
Charity, and bought her two Cotton Negligés—
She taught us all french capitally, and as Capit-
ally taught us to make Mushroom Soup and

Soupe Maigres—It was our chief Amusement
after our Lesson to gather Mushrooms and
Herbs for our Regale—With her good Will she
would have superadded Frogs &c but we declined that part of it.

Madame Bondagée being a parisian had a remarkable good Accent and a good Notion of
teaching french Grammatically—She was an
Enthusiast for her Pauvre Roi as she termed the
french King and gave us such an Account of the
Attachment of the french for their Sovereign
that none could suppose they would Murder
him and all his family shortly after as happen'd
in the French Revolution—Living so near Versailles she had all the Court Anecdotes by rote
and was really very amusing, but she fell into
drinking and there was then no bearing her
Temper and Vagaries.

| A private play | (CHAPTER 30TH) | Balls, Suppers, etcetera |

> " *But now a serious Word about the play*
> " *Auspicious smile on this their first Essay*

The young people at Castletown now acted a
play in the most Capital stile, for as they spent
every winter in Dublin they could not fail to
catch The Theatric fire at a Time when the
Metropolitan stage abounded with Capital Performers—No expence was spared in dress or

Scenery—The play was the Opera of Rosina—
Miss Butlar Lowe acted the part of Rosina—
Mr Cox that of her Enamoratta—They could
not be uninteresting performers, for Young as
they were they were glowing Lovers off as well
as on the Stage—But Miss Butlar afterwards
married Mr Wall—and Mr Cox Miss Prettie—
Miss Cox acted the part of Phœbe with uncommon spirit and grace—Her brother Richard
was equally excellent as William—in short they
got off with the greatest Eclat.

After this we gave a grand Ball which was succeeded by a round of Balls ending at Curraghmore where there was a most splendid one—
Miss Butlar was then the Rage for Beauty and
she certainly was a most beautiful Interesting
girl—Mrs Penefather gave us a Ball at Coolnamuck—Mr Butlar took it in his head the first
set not to let his Daughter Dance that Night—
One would think he had then the foresight to
reserve her for the Heir of Coolnamuck Mr
Wall, whom she married some Years after—
She was dress'd that night in a white sarsnet
slip and lookd indeed the picture of elegance—
Every one cried out at Mr Butlars whim, but
he was inflexible to the great Mortification of
young Cox.

Mrs Penefather now asked Miss Carshore and
Me to spend some time with her—Her Mother
& Sisters Mrs and the Miss Moores were there
at the time also a Mr and Mrs Gore and some
others—Mrs Penefather laid herself out to

make her House agreeable to Miss Carshore
and Me whilst we staid.

The Jephsons were now grown up beautiful
girls—They, their Cousin Miss Butlar and the
Coxes Made the neighbourhood famous for
pretty Girls—Indeed Carrick has been always
so for pretty females of all Ranks.

3d Parish Rebellion	(CHAPTER 31ST)	Our Men Mangled by the Right Boys

Whence is it? Those Barbarians here again!

In the Autumn of 1781 we had a Second Parish
Rebellion and this year (1782) it broke out a
third time with increased fury—All the Assistance we received from Lord Tyrone Lord
Desart and the gentlemen round could not quell
it till we were forced to call in the civil and Military powers—The Rebels had been foiled in the
Bishop's Court where a Combination was proved
against them and they were defeated in fifty or
sixty Lawsuits—This enraged them so that they
this year attacked a party of our Men who were
out at Night drawing Mountain Tythes—They
beat them most desperately, left them for dead,
and carried off the Tythe Corn—We sat up till
4 oclock for them and sent a second party to
reconnoitre, These also they beat and great was
our Horror to see them return Mangled and
coverd with blood without their Companions—

Whilst their Wives and Children came shriek-
ing for their Husbands and parents—We immediately sent for Mr Carshore and his Assistant, And had them all dress'd and bandaged in
the Kitchen—They were all badly wounded and
we sat up till 8 Next Morning in a situation
truly deplorable half the Men had not yet been
found And only at Noon Next Day could they
be picked out of the Mountain Ditches where
they had been tumbled half dead by their merci-
less Assassins—My Mother who had till then
battled it out stoutly No sooner saw the Men
cover'd with Blood than her spirits entirely sunk
and Next Day she was in one of her old violent
Nervous Fevers which lasted a long time with
imminent Danger to her Life—Indeed there
were four or five of us almost equally ill after
the Horrors of that Night—This provoked her
Friends to an Effectual Exertion against those
Miscreants—The Day following was the fair
Day of Carrick—Mr Cox and Captain Monck
of the 13th Light Dragoons with a party of
Military scoured the Country, surrounded the
Ringleaders in their Houses, and lodged them
in goal—Some of them were transported others
punishd by Law but our Wretched Carmen sold
their own Blood and did not prosecute as they
ought—However the Lads got a hearty surfeit of
their Doings and came that Year after many
Overtures to throw themselves unconditionally
on My fathers clemency—For three Days we
had the House full of them Weeping, begging

Pardon and signing Articles of Capitulation
with the Most abject Submission.

A Curious Circumstance happend during these
Affrays—The 12th Dragoons quarterd here got
the Route and a press Gang of twelve men with
a Young Officer at their Head came up here at
Night to press all our Horses and Cars—had
they succeeded it would have ruind us for all the
Tythe would have been gone Next Day—We
therefore baricadoed against them and kept
them out a long time—They at length stormed
both gates and enter'd sword in hand with a
Volley of Oaths, Whilst my Father and Brothers
in vain shook their Cudgels at them—The
furious Soldiers patroll'd the place but blind
with Liquor they did not perceive the Cars that
were every where cover'd with loads of Corn—
Our Men had the Address to carry off the
Horses into the Back fields so that they missd
them also and went off empty and enraged—an
alarm about the French caused this Commotion
—As for their little officer he stood outside the
gate where My Father and Otway found him and
promised him a good licking—He was a Mr
James Roe, Cousin to my Tyrant and then only
fourteen years of age, though in the Army.

Mrs Cooke's Departure for Dublin ended the
year 1782 and left all our Beaux in deep Dudgeons, especially poor Mr Rankin who was
really deeply smitten—He was an old Batchelor,
who came from the North to Carrick for the Air
—He having an asthma of which he died some

time After—During the three parish Rebellions
he never quitted My Fathers Side—Wet or Dry
he rode after him through Bog and Mire, and
shewed himself a most sanguine Steady Friend
on every Occasion.

Mrs Cooke was universally regretted here She
was as good a Creature as possible but had a
couple of Mischief making Servants who constantly tattled and put her Out of Temper—She
was a fine figure of a Woman, large, and handsome though not so beautiful as her Sister Lady
Burton whom she greatly resembled—These
two and Mrs Weldon were co heiresses to the
late Lord Desarts alienable Property—Mrs
Cookes two Daughters Sophia and Lucy were
young Children when here—so cut no figure in
the passing Scenes.

Those three Ladies had a Natural Brother Mr
Joe Cuffe he lived mostly at Desart but getting
sickly they prevail'd on my Mother to bring him
here—He was a mighty good Creature and was
much pleased with his new abode—I was then
a very young Child but a great pet of his and as
he had a great taste for Music, drawing and the
Belle Lettres he strove to engraft a like taste on
my Young Mind—He lent me all his Books,
gave me some chosen volumes and began to
teach me to draw, but falling into a deep decay
he left this and died soon after to the great
grief of all the Family who respected and loved
him as much as if he had been Legitimated
into it.

| Divers accidents publick and private | (CHAPTER 32D) | Deaths of several persons here |

Tis but a Night, A long and Moonless Night
We make the grave our Bed and then are gone

The Year 1783 was renderd remarkable by the Declaration of Independence to the Irish Parliament and the fall of Fishamble Street Hall by which great Numbers lost their lives—but what signalized it most fatally in our domestic Circle was the Death of poor Mrs Carshore who as before hinted died of a Putrid Fever—She was a rough, jolly, goodhumoured Woman the best of Wives, of Mothers, and of friends—We could not bear to be an Evening without her and Wet or dry she came up—In her Red Rug Cloak as they kept no Carriage—An Evening Party at Mrs Carshores was the greatest treat we could have—She was very fond of young people and laid herself out to make her House pleasant to them—She gave us constant Syllabub-parties at a House and Orchard they had outside the Town or in a Garden that lay behind their House in Carrick—In collecting for this Spot the most curious flowers from all quarters of the Globe—And in Rubbing her Tables that shined like glass did Mrs Carshore " pass the harmless Tenor of her way beloved and respected by all who knew her and equally

lamented at her Death—She was in all our
parties—And the Jephsons and we forming in
a Manner one Family we equally felt her Loss
—her Daughters and Husband indeed came
up as usual but though they were all agreeable
it did not make up for the Loss of our good
Friend.

Next to Mrs Carshores parties Mrs Nicholsons
of Wilmar was the favourite haunt of Mrs
Cooke and us young folks as there were always
remarkable Slim Cakes for Tea—And all the
gossip of the Country after it.

Mr Carshore soon became such a favourite at
Curraghmore that he seldom came as formerly,
to play Backgammon and dine on Beans and
Bacon here—He was established in the Curraghmore business by his Intrinsic Cleverness particularly display'd in attending Lord De la Poer,
Lord Tyrones Eldest son Who fell from his
Horse leaping the Iron Rails of their Court yard
just as Lady Tyrone was stepping into her Carriage to dine out—She saw her charming Son
fall and in a few Minutes he was brought up
stretchd on a door almost lifeless—He died in a
few Hours—He was a beautiful young Man
just grown up and adored for his humane and
Charitable Disposition.

The same year died Miss Beresford Daughter of
Commissioner Beresford—she was niece to Lord
Tyrone a beautiful young Woman—and Mr
Polier Lord De la Poers Tutor and Bosom
Friend—The three Deaths happend within

three Weeks—They were all buried in Clone-
gam Church in one grave—1778—One Very
handsome Monument commemorates this fatal
Event—And describes the affection the Victims
bore to each other—Soon after a grand and
beautiful Obelisk was erected on one of the
highest Hills at Curraghmore which rivals
ancient Architecture in its Colossal Height &
Dimensions — What made the Catastrophe
More Affecting was that Lord Tyrone and his
Brother received at once The News of their childrens Death at the Waterford Election where
Mr Beresford sat as Candidate—To describe
the Distraction of the two parents would be impossible—And the same election was rendered
still more ominous by the Death of Mr Power
Son to the opposing Candidate who was killed
in a Duel.

1783 The Bank of Ireland was established And
the Order of St Patrick instituted—Lord Tyrone
was one of the Knights and was soon after made
Marquis of Waterford—But it made up poorly
for their recent Loss though the Whole Beresford Family immediately got into power And
soon arrived at the Acme of Worldly grandeur
and prosperity—Curraghmore shone with encreased Splendour if possible—But whenever
My Father and Mother dined there En Famille,
the Noble Owners gave a loose to their feelings
on the Woeful loss they had sustained.

> " *Yet still ev'n here Content may spread a*
>   *Charm*
> " *Redress the Clime and all its Rage dis-*
>   *arm*

My Brothers Now came home for the Christmas Holidays and on Christmas Day commenced a Most terrible frost and Snow which
lasted to the 21st of February—Some Old
People said it was as bad as the Hard Frost in
the Year 39—At its commencement we were in
constant Alarm about the Boys who hunted over
the Snow fearless of Danger and the Dreadful
Event at Curraghmore often occurd to our
frighted Immaginations—but the Snow soon
became Mountainous high with consequent In-
undations that soon prevented Man or Beast
from stirring—Many Cottages were totally
buried in the Snow or demolishd by floods—
And all our people were continually employ'd
in keeping our Mansion habitable—sometimes
we were driven from the lower Regions by the
Water pouring in to every Room in deep lakes
—The Trees were one Sheet of christalized Snow
in which we lost all the beautiful Bays and ever-
greens that abounded in Our Gardens—The
Number of Lives lost and the Damage done
all over Europe could Not be Calculated—
Every Newspaper brought the most dismal

93

Accounts foreign and domestic—And all Nature
lay in Mourning.

The Snow however afforded great Sport to the
two Boys and almost made up for the loss of
their hunting—We sat the whole time wrapt up
in Great Coats over the fire when not dabling at
the snow piled windows—We had Mrs O Hara
a Music Mistress in the House—But to play or
do any kind of Work was impossible, and we
spent the Whole 47 Days while the cold lasted
playing Cards and roasting Sprats in both parlours for we were forced to divide and have two
fires—The Sprats were driven in in such plenty
that heaps were thrown out every where—It is
astonishing we did not die of Dysenteries for
from Breakfast till Bedtime we had plates upon
plates of them—Mrs O Hara and we playd
Cards for them which was near costing her her
Life in the following Manner.

The Boys and she fell out about them at Cards
and they swore vengeance against her—She was
a fat unwieldy Woman weighing sixteen stone
—She could not move from one Chair to another without Help being a Martyr to the
Rheumatism and gross humours—One Day
they caught her sitting alone at the Harpsichord
—And being Mischievous as possible, they got
a quantity of Wet Straw and set fire to it on the
hearth then locked her up in the parlour and ran
off—Her Screams brought the whole family to
the Door but finding it locked we ran to the
Window—and saw Mrs O Hara fighting the

flames with her Crutch, and half suffocated with smoke—by good luck we came in time to save her and the House together—She was soon near being revenged of one of her tormentors for one Night as we were sitting in her Room where she lay confined with the fright We heard a dreadful Noise as if the House had fallen, and at the same time Shrieks from below—On our running Down we saw my Mother laid seemingly lifeless on the Tythe parlour floor—My Father roaring and kneeling over her and Mr Dan Cuffe rubbing her hands and Temples—In Another corner was my Brother Otway as white as a Cloth and shivering and Shaking with old Mary and half a Dozen Servants rubbing him all over and screeching about him—In another Corner lay prostrate a heavy old fashioned Tall Boy and Bureau with all their motley Contents—Which explained all and more than had happend—At first we thought my Mother was killd and Otway badly hurt We therefore joined Chorus with the rest of the Company in a Yell that animated even Mrs O Hara to do what her friends thought her incapable, namely to take a leap down five steps of the Stairs as far as the Landing place—Meanwhile my Mother slowly recover'd and had the pleasure to see that her Son was Safe with only the loss of a fine set of India China of great Value that she brought over from England.

It happen'd that Master Otway had climbed on the Bureau and caught hold of a Shelf of the

Tall Boy when the Holdfasts gave way and all
came Tumbling down together—Luckily there
was a patent steel Mill in the Way and his Neck
caught between two of its Iron Horns which
broke the fall of the Tall Boy—There he stuck
with scarce a hairs breath between his Head and
the Massive Oaken Tall Boy—My Mother ran
in at the Noise and on seeing the Situation of
things fell lifeless on the floor whilst My Father
and Mr Cuffe in a state little better franticly
strove to help her—Otway was taken from the
heaps of Rubbish (Wonderful to tell) Whole and
unhurt except the Shock his Nerves sustaind—
The Next Day we all kept our Beds with the
fright but none sufferd so severely as poor Mrs
O Hara Who never stirred off the Broad of her
Back for some Months After it—Mr Cuffe replaced the China sometime after when he went
to England by sending over another set somewhat like but much inferior to the former—
These he very genteely sent as a present for as
Otway was his God Son he thought himself
bound to answer for his Misdoings.

A Miraculous Escape	(CHAPTER 34TH)	Power of Music

" *All Chance Direction which thou canst not
see*

Two Days after this on New Years Day 1784
My father after officiating at Church was stand-

ing opposite the Bellfry when some one observed
the Steeple Shake and pull'd him away, which
was scarcely done when the Whole Gothic
fabrick with its Bells and appendages fell to
the Ground and a large Fragment tumbled at
my Fathers feet—The Steeple was of the Most
Massive Stone two or three hundred years old—
Though the people had not yet dispersed from
the Church No one was hurt—And two such
Miraculous escapes in our family in the course
of two days was thought to be a peculiar Inter-
position of providence for us.

This year set in propitiously for at its commencement the long American War was terminated
after lasting ten years and Peace was also signed
with France and Holland who aided the
Americans.

When the frost was over We resumed our
Music—Mrs O Hara had a most enchanting
Voice—loud, clear and Harmonious—She could
pitch it to every Key and Modulate it as she
pleased to the most difficult or most simple
Music—for besides great taste and judgement
she could thrill the Heart to tenderness and
Rapture—We sang every Sunday at Church
joined by some of her Town Scholars and enchanted the Congregation with the Variety of
our Hymns and Plsalms—At home we hardly
ever quitted the Harpsichord—Mrs O Hara
had an unbounded Variety of the finest and most
touching Airs—which she sang for me whenever I pleased, and we often sat whole Hours by

Moonlight at the Harpsichord—She Singing
and I listening " In Rapture Wound—I was
then of a romantic Age—All around Me was
Romance in a Retreat beautiful as the Garden
of Eden, and inshort every thing conspired to
encrease that Sensibility, keen and Sharp as a
Two Edged Sword which ever attended me from
Youth to Age, and always prey'd on me whilst
I nourish'd it with the blindest Vehemence, and
fondly cherished the Viper that made succeeding Misfortunes intolerable—I often left the
Harpsichord in hysterical fits of Crying without
knowing Why or Wherefore, and Mrs O Hara
pleased with an Auditress who felt her Music,
indulged my foible Even to Madness—thus
pass'd the first part of this Summer.
We Now received a Letter from My Aunt
Blunden entreating us to pass a good Part of the
Summer at CastleBlunden, which we promised
to do after My Father return'd from the Visitation of Cashel where there was a New Arch
Bishop, a New and Elegant Cathedral, And the
first Choir in the Kingdom, appointed by the
Arch Bishop (Doctor Agar), who was a great
Amateur and Music Mad—As we always went
with my father we packed up our best Duds for
the Occasion—The Evening before we went, a
Rap came to the Door, and a Young Clergyman entered who was a perfect Stranger—He
announced his Name as Gwynn—said he was
just come from the North Country and delivered
a letter from the Bishop of Ossory (brother to

Lord Waterford) recommending Mr Gwynn to
my fathers Care and protection as a Young Man
of unexceptional Character and the Bishops
particular Friend—My Father freely welcomed
him, and finding he had not yet taken Lodgings,
beg'd he would make this House his residence
till we returned — When My Father would
consider what Lodgings he would most recommend to him—Mr Gwynn all Gratitude
accepted the Offer, and Next Morning we set
out for Cashel leaving the Girls to take Care of
Mr Gwynn.

Mrs Clarke and the Boys received us with Extacy and the Hares treated us in the Most
friendly Manner—They all lived in one large
House divided into two—Mr Hare and family
lived in one half and Mr Clarke and his
Boarders occupied the other—This Double
Mansion was just near the Cathedral John Street
Cashel and had all the benefits of the New Improvements round that noble Edifice.

| Oratorios Dinners | (CHAPTER 35TH) | A domestic Escape |

" *To heavenly Themes, sublimer Strains belong*

I had Never heard any powerful Music before
—but the Oratorios no sooner began than I felt
Myself quite overpower'd—I wept and laughd
with secret Rapture—My Head Swam and I
found Myself fainting Away and just on the

wing to Heaven as it were—I knew not what
passd till I found Mrs Hare holding a Smelling
Bottle to my Nose which the ArchBishops Lady
Mrs Agar had humanely handed over the Pew
—I was quite Shocked at My Own behaviour,
recollecting the Lecture Mrs Fleming gave me
once before on an Occasion somewhat similar—
The archbishops Throne was just over our Pew
—He noticed all that passd, and seemd delighted at the Effect his Music had on a Novice
—After Service Mrs Agar asked My Mother if
I was her Daughter declaring herself much
pleased with My Sensibility—" Comfort Ye My
people, " Every Valley shall be Exalted, " and
the Trumpet shall sound " were the three principal Oratorios and I do believe there never was
a more Capital Performance As the ArchBishop
spared No cost or pains on it—Mr Hare rallied
me a good deal on My feelings, the Effects of
which were too obvious not to be seen by the
Whole Congregation.

We were Now introduced to Mr Clarke our
friends Husband—a very handsome Agreeable
young Man—Mrs Clarke never quitted our side
whilst we staid—We dined that Day at Mr
Hares—The next Day at the School with Mr
Clarke who got it as a Portion with his Wife—
The third Day we took leave of them and set off
with Tears in our Eyes for Carrick—Mr Clarke
promising to bring his Wife to Carrick the Next
Vacation.

On our Return the first News we heard was that

our New Guest Mr Gwynne had in our Absence
broke his Leg——However on Enquiry we found
it not quite so bad though he had received an
ugly Cut and Bruise——They were rolling the
Gravel Walk, and coming to the Slope the Men
were not able to stop the Rolling Stone——My
Sister Lucy was in the Way, and Gywnn seeing
her danger, threw himself in the Way and received the Stone on his Leg which would have
crushed her to Atoms——We were all very grateful for this Knight Errantry, and he was so
well Nursetended that in a few days he was able
to receive the family in his Room where we constantly drank Tea till he was able to come down
Stairs.

Gwynn made himself very Agreeable both to
Parents and Children, And my Father gave him
an Invitation to prolong his stay at our House——
He had always a Book in his pocket for Me——
And a Leaf of gooseberries for the Gaffers as he
provincially call'd the Children——He was Young
and very romantic, with a great deal of Learning——a great deal of Goodnature and very little
Money——He was more Music Mad than any
Man I ever met with——Handels Water Piece
which Fanny and I play'd double Made him
bounce like a Crazy Man——" The Soldier tired
and God Save the King had the Same Effect——
but if I ventured on the Rapture " Gramachree
——" Delia or " Come live with me " he was quite
frantic whilst Mrs O Hara sat ready to burst her
fat Sides laughing——He made the House very

pleasant, brought us up all the News of the Town
and read to us every Evening—Thus we passd
our Time within doors—We breakfasted, dined,
and Supped under the Green Shade on a Grass
Plot beneath the parlour Windows—Gwynn
was overhead and Ears in love with the whole
Family, When to his great annoyance as he express'd it we received a second Summons to
Castle Blunden.

| 2d Visit to Castle Blunden | (CHAPTER 36TH) | Various Events there |

" *And Morn With welcome Lustre Shines* "
" *And Evening unperceived declines* "

On Our Arrival there, We were Received with
Loud Shouts from the Gentlemen and Many
hugs from the Ladies—The whole Family were
assembled to Meet us and we found the Girls
much improved in Beauty and Vivacity with a
Valuable Addition to their Train in the person
of Mr Matthews a young Man of large fortune
just return'd from his Travels and a profess'd
Admirer of Miss Charlotte Blunden—The
House of course was now more gay if possible
than ever—The Bishop of Ossorys family with
Lord and Lady Westmeath and many others
were to dine there the day after our Arrival—
We lay in a large Room with two Beds my
Father and Mother in one and Fanny and I in
the other, just opposite the Old Closet Occupied

by Betty Hare and I and next Door to the
Gentlemens Barrack at the Other Side.

We had not been an hour in the House, when
Sir John began to play his old Tricks and sent
Mr Matthews in for his knee Buckles—we
were all dressing and half Naked and this being
our first Introduction to him Nothing could be
more whimsical, Whilst a roar of laughter from
our wicked Neighbours expounded the Con-
trivers of this awkward Rencontre—The Next
Day all was Bustle and Hurry—Every Bit of
Plate in the House was set forth to shew off
Charlotte's New Beau to advantage—This
passd as well as such Days generally do—We
had a great Croud and a most sumptuous Entertainment with Cards Dancing Supper and
Songs.

This being over we found the family resolved
to make the House ten times more pleasant if
possible than ever—The Weymeses, Bakers,
Boltons were all there—We Nutted, Boated,
fiddled, danced, Romped from Morning till
Night—Mr Matthews read Plays to us and Sang
Songs till one or two oclock after Supper—He
had a Pleasing though not a fine Voice and inspired by his fair Mistress he sang the Most
Charming Songs with all the Pathos that Love,
Wine, and a perfect knowledge of Music could
produce—The Evening We arrived, Catty
Whelan the Housekeeper an Old family fixture
enter'd to undress us and after carefully Shut-
ting the Door whispered two important Secrets

in our Ears—The first was the intended Match
between Miss Charlotte and Young Mr Matthews and the Next that Sir John at the Desire
of the whole family had proposed for Miss
Robbins a rich Heiress and their tears had prevaild on him to renounce Miss Semple to whom
he had been much Attached—Miss Robbins
had Six thousand a Year and Miss Semple had
only a pretty face and the Earnings of her father
who was an Eminent Physician—There had
been Great Work about it—Sir John was at first
quite Mad but the Tears of his Mother and
family at last prevaild.

Sir John was quite the Sir Charles Grandison
of his family—to whom they all look'd up with
fear and Reverence and this bold Interference
was a last desperate stroke of Courage in the
whole family, with Matthews at their Head—
He had always been remarkable for his Gaiety
and goodhumour amongst them but now he
grew quite snappish and fretful—To us he was
the same thing as Ever always free affectionate
and polite—I had good reason to say so for he
always made it a point to protect Me against any
rising Satire or ill humour—When any part of
My Dress did Not please him he candidly told
me what faults he found and how I should
rectify them, but he would allow no one but
himself to Criticize Me—He always said I was
a Meek Angel amongst them and he must take
care that his little Cousin was well treated, this
picqued them Not a little particularly Charlotte

who was a bit of a Tartar and knew his Inuendoes chiefly referr'd to her hasty temper—and petulant smartness.

| An unpleasant Event | (CHAPTER 37TH) | Consequent Bickerings |

To failings Mild yet zealous for Desert
The clearest Head, and the Sincerest Heart

In the Midst of our Gaiety—My Sister Fanny fell ill of a violent feverish Cold, and continued so ill for a Week that we were greatly alarm'd for her—They all shewed the greatest Concern —However one Night that she was very bad and Doctor Butlar had pronounced her life in Danger, they forced us down to Supper—My Mother sat crying at the Table whilst they strove to force a poach'd egg down her throat— Every one eat away in Melancholy silence but something being said that vex'd Sir John he sat growling at My Aunt and the Girls—They not daring to answer him turned all their Ill humour on Me, and began to scold me for not being More conversible which was a usual Trick with them when out of Sorts—Sir John took my part—commended My Modest Diffidence and said it would be a happy thing if they all followd My Example—Then looking angrily at Charlotte, he severely animadverted on Women whose Tongues were continually going like the Clappers of a Mill—She was fired and this

rouzed her Beau Matthews but both sat in
Silent Sulks—Sir John observing that they had
neglected to bring Me My Milk, Sternly asked
the Servant Why Miss Herberts milk was not
brought as usual—My Aunt replied that Nurse
Shortal who had the Key was out of the Way—
He swore it was all a Contrivance and that no
such Tricks should be play'd in his House, Vowing that if it was not brought up he would dismiss Nurse Shortal the next Morning—Ovrington Blunden began a Harangue in favour of his
old Dry Nurse, which provoked Sir John still
more, and he was going to strike Ovrington—
They all pouted, wept, and sided with Ovry and
their Nurse, which brought on a general Battle
whilst I sat by sobbing for being the Innocent
Cause of it.

The affrighted Servants ran for the Milk, but as
ill Luck would have it one of them ran against a
beautiful Chandelier in the Hall that cost twenty
Guineas the Day before and broke it to Pieces—
This Accident did not add to our Good humour
and We parted for the Night in high Dudgeons,
and Mutually disgusted with Each Other—
Fanny soon after began to recover, but no
Sooner was she down Stairs than my Father was
taken ill of the same Complaint and forced to go
to his Bed to the great terror of my Mother and
all the family.

Sir John doated on My Father and was Miserable about him—He was continually popping
into the Room—As I nursetended My Father

whilst the Ladies were at Cards, he gave Me
Many Praises for my Attention whenever he
enter'd, declaring I was the best of Daughters—
When My Father recovered we were again all
Life and Gaiety—One Day after Dinner as we
were patrolling the place, we saw a Horseman
Galloping down the Approach—I was surprized
at recognizing Mr Gwynn Who having been at
the Kilkenny Visitation gallop'd out to see his
Old Friends—He was overjoyed at Meeting Me
and Alighting from his Horse Saluted Me with
so much Warmth that Araminta Blunden reprimanded me severely for suffering so young a
Man to Make so free with me—They were very
inquisitive about his fortune and family and investigated me with such prying looks that I was
on thorns every time he approach'd Me and
heartily glad when he went away the Next
Morning.

| A family Breaking up | (CHAPTER 38TH) | Various Frolics |

" *Trace Science then With Modesty thy Guide*

Ovrington Blunden was now preparing to get
into the Army, and expected immediately After
to be orderd abroad—which was a great damp
to My Aunt and the family—William was
entirely devoted to his Books, and Was training
himself to become a Farmer, as He, My Aunt,
and Araminta were to live together when Sir

John and Charlotte were married—It made us
all Melancholy to think that so happy a Set
would soon disperse in a Manner for Life—
Every one strove to detach William from his
Books And my Aunt and the Girls forced Me
every Night to ask the Honour of his hand to
dance, but the ungracious Swain always refused
—As we were the two Modest ones of the family
We felt equally Awkward, I at being refused,
and he at his own rudeness, but he knew the
raillery he would undergo if he relaxed from his
Stately Gravity—and that he would besides be
continually pesterd to make up a set.
On those Occasions he always fled to his old
Haunt the Nursery where Mammy Shortal kept
a vacant Chair at the fire for him which None
but himself durst invade—However after the
Dancing the whole party powderd up every
Night to plague him—I was always an immo-
lated victim for Sir John at the instigation of his
Sisters romped and kissed Most unmercifully
whilst in Vain I roared for Succour from my
friend William and Mammy Shortal—Neither
durst interfere and Could only Growl and turn
up their Eyes at a Distance—My Wild Cousin
not content with his Nursery freaks was continually Mistaking our Door for his, and indeed
one night riotously burst in as we were popping
into Bed and Clamorously demanded where his
little Cousins were—and railed that we were
Not forthcoming — We stood En chemise
peppering behind the Curtains—being very

tipsy he searchd the Bed swearing he would Not
leave the Room till he saw that we were safe
lodged—at length he found us wrapd up in the
Hangings and held us fast till My Mother
draggd him away whilst we in the greatest fright
expected every Moment he would make us
figure out in our primitive loveliness.

Every Night after boating I was left in the lurch
by My female Companions who scamperd off,
leaving Me in the Boat at his Mercy—After
supper I was left in the rear to be locked up with
the Gentlemen who never let me Out toll free—
But their greatest amusement was to force a
Song from Me for My Modest Tremors and
quivering Voice afforded the wicked Set the
greatest Merriment—One Night after dancing
in the Court yard Sir John and Mr Matthews
had a dispute about their Buckles—They left
their Quarrel to my Decision and I gave it in
favour of Sir Johns plain buckles over the dashing Macaroni Buckles of his Competitor saying
Sir Johns were handsomer but Mr Matthews's
More Beauish—This Term before his fair One
Nettled him a good deal, and he stalked off disconcerted amid the Shouts of his Companions—
Whilst his triumphant Antagonist thanked Me
for Smoking the Beau—However in the Evening Charlottes Beau was revenged for he found
out that my Petticoats had stuck up behind
whilst I sat at the fire—This Discovery and Sir
Johns throwing himself Across the Sopha to
take a full View soon excited a general roar of

Laughter at My Expence—which was a Riddle
to Me till My Aunt call'd over and begged I
would not shew My Legs so much to the
Gentlemen—This was no sooner over than
Charlotte afforded them a fresh subject of Merriment by drawing the Chair from under Frank
Shearman a very big Man who was a Constant
Inmate at Castle Blunden—poor Franks heavy
Skull came to the ground with a dreadful Noise
and we left the Old Ladies to bind up the
Wounds of their Goliath, as he always made one
at their Whist Table—where he would have
been a irreperable Loss—Whenever My Aunt
asked Frank Shearman how many honours he
held his Answer was two or four by honours but
it generally came out that he patchd them out
with the honour of Playing with her Ladyship—
I Every Night playd the piano forte for Sir John
and Mr Matthews—sometimes we sang Catches
—All the Morning the House resounded with
their fiddles, and After Supper Mr Matthews
sang Songs so that it was Harmony from Morning till Night, and from Night till Morning—
At length the Time came for our Departure
from this Gay Scene, and we seperated to the
Mutual regret of all parties—The Night before
we left it Sir John grew again Obstreperous, and
Swore he would never Marry Miss Robbins but
it was only the last struggles of a free Spirit sighing for its native Liberty for he soon after
yielded to his Mothers remonstrances to visit
Miss Robbins in form.

" *Where gates impregnable, And coercive Chains*
" *In durance strict detain him, till in form of*
" *Money, Pallas set the Captive free*

On our return we found that Mr Gwynn had
left our House and taken Lodgings in Carrick
—My Mother assisted him as far as she could
in Housekeeping—He however lived here all
the summer only going home at Night to his
Lodgings.

About this time my Father made a New pur-
chase of an Estate in the Co Waterford—The
Heirs were so numerous, and so Obscure that
it cost wonderful Patience with a great deal of
Time and Money to make them out, and the
pretended Heirs who were full as numerous as
the real ones, kept him at Law for many Years
and tormented him, with false Deeds, false Possessions, and all the Arts that their quibbling
Attorneys could devise—So that he was forced
into such expence that the Suit became Neck or
Nothing with us—After some Years of un-
speakable trouble and Difficulties My Father
compleatly defeated them in every Court and
got into full possession—We had nothing but
Bonfires and Rejoicings for some Days for our
Success—Thus ended this disagreeable affair
after our being forced to bring Witnesses from
the County Kerry, England and every part of

the globe and to maintain them here at great
charge.

We were now at full Liberty to follow our
Amusements—We had Many flaming Parties
this Summer particulary one Given by Mr
Simon Osborne of Annfield (a Widower) to a
Miss Dodd with whom he flirted, and who
pestered him out of a Fete Champêtre—Every
one within twenty or thirty Miles was invited—
We dined under Tents and Marquees in the
Lawn—Nothing could exceed the Elegance of
the Entertainment, and there was no counting
the Company—But the chief Heroines were two
Miss Kenedys both newly Married—They were
just come from the assizes of Waterford where
they prosecuted to Conviction three Men who
ran away with them a Month before from whom
they were rescued by their present Bridegrooms
—The Men were hanged and every one was
disgusted at the Ladies appearing so soon in
Public after so horrid a Business—The Eldest
Sister at the Tryal fainted several Times and
wished to evade the Prosecution, but was urged
on to it by the Youngest who was hardend and
inexorable—This fair Termagant was a very
fine handsome Woman and came to the Ball
dressed in a great display of Bridal Finery—
pure Virgin white, trimmed all over with Silver
Coxcomb whilst many cursed her Cruelty in
hanging three very handsome young fellows of
good Families Who treated her with Respect
whilst she was with them—The Eldest a pretty

Woman was more Moderately dressd in a brown
Lustring quite plain.

We had Now a Visit from Lord and Lady Maxwell and my Aunt Cuffe——They staid some time
with us——Lord Maxwell was a well disposed
Good Natured handsome Young Man and did
not disdain to help us in Haymaking and romping under the Haystacks and so forth——This
party left us and were succeeded by Mr Henry
Herbert of Muckrus who brought over his
Young Wife for the first time from England——
She was Daughter to Lord Sackville, better
known by the Name of Lord George Germaine
——Of all the bewitching Beauties I ever beheld
She was the Most fascinating——Though some
and amongst others Gwynn did not think her so
handsome on account of her Skin which was
quite like an East Indians, but for my part I
was quite charmed——Her beautiful black Eyes
and Eyebrows under a handsome forehead Her
long dark Eyelashes and Ebon Hair which fell
in thick Tresses below her Waist renderd her
Irresistible——Her mouth, her smile, her Dimples
were Enchanting——Her skin was the Clearest
Brown——Her Legs Arms and whole person
exquisitely turned and her harmonious voice
would have Melted the Most frozen Apathy——
Every part was Beauty Every Action Grace——
They staid here a Week, and she frisked down
every Night to Carrick where she amused herself with every Triffle that Occurred——We had a
round of Dinners for them of Course everywhere.

When they left us Mr and Mrs Clarke
arrived and spent a week or fortnight driving
about and viewing the Country—He was more
just to Curraghmore than his Wife had formerly
been and own'd that it quite surpassd his Ideas
though he had heard Much of it—Indeed even
English Mrs Herbert in her playful Manner
allowed it its merited praise, though well inclined to be satyrical on every thing Irish—Her
own place (Muckrus) She had not yet seen of
which a certain Bishop pronounced that a King
of France might Make another Versailles but
God alone could make another Muckrus—This
Year was signalized here by the Marriage of
Mr Sutton a very handsome young Clergyman
without fortune, to Miss Jenny Shaw of Figlash
with a large one—The Ladies were all breaking
their hearts after their elegant Sutton and mad
that he should bestow himself on long Jenny as
she was called or to live on Home kill'd Mutton
with her father and Brother long John—but
Jenny in her fortieth Year buried them both
and carried off the property and her Young
Husband to the Mountains of Kilmoganny
Where she reform'd him into a compleat good
Husband and lived many Years happily with
him and an only Daughter that blessed their
Union.

Oh Days of Youth! Oh careless Days! Untaught To Weep, if Love shed Not the pleasing Tear

We Now sat down quietly in the Domestic Way, with no other Company than Mr Gwynn—Our Days as usual Spent under the Shade with peace and plenty at our Board—Mrs O'Hara singing every Hour that I was not at the Harpsichord— We read Poetry, Novels, Sermons, History, hickledy pickledy as they came in our Way without any regular System except a smattering of English and french Grammar—Fanny embroidered, and I drew an occasional Picture, but as bad Workmen have always bad Tools we spent more of our Time in Laughter and Idleness than to any profitable purpose always wanting brushes, paints, Silks or Copies—As for Mr Gwynn he was entirely spoiled for any useful Study, except pondering what song he should ask for, or What Play he could invent to amuse the Gaffers (his North country term for Children)—The time now came to set a going a small Kiln we built in a back Kitchen—Our great Amusement then was to listen to Terrence Walsh the Mason who used to divert my father with his odd Stories and make him laugh by the Hour—One Story I remember was of Mr Wall

who being out of his reason for Many Years,
once Sent to buy up all the Soap in Carrick—
on Terrys assuring him the Castle of Coolnamuck Might be moved down to the River if he
bought Soap enough to smooth the way down—
My Father used to invite us all to Sup en
famille about his Kiln and had always the finest
white potatoes roasted for us cooked by himself on the hot Lime And plenty of the finest
Bonny Clobber (Thick Milk) from the Dairy
—Miss Butlar used to come in from Next
Door and she and Gwyn kept us in a Roar
with anecdotes fresh imported from Carrick
where they spent a couple of Hours each
Evening.
To compleat our regaling my Father Made
Terry Walsh build a Wall round the Well in the
field with a Door to it—And no WineCellar full
of Champagne was ever More carefully locked
—He perswaded the Children and Servants that
there was a Particular Virtue in the Water and
they were constantly applying for leave to get a
Glass of [it]—Every Night he had a Quart of it
brought home for Supper and it was handed
about in Wine Glasses as a thing too choice to
be swallowd in large Gulps—We sometimes
drank Tea at Wilmar to vary the Scene and Mrs
Nicholson had always the finest Slim Cake for
us—Sometimes we sat out under the Windows
till 12 oclock, telling Stories or listening to Mrs
O Hara singing.
At length we got a letter from Castle Blunden

with the disagreeable News that old Mr Matthews had broke off the Match between his Son
and Charlotte Blunden on account of Money
Matters and that they were all coming here to
avoid disagreeable Comments—Just then Ovrington Blunden had got his commission and
Carrick was almost his first Quarters His Regiment being Station'd here though he had not
yet joined it—None but my Aunt and the two
girls came which was a Great Disappointment
as the Gentlemen all promised to Come—We
got an Assembly up to dispel Charlottes Gloom
—but she was too proud to let it appear and
flirted away immoderately with Ovy's Brother
Officers—We went to a Waterford play to hear
the delightful Mrs Billington sing—but Mrs
O Haras voice pleased me Much better—After
a Weeks Stay the Blundens went home.

Family Fireside	CHAPTER 41ST	Miss Carshores Marriage to Mr Curtis

" ——*Where all the ruddy family around*
" *Laugh at the Jests and Pranks that never fail*

The Winter came on Pretty hard, and we all set
diligently about our different Occupations to
make up for our Summers Idleness—Mr Gwyn
made it a Rule not to come up from his Studies
till Eight oclock struck and every Night regularly at that hour his Rap came when we sat till

Eleven reading, working, telling Stories, or
playing small Plays.

It is now time to introduce My youngest
Brother Nicholas who was then beginning to
Speak——He was really one of the prettiest Boys
possible and he generally slept across my Lap
in the Chimney Corner where we all admired
his fair Curling Locks and long Eyelashes the
finest I ever saw——Mr Gwyn used to Nurse my
Sister Sophy——He had her constantly in his
Arms tossing her up to the Cieling to the great
terror of all present or Making her Spout plays
on a Table——He christen'd her Poor Yorick,
she had so little many droll sayings.

Matty was my Chum——Fanny my True Yoke-
fellow at Handels Waterpiece, the Battle of
Prague and other Double pieces which we playd
together——Lucy was Fannys Bedfellow and her
Working Companion and voluntary Factotum
in every thing——Otway and Tom were Objects
of Adoration to the Whole family——We pass'd
the long Winters Nights in the Merriest Manner
whilst My Father took his Nap at one Corner
and My Mother settled her Accounts at the
other Corner of the fire——We now heard that
Charlotte Blundens Match was come on Again
and soon Got a Summons to hold ourselves in
readiness for the Wedding——This was hardly
published when my Mother got a Note from
Mr Carshore informing her that all matters
were settled between him and Mr Curtis for the
union of his Daughter with the latter——and re-

questing the presence of Our family at the
Wedding—Accordingly we attended and had
the pleasure of wishing Miss Carshore Joy as
Mrs Curtis in her eighteenth Year—Miss
Blunden of Kilmacoliver and I stood Bridesmaids—The Bride looked famously and dress'd
in an Azure Sarsnet with white ribbons—Miss
Blunden was dress'd the same way but for fear
of Mistakes wore brown Ribbons—and I
sported my Straw colour Lustring—Ceres like
in the Azure Throng—The Wedding was in a
Private Stile and we had Nothing but Cards and
a Supper with a few Jokes about the first kiss
from Mr Rankin—The next day we visited the
bride in form and were received with Modest
Gratitude.

| 3d Journey to Castle Blunden | (Chapter 42d) | Our Reception there |

" *The Officious Daughters pleased Attend*
" *The Brother adds the Name of Friend*

I was soon to have two More Weddings on My
hands whilst the Genius of Goodnature pitied
my situation and Wished Me a better Office
than standing as an Uninteresting Bridesmaid
at the train of Hymen—My Mother now
brought Me a White Lustring for Charlotte
Blundens affair hoping that it would be more
lucky than my Straw Colourd one—She and
Mrs Jephson then paid a Visit at Curraghmore

where they laid their whole Budget of Intelligence before Lord and Lady Waterford—Lord Waterford asked who was to be Charlotte Blundens Bridesmaid They told him I was to have that Honour—He jocularly asked what Dress I was to wear and hearing I had got a White Lustring affected Great uneasiness lest Mr Matthews should mistake me for his Bride—Lord Waterford was always pleasant and Jocose especially in his own House and took great Delight in joking with My Mother and Mrs Jephson about their Daughters—My Sister Fanny Got a pink Slip and Leno Frock on the Occasion and thus equip'd We Set off for the Wedding.

The whole Family were assembled on this important Business Mr and Mrs Weymes, Mr and Mrs Baker, Mr and Mrs Bolton, Two Miss Weymeses, Frank Shearman—The family of the House and ourselves were the party in the House—Besides them We had Mr Matthewses Father and Stepmother—Miss Emma Matthews his Sister and his two Brothers Messieurs Joe and Arthur Matthews besides many others less relative—We arrived there some time before the Writings were finished as old Matthews crossly threw in many delays—But it was no more the Same House as formerly—My Aunt and the Girls were continually Occupied—and Sir John who had always been the Life of the Circle was no longer the same man—He grew quite grave and thoughtful, and had already the appearance of an old Married Man—We seldom saw him and when we did he was always encumberd with Deeds and Settlements for his own and his Sisters Marriage—At Table he was quite Silent and lost all his Vivacious talk—He sometimes when Sick of Business took a Gallop to Waterford to hear Mrs Billington so that we had very little of his Company—as for Charlotte she grew quite cross and fretful as the awful Crisis approached—She and Mrs Bolton had Perpetual Squabbles as the latter plagued her most heartily—Mr Baker was Jealous of every Man that looked at his Wife—and Mr Bolton was laid up in the Gout so that Araminta Fanny and I were the only goodhumourd solid people of the whole set.

Mrs Matthews Wedding	CHAPTER 43D	Company and Occurrences

See Hymen Comes! How his Torch blazes!

At length the important Day arrived—The Bride was dress'd in a White Sarsnet and a White silk Bonnet with a very long Veil to it—Her Dress was very rich with fine Lace and costly Trinkets but I thought I never saw her look Worse as she was quite disfigured with continual fretting and Anxiety—Miss Emma Matthews and I were dress'd in White as Bridesmaids—Araminta in a strawcolour Lustring Fanny in pink, as for the Married Ladies it

would be impossible to describe the Number
and richness of their Ornaments as they vied
in the profusion of their Jewels and other
Finery.

The Young Couple were married some time
before Dinner and after sitting in form for Wine
and Cake we assembled in Groupes about the
Room—Sir John came up to me and took me
by the Hand thanking me for his Sister Charlotte—I thought I never saw him appear so
amiable as that Day—acting as the father of his
Family at his Sisters Wedding—to whose fortune he made a handsome addition and promised
Araminta a like Sum—Indeed he shewd great
Sensibility on the Occasion—and taking hold
of my Hand he seem'd ready to burst out crying
as if to say The happy past is over and the Future
is uncertain—He was dress'd in Scarlet faced
with gold a very rich Dress but it did not become him—Charlotte Araminta Fanny and I
were so affected that we were forced every
Moment to shift our places that our Tears
should Not be observed—We sat down to
dinner at two very large Tables—Mr Weymes
made the Side Table very agreeable but the first
Table was silent and formal and they borrowd
all their Wit from our Merry Board—We had
a most Sumptuous Entertainment of every thing
the Season afforded—In the Evening the
Tenants Assembled and danced before the
Windows—and were afterwards freely regaled
and Money thrown to them—At Night we had

a Ball and Music from Kilkenny and the Day
ended with a flaming supper and Concert—
Next Morning the Bride shone forth in All the
splendour of Beauty—A highly Glazed white
Linen Gown white Ribbon and a large handsome French Night Cap, made her look indeed
according to Mr Matthews application of the
Song of Phœbe to her—" Beauty's Fair Queen"
—whilst all around " paid homage to her
Charms".

Meanwhile Mr Barnes an old Uncle of Miss
Robbins came with a Budget of Rent Rolls—
The greatest Respect was paid him but for my
part I thought he looked more like a Hang-
man than the acting Parent of a rich Heiress
—Sir John used to Liberty seemd tired of
paying attendance and defference to the
Opinion of this Man of Business, and was
like a Bird let loose when his Mentor in Law
went away.

Mrs Matthews Wedding was succeeded by a
Multitude of Visits and Entertainments—But
we did Not Stay for the latter as My Father
received a Letter from his Niece Fanny Blennerhasset informing him she was going to be
married to Mr Browne a Clergyman and a Man
of Great Property in the County Cork—And
begged My Father and we would hasten up as
she could not bear to be married by any Other
Clergyman—We were Not sorry to Miss the
Kilkenny round of Dinners and on many Accounts gladly answerd that we would obey the

Welcome Summons and post it up to Dublin—
having fixed to set out Next Morning.

In the Evening Sir John now disengaged from
Mr Barnes and his armful of Rent Rolls drew
me to the Forte piano for the first time this last
Excursion—He made me play push about the
Jorum with my own Variations—a Tune that
obtained me much Celebrity at that time—He
placed himself vis a vis—and swore in Raptures
I surpassd Mrs Billington in Taste and engaged
me to play and Sing for him the rest of the Evening—Accordingly we amused ourselves at the
forte piano till Supper was Served—He made
me sing for him Many old songs such as Molly
Astore and how Sweet in the Woodlands declaring my soft plaintive Voice and Collection of
plaintive old Tunes pleased him more than the
finest Opera Performance And he Encored Me
over and Over saying it was the last time perhaps he should ever ask me to sing for him—
His Sisters sat round us and Made him Give
a full Account of his Intended—He told them
she was much the size of his little Cousin—
She was compleat mistress of Music—Drawing
—Dancing—And understood Greek, Latin,
French, English, and Italian as well as her
Masters—Wrote Capitally and was in every
Respect a most accomplishd Pretty little Creature—His Sisters were all quite frightend at
such a learnd Lady's coming amongst them, and
he himself laugh'd as if on his good behaviour—
His Father not having given him a public Edu-

cation I believe he would have liked his fair One
as well without her Greek or Latin—He was to
set off Next Day on his Courtship and seem'd
that Night taking a last pathetic leave of Youthful folly, and his former Playmates.

The Next Day we set off for Dublin with heavy
Hearts and weeping Eyes foreboding from the
Changes that were to happen that we should
never again spend such happy Hours in the old
Family Mansion of Castle Blunden.

Mrs Brownes Wedding	(CHAPTER 44TH)	Portentous Accidents

Marriage amongst Men is an Evil much desired

On our Arrival in Dublin we stop'd at Lord
Maxwells at My Aunt Cuffes old House No. 7
Glocester Street Now given up to him with his
Wife And within a few Doors of Lady Anne
Fitzgeralds the Scene of this new Wedding
as Miss Blennerhasset then lived with Lady
Ann.

We now Learned from the Mischievous Lord
Maxwell, all the Intricacies of the Courtship—
Mr Browne had been refused seven times and
had in despair Embarked for England—But By
the Interference of Lady Ann he was recalled
when on board the Ship and all Matters Amicably Adjusted—Lady Ann would now hearken
to No delays and Made Fanny Hasset write off
in all haste for My Father—However after we

got to town the Bride Elect so piteously demanded a Respite that it was granted though all
acknowledge she deserved none after her seven-
fold Refusal—Meanwhile we were invited every
Day to Lady Anns to meet Mr Browne who
was a plain Sensible Man between thirty and
forty years old with a pair of beautiful black
Eyes to recommend a person otherwise not at
All handsome—We had Miss Fanny Hasset
quite in Stew as her Friends did not spare her
after the Many Good Offers she had refused and
her frequent Rejection of her present Lover—
However he gave her a small panic the Night of
the Wedding, for though we all Assembled
early to Tea Eight Oclock struck and no Bridegroom appeared—The Whole City was ran-
sackd for him but he was not to be found—
However about Nine Oclock he enter'd saying
he had been shoping and could not fit himself in
Gloves—but as he was a sensible little man
every one thought it was a piece of Satyrical
Revenge on his long demurring Spouse.

It was indeed a Night of Ominous Disasters
and all the Old Ladies were terrified with fore-
bodings—At the first Onset Lord Maxwell
fiddling with the Brides Diamond Watch (a
costly Present from her Lover) let it drop on the
Marble Slab and it was smash'd to pieces—
Next the Bridegroom himself was not to be
found—thirdly my father lost his place in the
prayer Book Just at " I take this woman to be "
&c—fourthly the Bridegroom dropd the Wed-

ding Ring and was forced to send out for
another—Lastly Lady Annes four Darling Pet
Dogs which she had dressd in White Ribbons
and Collars set up such a Yelling that my Father
was forced to lay down the Book till they were
turned out of the Room—So many awkard
Accidents in such a genteel Assemblage was
looked on as a Lusus Naturæ and caused general
Consternation—However the Brides appearance presaged a More fortunate Denouement—
She was dressd in a plain thin Musline trimmed
with fine lace and pale blossom colour Ribbon—
with a Handkerchief elegantly pinned on her
head—with flowers and ornaments of that delicate hue—There was such a Mixture of Modesty
and Chearfulness in her that all her friends were
charmed—She looked quite an Angel and to the
Credit of her Education acted like One throughout the whole Ceremony—Lady Ann was all
Exultation—and My Aunt Cuffe and Lady
Maxwell declared they could form No Idea of
half her perfections till then—As for Mr
Browne he was quite lost in Adoration—We
play'd Cards all the Evening in a sober Stile
Suitable to a Clergymans Wedding And at
twelve oclock Sat down to an elegant fancy
Supper.
The next Day the happy pair left Town without
waiting for Visits—And after a Weeks rest we
left Dublin and returned to Castle Blunden—
We did not stay long there, and returned home
quite jaded after our round of Weddings—

Fanny Blennerhasset was the fifth of my Friends
I dispatched to the land of Matrimony.

| A Carrick Assembly | (CHAPTER 45) | A Sad Elopement |

At length repose the weary Head
Safe on our old acquainted Bed

We found the Town of Carrick preparing for a
grand assembly for Mrs Dobleses Benefit a poor
Widow who was often at our House and was
fallen from an Affluent State into extreme In-
digence—We went there quite dress'd à la
Mode but reaped no other Advantage than being
asked to dance by the Charming Watts then
much admired amongst the Belles whose general
Toast was " The winning Ways of Willy
Watts "—I had likewise the felicity to hear
from Mr Gwyn that his friend parson Stephen-
son (Another Admired Beau) reckond me to be
the best and most fashionably dress'd Woman
in the Room but these were Small Encourage-
ments after figuring away thrice within a Month
as an humble Bridemaid—however my friends
perswaded Me these were ominous Circumstances but though I brought home two New
Tabbinets and other finery, I past the Winter as
Spinster

{
" *Like Yon Neglected Shrub at random cast*
" *That shades the Steep and sighs at every*
   blast
}

128

Whilst we were thus engaged about honest
Matrimony making our friends at Muckrus
were far differently engrossd—The enchanting
Mrs Herbert bewitched every heart, and was
equally bewitched by our Cousin Captain
Hedges then a Visitant at the house of his bosom
Friend the Master of Muckrus—The beautiful
Mistress was soon much talked of with him and
the Abbey mentioned as the place of rendezvous
—Her distracted Husband carried her off to
England where her father locked her up for
some time and fed her on bread and Water—
Her doating Husband became her advocate and
at his Intercession She was liberated after a
rigid penance—They lived for some time after
on good terms and had a Daughter and two Sons
nearly as beautiful as their Mother but horrid to
relate their Eldest son was burned to death at
Muckrus—Mrs Herberts restless Mind could
not content itself with being Mistress of that
Elysium and all its Delights and after various
imprudencies She eloped with a Scotch Major
—Her Husband then sued for a Divorce and
Damages but the Guilty Pair Secreted themselves and traversed the Continent till Major
Dunn Got a Paralytic Complaint which deprived him of the use of his Limbs and his faithful partner carried him up and down Stairs on
her back to the tune of All for Love or the
World well lost—So the Story Goes—here I
have a little anticipated Events but it all came
to the Same thing for Mr Herbert lost his Wife

and she her Character whilst every Newspaper
echoed their misfortunes.

| State of the Vicinage | (CHAPTER 46TH) | An Expensive Establishment |

See future Sons and Daughters yet unborn

Mrs Curtis now went to settle in Dublin—
where she put forth a fair Daughter—but After
a time she perswaded her Spouse that Carrick
was the most eligible of All Situations and she
returned to give Birth to a Son and Heir.
The Jephsons were all in Statuquo still though
constantly going about on different Excursions
—but their encreasing Loveliness left them No
fears of lying long on Hands.
The Coxes were figuring away every Winter in
Dublin universally admired for their Beauty and
Haut ton for they spared No Expence on their
appearance—to the tune of 8000 a year and a
vast accumulated Debt whilst fifty Servants in
Livery Graced their train besides others of all
Ranks.

| Rural pleasures | CHAPTER 47TH | A Grand assembly |

Oh Woods! Oh Fountains! Oh delightful Meads!
That lent us Flowers the prime of blooming May
To deck our Tresses—

As for us we were still feeding on Potatoes and
Milk at home, and enjoying all the calm Delights of a Young Summer in our Natural Soil—
Beaux we had none but Heck Young, and Mr
Gwyn who grew every Day more Attached to
our family and the Towns people used to make
their remarks saying, that Mr Gwyn could
Never visit them unless Miss Herbert pleased
to walk into town and all that—However we
amused ourselves very innocently and left them
to enjoy their Speculations solacing Ourselves
with Books, Musick, Rural repasts and fruit
Eating—We spent our Days in the different
Bowers as they Afforded Shelter from the
scorching Sun and our eternal Laughter gave us
no room to suspect Cupids Darts—Once indeed
Mrs O Hara cut off a Lock of my Hair and
bestowd it on Mr Gwyn who placed it in his
pocket Book but returned it on my remonstrances though he was much huffed with me
for taking it from him—Tis true his encreased
attention became evident—during the Winter
he only spent two Hours each Evening with us
—then he commonly brought a Book in his
pocket and read to us—finding I had a taste for
Poetry his chief care was to select such poetry as
he thought I would like—he often lent me
Books and pointed out to me the chief Beauties
in each Volume—The cool Arbours and fragrant
Bowers made our Book doubly delightful in
Summer—Gwyn had great Sensibility and was
charmed to find me Susceptible of the Beauties

he rapturously Indexed—I own I had the
greatest friendship for this young Man whose
affectionate attention to me meritted My Gratitude—and he was so pleasing to us all, that we
missd him Greatly when he Left Carrick, which
happend on the following Occasion.

He was offerd the Curacy of Feathard about
fourteen Miles from Carrick it being vastly preferable to the Curacy of Whitechurch—he consulted us on the Occasion, and we advised him
not to lose so favourable an Opportunity of rais-
ing his small Income and future Expectations—
He accordingly left Carrick but without taking
leave of us, as he could not bear that Tryal.

Some time after we had an assembly and Concert for the Benefit of Mrs O Hara who had
also left us and settled amongst her Scholars in
Carrick—as my Mother and her other friends
strained every Nerve to procure her a good
Benefit the Rooms were as full as they could hold
of people from all Sides of the Country.

| An Assembly | CHAPTER 48TH | A poetical Effusion |

---

*You took her up a little tender Flower
Just sprouted on a Bank; which the Next Frost
Had nipt—*

We had not been long Dancing when Mr Gwyn
enterd—After speaking some time to My
Mother, he came over to the Set where I was

dancing and his joy at seeing Me again seemd
quite uncontroulable—Though this Appear'd
quite natural to *me*, I dreaded the Comments of
the Commentators of all sorts round us—He
kept at my Elbow till the Set was over, and
asked me for the Next, to which I chearfully
Agreed—during the rest of the Evening he
seldom quitted My Side but followd Me even
whilst I danced with Others.

He staid with us all that Week—Old Madame
our frenchwoman often joked with me about
him and shook her head crying—Ah Le pauvre
Gwyn! A Speculation I always laugh'd at but it
now seemed realized for it was really evident he
had sober serious thoughts of me—or rather
frantic Phrenetic Ones for his whole behaviour
was tumultuous to a degree—His Eyes were
ever fixed on Me with the strongest Emotions
in his face and an evident struggle to impart
some inward Secret—His Manner was sometimes so violent that he really terrified and per-
plexed me—From this Time his visits became
frequent—He generally came early in the Week
wet or dry and Staid till Saturday forced him
home—One Day he caught Me nursing a
foundling that had been left at the Door and
warmly observed What a charming little Nurse
I would make—Fanny insisted she would Make
a Much better one—and they had a fierce Contest about it whilst Mrs OHara and the rest of
us sat in laughing Neutrality—at a Dispute
really inveterately handled—after one of his

visits the following fragment was found in his
Room and handed to us—

Fragment—April 85

Thoughtless! Unguarded! in the World untried
No light to mark my Course! no friend to guide!
Pensive and careless, Journeying all Alone
To Southern Climes unknowing and unknown
I who am wav'ring, Ignorant of the End
Where shall I couch in Peace? Where find a faith-
    ful Friend?
Such gloomy Thoughts engrossed my anxious Mind
When first I left the busy Town behind—
From Parents, Kindred, tore Myself Away,
And yielded struggling to commanding Sway
But when once wafted to the destined Ground
For painful Thoughts no longer Room I found
At Night my Guardian Angel o'er me stood
Whispring, Let me direct thee for thy Good
The world a fickle, dang'rous babbling Stage
And Thou unpractised through unseason'd Age
In haste to H—b—t's peaceful seat repair
And see what Happiness awaits thee there
There unanimity and virtue dwell—
Pleasures unbounded more than tongue can tell
Domestic Joy has there set up her Throne
Fraternal Love has mark'd it for its own
There's Mirth, and lovely Sweetness unconfined
Glad Music too to charm the feeling Mind
Go then, a Welcome there youll find, and Stay
Till three full Moons or more have rolled away

There rest secure and from Example try
Discord to quell and Stop the Needy Cry—
The Happy Summons gladly I obey'd
I went, and found the Modest Seat arrayd
In Grand Humility, Attractive Ease
And every Virtue inly formd to please—
Here the fond Sire, by Profession Grave
With Heart that still adorns the Just and Brave
Oft a Companion acts to childish Minds
Indulges them in Sports of Various Kinds
The Genuine Parson, Duty's call t'attend
The tender Husband and the Steady Friend—
Here the Sage Mother with unwearied Care
'Gainst future Ills doth every Fence prepare
With her humanity still finds a Nurse
Religion Steers the pilot of her course
Her noble Birth the Meanest ne'er oppressd
And Modest Merit is her welcome Guest—
The gentle Daughter! soft, attractive, sweet
With awful Modesty commands Respect
With undesigning, unaffected Grace
In every generous Heart she holds a place
Her Modest Eyes unconscious of their Charms
Fill the fond Soul with ezquisite Alarms
Whilst from her fingers, Music's softest Strains
Come mended—on the Sepse their force remains—
The others all in diff'rent Ways conspire
T'attract Esteem, and Gen'ral Love t'acquire
Whilst Genial Sympathy reigns unconfined
And mutual Tenderness swells in each Mind
Thou Seat of Hospitality and Rest
How often have thy chearful Rays Me blest

How often was thy friendly Summons sent
And my dull mind with gloomy Care unbent—
How often—

Here the Fragment was left unfinish'd but in it
was another short one on the Indisposition of a
Young Lady.
After this we did not see Mr Gwyn for a long
time though we longed for his Return to make
him finish his pretty Eulogy of which we were
one and All not a little proud.
One desperate Night however he enterd the
Room whilst we were assembled at Tea—
Though wrapd up in Oil Cloth he was wet
through and through—When he had dried himself he walked about the room and seem'd much
flurried—By chance a pair of New Shoes of
mine lay on the Harpsichord, he took them up
exclaiming Oh What a foot, sighing and
cautiously Replacing them—The Next Day we
were all assembled as usual in the Music Room,
after Breakfast we produced his poem and
begged he would finish it, he attempted to snatch
it away, but at length promised to transcribe it
with Emendations and Additions he had Made
—He retired with it to his appartment where he
staid till Dinner—He then said the poem would
be ready in the Evening—and Mention'd that
he must Go away next Day—His Eyes were
swelled as if he had been weeping and he Expressd his Sorrow at leaving us in such forcible
Terms that I was forced to say I hoped we

should soon Meet Again—In the Greatest Per-
turbation he said it depended on one Circumstance whether we should ever Meet again, and
that a single stroke would decide and Mark him
for ever happy or Miserable.

A Love Letter   CHAPTER 49TH   An Angry
                                   Adieu

" *Ev'n He whose soul Now melts in Mournful
    Lays*
" *Shall Shortly want the generous Tear he pays*

Though I knew nothing of Gwyn's Intentions,
My Blushes pleaded Guilty to his distress, but
decorum would not let me understand more and
really I thought he had besides got into some
terrible Scrape by the frightful Convulsion of
his features, and was much affected at his Agony
—After Dinner he again retired to his Room
where he staid the whole Evening excusing himself by sending Word he had some business to
transact—I was crossing the Hall after it grew
dark when Gwyn rushed down stairs, put a
Sealed Packet in my hand—wrung it with the
greatest Vehemence and darted up stairs again
like Lightning—I stood for some time in
Amazement and then proceeded to get a Candle
supposing his packet to contain the Copy of
Verses he promised—On opening it however
the first words I saw were " my Dear and lovely
Miss Herbert—at the Head of two long Sheets

closely written Not containing the poem as I
supposed but a Declaration of his passion which
he said had subsisted ever since he first came to
Carrick—that he had suffer'd inexpressible torment in Struggling against it—He said he
would supplicate on his knees the Consent of
my Father and Mother if I refused him, and
would petition Lord Desart to interfere and
threaten'd the most desperate Consequences as
he knew I could never be his, though despair
had prompted him to write thus—warning me
I should soon hear of some fatal Event and must
answer for the Consequences—inshort his whole
Letter seem'd dictated by the wildest Phrenzy
—Reluctantly I shew'd the Letter to My
Mother not daring to act uncouncel'd Young
and inexperienced as I was—She sent it back by
My Sister Fanny with a Message that had I
known its contents I should Not have open'd it
—On seeing his Letter returned he fell into the
most frantic fits of passion, tore it in her presence
and threw it into the fire telling her he knew My
Mother had dictated the cruel Answer—He
then threw himself on the Bed, Wept like a
Child wringing his Hands and declaring he was
undone, Whilst Fanny stood transfix'd, afraid
either to go or Stay—She however at length ran
off and left him—My Mother Now acquainted
my Father with the Transaction—He was
greatly shocked as he had always a great Love
for Gwyn but he was now much enraged against
him—My Brothers who were then big School

Boys vowed Vengeance against him—but next
Morning he went off before any of us got up—
I own I was greatly vexed that I had exposed
him to my hot headed family—He had com-
mitted no fault but honouring me with his
Esteem—and declaring it in an unguarded hour
—by which he had lost the friendship of the
only family he regarded here—Indeed I was
quite Miserable at thus banishing him from his
Eden—And my Conscience was never easy till
I heard some Months after of his Marriage with
a Miss Rolleston a Lady of large fortune near
Feathard—who besides got him good church
Preferment being related to some Person in the
Ministry—As I heard he was perfectly happy
with his Choice—I thought myself quite Ex-
honorated from all further feeling on his
Account.

| A Baronets Wedding | (CHAPTER 50TH) | A farewell to Childhood |

For it is hard to wear their Bloom
In unremitting Sighs away

We Now got an Account of Sir John Blundens
Marriage with Miss Robbins—He Got a delightful Estate in the Co Kilkenny with her and
several other articles amounting to a clear 8000£
a Year—We sent a Letter off to congratulate
them on their arrival at Castle Blunden—My
Aunt wrote back their thanks and sent two

pieces of Silk one for My Mother and another
for Me, Sir John having given her a Charge to
search every Shop in Dublin for the most
elegant and becoming patterns as a Wedding
Present from him to us—she accordingly sent us
fifteen Yards each—My Mothers was sattin
with Stripes and flowers of Browns and pink—
mine a rich pink Tabby with Sattin Stripes—
This was a fresh proof of his Attention to us
when we were at a Distance from him—And his
Mind So occupied—I own I did not live three
Summers in the same House with this amiable
Cousin without feeling a strong Biass towards
him—There is a Sensibility in Youth indepen-
dent of Love which inclines the unpractised
Heart towards each fascinating and amiable
Object—Sir John ever pleasant at the Head of
his family and good and generous to every
branch of it was a dazzling object to a young inexperienced Mind but they say Love can't live
without Hope, and I believe nothing saved me
but the Certainty that he was far out of the
reach of my humble Expectations——All the
time I was at his House he seem'd to Make it
his chief point of Duty to befriend protect and
direct me and indeed to think that a Wild
Young Baronet flushd with Prosperity and the
Reception he every where met with, should
think at all of So insignificant a Being as myself
was too flattering to be observed without Gratitude by me—Besides he had a peculiarly Graceful Manner of Doing and Saying, that made

every thing he did or said pleasing to a Young, timid, humble Mind.

I shall now take leave of my more Childish Days which I have never forgotten, and which Yield me a Recollection of Pleasure Mixd with pain to think that they are pass'd never to return.

Adieu then all the Dear Delights of Childhood!
Adieu Mrs OHara and Madame Bondagee!
Farewell my Kids, my Dogs, and My feasts!
—Farewell my Friends and Youthful Companions!

Old friends   CHAPTER 51ST   Rural Apathy

Heav'n from all Creatures hides the Book of fate
All but the page prescribed their present state

I may say that the Marriages of my old acquaintances fixd the first Epoch of My Life—New friends, New Relations Started up every Hour, but I felt not the same warmth for them as for the former Race who being Now all Married and Settled were too much occupied with their Families to be what they once were.

I pass'd the Next four Years of My Life in a kind of Calm Apathy little interested about passing Scenes after I had conquerd my early Penchants unless some Family occurrence called forth my Sensibilities—When Gwyn ceased to visit us we had No Men here but Officers and Strangers who generally Attached themselves to

{ 1785 }

our beautiful Neighbours the Jephsons—Our
Female Friends were scatterd about the World
with their Husbands—We were in Ourselves a
happy family and the Rubs of Life did not then
wound deeply whilst

" *The World was all before us where to chuse
Our place of Rest—and providence our guide*

END OF BOOK THE SECOND

142

" *For who to dumb forgetfulness a prey*
" *This pleasing anxious Being e'er resign'd*

I spent the former part of My life improving
Myself for Society as well as Solitude—The
present afforded me no Opportunity of displaying my little stock of Accomplishments, but still
I was not without the flutter of Hope and Expectation—However the time was to come when
a Passion so strong and violent seized Me that
I lost both Society and my few Accomplishments
together—A Passion so forcible that it shook
every Sense and Shatterd every Nerve—And so
lasting that it wore away all the prime of My
Life in Embitterment and Disappointment.
The present period I might call a Non Entity in
Existence being quite disengaged from any particular pursuit and divested of any interesting
Passion—The Thing that first aroused us from
this torpid State was the happy termination of
the Ballysallagh Lawsuit—We had Bonfires and
a May pole set up for it—and after the long
anxious dreary Winter it was an Agreeable Sur-

prize—And the best Maying we could enjoy—
All the people of the lower Class round us Assembled dressd in May dresses and we had two
Days continual Dancing in the Field whilst they
were orderd a suitable Treat—The Jephsons—
The Officers and other Odd Company drank
Syllabub with us and we danced on the Gravel
walk almost as jocund as the Quality in the May
green—The Officers then here were a Captain
Mellifond, Mr Nugent &c—Mrs Mellifond
and the Officers gave us a Ball which though not
very grand pass'd off very pleasantly—We had
a Good Many officers of the Regiment at it and
a handsome Supper—This was followd by a
Syllabub party given by Mrs Jephson—We
regaled in the Dark Walk a Cool shady refec-
tory where we generally drank Tea in Summer
when with them—Mrs English then gave a
Ball on the Occasion though she was related to
our Adversary—Inshort we had nothing for
some time but Junketting which made Time
pass deliciously.
At that time a Miss Howley lived with Mrs
English a remarkable fine handsome Young
Woman but as remarkably vain proud fierce and
intractable—In the Winter I got a little fancy
Watch—And the Jephsons immediately after
sent to London for one apiece—They braggd
so much of them to Miss Howley on Purpose
to vex her, that she resolving to outdo them
sent to Paris for One—The Officers and we had
great laughing about this new prodigy that was

to appear to the total Annihilation of our Vanity
—April Day I rose early made a very pretty
Turnip Watch—and sent it in a nice little packing Box with a Dozen sheets of Brown Paper
and as many Seals, with the Box tied and seal'd
in like Manner—Round the Watch was a Paper
written—A Paris Watch for Miss Howley and
lines to the following Effect—" Beware of the
Ides of March said the Roman Augur to Julius
Caesar—" Beware of the Month of May said
the British Spectator to his fair Country Woman
—" And Beware of the first of April says the
writer of this to the fair Miss Howley having
the Honour of calling her—An April fool.
Officers, Jephsons, All were assembled at Mrs
Englishes usual Levee when the Packet arrived
—Oh God said Miss Howley (bouncing up)
" It's My Watch!—My Paris Watch!—In
transports she began to unpack—Ay! It's easy
to know french Packing from english she cried
—casting a triumphant Look at the Jephsons—
She went on unpacking Paper after Paper till
quite out of patience she call'd to Melifont for
his Penknife—Words cannot express her Rage
at the Disappointment—She Wept, stamp'd,
and tore her hair nor could be pacified till
Mrs English promised to find out the Author
of this Insult—Immediately Mrs Bab Butlar
was dispatched at the head of half a Dozen
Old Cronies to find out who had dared to insult Miss Howley—but hearing of the Racket
it caused we let none but the Jephsons into

our Secret—They to be sure enjoyed it with
mischievous Sport.

They had however Scarce vented their Laughter
at Miss Howleys Expence when I play'd them
a Trick which though not so vexatious compleatly duped them—I dressd Myself as a raw
Country Girl and went in one Night with a
Letter which on rapping at the Door I delivered
to Old James Meaker the Butlar and he presented to his mistress—In it I complained that
I was a poor Country Girl who had the Misfortune of having a Merry begotten Child, That
I complained to Mr Cox the Magistrate of the
Young Man who had quitted Me—but that he
order'd me to be turned out of his House and I
threw myself on her Honours Mercy to speak to
Mr Cox as I knew she was intimate with him,
and he could refuse her Nothing she asked—It
was a long Letter and so compleatly disguised
in the Hibernian Dialect that She never once
suspected the Forgery — Meanwhile James
Meagher came to the Door and was very inquisitive to know what brought me there so late
at Night — He questiond me so hard, and I
made such pert Answers that he called Nurse
Dwyer who advised him to kick me out of the
Hall—In a little time the Bell rang violently—
and I heard Mrs Jephson in the greatest passion
crying " The Audacious Creature! How durst
she presume to think I would speak to Mr Cox
on such a Business—Our family all drank Tea
there on purpose to witness the Joke—When

they had worked up Mrs Jephson sufficiently, the Boys came out to me and we had such a Sham Battle of ill Language that James, Nurse, and Mrs Jephson were compleatly transmogrified into Furies—They shook me and threatend Me with so many Grimaces that the Boys and Girls screech'd again with laughter—I was at last kicked out of the House and the Door clap'd in my Face—Mrs Jephson kept the Letter and shew'd it to the Gentlemen about—They offerd a Reward for Apprehension and Not till a long time after did we inform Mrs Jephson who her Petitioner was.

Sometime after this Mrs O Hara our Music Mistress left Carrick—I remember it was she who transcribed the above Letter that the Hand should not be known—She settled in Thurles and died some time After—Old Madame Bondagée the frenchwoman had left us a good while before—They both turned out Drunken, but they had pass'd through many and various Scenes, and were very entertaining as well as clever in their Business.

Mr Wimpe our writing Reading and Grammar Master was forty Years Clerk of the Parish and our Prime Minister on all Occasions—Our Chief adviser on all important affairs—Our Consoler in Misfortune—Our Felicitator in Prosperity—He visitted us daily for forty Years in the Capacity of friend as well as Mentor and we reaped all the Benefit of his Sage Counsels and Observations.

{ 1786 }

A trip to
Killarney

CHAPTER 53D

Delightful
Excursions

" *Dear is that Shed to which his Soul conforms*
" *And dear that Hill that lifts him to the Storms*

It was now resolved that We should pay a Visit
to Killarney to visit Mr Herbert and his Wife
who having made up all Quarrels were lately
returned from England to domesticate once
more at Muckrus—Our Journey was tedious
but nothing material happend till we came to
Newcastle, where we ran over a little pig—The
Owner came to demand Payment and my
Mother offerd him half a Guinea, which he
would not take—She then bid him go about his
business but he gatherd a dreadful Mob about
us, just at the time the Right Boys were rising,
which frightened us beyond Measure, and we
gallop'd out of the Town with the loss of the
Coachmans Great Coat which they seized—We
called at the Magistrate's Seat (Mr Meredyth)
and complained them—He was related to my
Father but said, he could not venture to stir
about the Business—We traveld over the dreary
Mountains till we got a View of Turk, Mangerton, and all the wonders of Killarney—Words
cannot express my Father's Joy at once more
seeing his Native Place—He felt his Youth
renewed, and acted the Child weeping and
laughing for Joy—See here Mrs Herbert!—
Look at that Mountain Miss Herbert!—Do

you see the Lake now Young Gentlemen? were his joyful Exclamations—We were as delighted as himself at seeing the way he enjoy'd it—When we got to Muckrus we were kindly received by Mr and Mrs Herbert and his three sisters Fanny, Mary, and Peggy Herbert—but Mrs Herbert soon grew weary of form and slip'd out of the room on pretence of seeing our Beds well aired but it was to play with the Children in the Nursery—We had very little of her Company, for she preferr'd racing on the Lawn with My Brothers and any gentlemen that drop'd in and constantly strip'd off her Habit running races all the Morning in that Trim—Besides the family of the House there was a Miss Cherry Saunders there and Major Herbert an old Cousin with two or three Scotch Officers who constantly came out—Our Arrival brought on Dinners and Assemblies at Killarney—all which we dispatch'd that we might view the place without interruption—My Father and Mother, Otway and Tom, Fanny and I were the Carrick Set there—After Viewing every thing about Muckrus and daily straying amongst its gardens, wilds, and the enchanting Nut Grove of Money Beg—we took Boat and the first Day saw a Stag let loose under Toamis and Glena Mountains—Whilst a Multitude of Boats cover'd the Lake with French Horns and other Instruments—It was a delightful Sight which has drawn Travellers from all parts of the World—We had that Day a party of Spanish grandees come purposely to see the Lake and its Environs—Our Boat's Company landed at Toamis—There we had a cold Dinner at a convenient Distance from it's beautiful Cascade which consists of three large falls of Water each of which is a Wonder in itself—It was then in full Beauty—The Body of Water was immense—The Noise of it's fall most tremendously pleasing if I may so express Myself—The Foliage that overshadow'd it, in its greatest Luxuriance, and the Wild Strawberries on its Magnificent Rocks fully ripe—They were brought down from the awful Precipices that enclose the Cascade by little peasant Girls, who for a small Gratuity sold us more than we could Eat—To give any Idea of Toamis Cascade on paper would be a Vain Attempt—but I liked it better than Mangerton though the latter was much more celebrated, being larger and more magnificent—but Mangerton has since acquired What it then wanted viz: Plenty of Wood and now far surpasses Toamis in Beauty and Variety—We came Home at a reasonable Hour that Night with our Heads quite turned with the enchanting Scenery.

| Island beauties | CHAPTER 54TH | Upper Lakes |

Whatever sweets salute the Northern Sky
With vernal leaves that blossom but to die
These here disporting own the kindred Soil
Nor ask Luxuriance from the planter's toil

Our next Excursion was amongst the Islands—
Ross and Inisfallen are beautiful and can only
be surpass'd by Dinish the fairest Sister of the
three—It is adorned with Mountainous Piles of
the most delightful Rock Work cover'd with an
unbounded variety of Trees and Shrubs—Now
a beautiful Pine Grove rises then a plantation of
Oak—Here you see on the bare Rock a Lawn
spread that surpasses the finest Velvet in Ver-
dure and Smoothness, there a Shrubbery of
Arbutus coverd with Shining Leaves White
Blossoms and Scarlet Fruit in one Season and
growing Spontaneously with other curious
Shrubs from the Rocks—The Whole is inter-
sected with the most delightful Walks—sometimes winding Sometimes in Vistas borderd with
every kind of Heath—Now growing Wild Now
regular as in the Most beautiful Parterre.

We dined and spent our Day in this enchanting Spot with the addition of Mr and Mrs
Richard Herbert of Cahernane and the Scotch
Officers to our Party—We eat our Meal of Cold
Meat in a Cottage on the Island—At length a
Day was fix'd to visit the upper Lakes which
being a long Days voyage required larger pre-
parations—We sailed safely up the dangerous
straight pass'd the famous Eagles Nest (the
Name of a beautiful wooded mountain forming
a perfect Cone to the Clouds) and landed on the
wildest part of the upper Lake shore—Here the
Rocks and Mountains are piled in such grand
Confusion that they set the Head quite giddy to

look at them—It seemd as if there had been a
Battle of Giants there and Mountains torn up
by the Roots and hurled in dread disorder—
After our first surprize we spent the Day in the
utmost Glee only interrupted by My Cousin
Fanny Herbert losing one of her shoes in a
Quagmire and Miss Cherry Saunders and one
of the Scotch officers tumbling headlong in the
same as they attempted a leap over it lovingly
together—The french Cook dressd our Dinner
under the Trees which we eat very Merrily till
the fire caught some combustible Matter on the
Mountain which blew up about us with a
Hideous Explosion and dispersed us all over the
Rocks—We were so taken up with the Novelty
of the Scene that we did not think of returning
till the Darkness convinced us we had im-
prudently out staid our time—We enterd two
Boats—Mr Herbert and us Ladies in one, My
Father Brothers and the Gentlemen in another
—as we thought my father worth a whole Shipload of us we left him in the Rear and bravely
faced the Dangers of the Night through the
narrow winding Straight exhorting him not to
fall back more than three Yards from us—Thus
Marshall'd with fear and trembling we commended ourselves to the Protection of Providence—We at length came to a frightful Pass
and got over it with such difficulty and hazard
that we were in Agony about the other Boat—
But what was our Consternation on hallooing
not to receive any Answer—In vain we roared,

and implored—Nothing was heard but whistling Winds which encreased to a Storm and the Rain fell in torrents—All was black as Pitch round us—My Mother, Fanny, and I gave up our Treasure as lost—And even Mr Herbert though used to continual Pilotry there confessd his fears for their safety—We three clung together in Tearful Agony Wet to the Skin—and shaking all over with cold and Terror—On landing at Muckrus, my Mother was carried more dead than alive to the House, and we walked by her Side screeching and roaring for our dear Father and our two dear Boys—We loudly rapped and heard the approach of footsteps—The Door open'd, and Lo! my Father and Brothers appeared with all the friskiness, that a good drying at the fire and a good Supper after it could inspire—The Gentlemen piqued at our affecting Superiour Bravery overshot us in the Dark and got a short way by Land to the House—Whilst we we[re] buffeting the Waves they were giggling at the Trick they had play'd us—When our first Joy was over they got a General Volley of Abuse from us all, and were in Disgrace for a Week after.

| A female Phenomonen | CHAPTER 55TH | An Old Abbey |

All Sweetness, Smiles, and Seeming Innocence

Mrs Herbert now got into a strong flirtation

with a Captain Baird but her Playful Wildness
and Innocent Appearance would have tranquil-
ized the most jealous pated Wretch into Security—She display'd all the simplicity of a playful
Child in every giddy Action—And None that
pass'd an hour in her bewitching Society, could
think her really Guilty—She was not fond of
Womens Company, but her Manners were so
charming to all that she fascinated every Sex and
Size—She studied every one, and Adapted herself to every ones humour without appearing to
do so, or laying aside for a Moment her own
Eccentricities—Her House was perfectly well
managed whilst She seemd totally to disregard
the Management—Inshort in profound Policy
and knowledge of the World she proved herself
the Daughter of a Great Statesman in Theory
and practise—She knew every thing understood
every thing, was deeply read without the Affectation of learning—and more deeply practised
under all the Appearance of Simplicity and
Childishness—Inshort her ready Capacity was
equal to every Acquirement and every undertaking.

In enumerating our Peregrinations round
Muckrus I should have mention'd one we made
to its famous old Abbey, a spot prohibited in
Conversation since its being Named as the
Rendezvous of Mrs Herberts former Gallan-
tries with Captain H—— The Boys, Fanny
and I were dying to see it and chose Nightfall
for our Walk that our visit to it should not be

known—Too late we repented, when traversing
the rocky Windings of the immense Garden we
frequently lost our Way in the Wild Labyrinth
—We at length groped our Way to a tall Melancholy Avenue of Elms that leads from the Garden
to the Green Enclosure where stands the gloomy
Pile—A Monument of Ancient Magnificence
—We enterd the Enclosure by a wicket, and
drew back with Horror whilst the Bats and
Owls clap'd their Wings around us—The
Abbey is surrounded by Trees and consists of
a variety of Squares above and below which are
environ'd by long Ranges of Cells and Cloisters
gloomy as Death—In the Grand Square stood
a famous old Yew Tree of immense Height and
Circumference—It was long the Admiration of
all Travellers but I forget it's Dimensions—The
outside of the Abbey is adorned with Battle-
ments of human Skulls and Bones piled as high
as the Building which though they shew its
former Celebrity are a most terrifying Spectacle indeed—We did not return till twelve at
Night to Muckrus, and were in the deepest perplexity how to account for our peregrination, or
rather Pilgrimage to this forbidden Spot.

The Beauties of Muckrus did not let us stay
much within Doors but in wet Weather we had
a large Library though in a ruinous state—and
every kind of Chance Games—Mr Herbert
mostly amused himself drawing sketches, there
were many good pictures in the Rooms—
Music was the only Deficiency there.

We at length took leave of Muckrus fully convinced of Mrs Herberts Innocence and quite charmed with our delightful Excursion.

| Return to Carrick | (CHAPTER 56TH) | An Extravagant Heir |

One prospect lost, Another still we gain
And not a Vanity is giv'n in Vain

We arrived at Carrick the Second of August 1786, and then got a New Neighbour whose coming soon alter'd the whole usual course of our Lives—This was my Cousin Edward Eyre Nephew to my Father—One of the greatest Oddities that Nature or Art ever produced—I say Art, because he studied every possible Method to make himself diverse from all Other human Beings—He was Heir to an immense property but spent and dabbled amongst Usurers to the tune of one hundred thousand pounds which kept him at Law and in poverty all his Life—He had a glass Coach and a glass Vis a Vis where he sat dress'd out from Top to Toe in a Suit of the Gayest Colour Silk or Sattin lined with Persian of a different Colour—He wore Sattin Shoes and Set Buckles had two or three sets of paste Buttons that cost an immensity—His Hair was dress'd like a Womans over a Rouleau or Tete, which was then the fashion amongst the Ladies—He sometimes carried a Muff, sometimes a Fan, and was always painted

up to the Eyes with the deepest Carmine—
His Manners and Actions were as Outré as
his Dress and he was for ever engaged
in some Novel Enterprize—Every Year he
bought 200 pounds worth of Lottery Tickets
though he seldom or ever got a prize of any
Value.

We all doated on him, and his settling here gave
us infinite pleasure—After searching out every
old ruined Seat about, (for such only would he
take) He at length took Linville a beautiful Cottage by the Side of the Suir—Six Miles from
our House and half way between Carrick and
Clonmell—There he lived in most romantic
Retirement with half a dozen favourite Servants
and two very large spotted spaniels of the
Leopard Breed which He called Miss Dapper
and Miss Kitsy and adopted as Daughters and
Co Heiresses—His Books, writings and Lottery Tickets engrossing the Hours that he did
not spend with those Ladies or at the Card
Table with his Mother Aunts, Cousins or
Cronies—He was continually planning some
ludicrous Exploit or Excursion and spared no
Expense in its Execution—We all lived mostly
at Linville with him, for he was quite affronted
if he had not two or three of us there Every
Week—He kept his Room all the Morning and
only came down to Dinner and Cards—Tea and
Cold Water were his only Beverage and Sweetmeats or Pickles of every kind his constant food
—When he was in good humour we always

came in for a share of his Goodies and even when out of Temper he treated us with the utmost Civility, and left us full possession of his House, Gardens and all they contained—He had not been long settled when we determined on a Round of Excursions to all the waste places of the Neighbourhood, where we drove with the coach and vis a vis full and a Cart following with all kind of provision through Bog and Mire, Thick and Thin, and many a disastrous Event we had to encounter to his great Delight.

One of our first visits was to Etm Ville the residence of Old Counsellor Butlar who we heard was from home at that time—The two Carriages and the Cart with provisions drove up to the Door with all immaginable freedom—but to our great Annoyance the Old Counsellor himself was the first Object we met at the Door—He came out, and with his hand to his Eyes very narrowly pored into all the Circumstances of our Visit—after pressing us in vain to alight, for we were rooted to the Carriages with Surprize he questiond to know What brought us there, Where were we going, And Why his friend Mr Herbert would take such a Journey without refreshment—He then hinted that he could Not make out what our Cart meant—And we were so dumbfounderd we could not answer a Single cross Question—We departed in a Roar of Laughter, leaving the Old gentleman in uncertainty and Amazement about us.

After dining at Kilcash, Two mile Bridge and
Many other places we began to be at a loss for
amusement when a famous Source of Enjoyment occurr'd—Ned Eyre had an Estate in the
Co Galway which he now determined to Visit—
And reading in the Newspaper that his Cousin
Giles Eyre of Sporting Memory, had a Horse to
run at the Ensuing Races of Loughrea—He
resolved that we should Post it off to Galway—
pop in on the Races of Loughrea and reimburse
the Expence by making up a Match between
his Cousin Giles and his Cousin Dolly—The
Idea got so strongly in his Head, that he already
was busy planning out our Cloaths, Equipage,
and future Visits—In the Interim his nephew
Sim White came to pay him a Visit, and was
quite surprized to see the fuss we were all in—
but we soon enlisted him for our Journey and
he wrote to his Mother not to expect him for
some time—Sim White was third Son of Mrs
White Ned Eyres eldest Sister and Brother to
the present Lord Bantry who got his title by
repulsing the French when they landed at
Bantry—There were four Brothers of the Whites
all Estated Men and three Sisters all Beauties
and Married to men of Rank and fortune—Sim
White was then a mighty pretty young Man of
genteel manners Sallow complectiond but had
beautiful Black Eyes with fire and Expression
of Countenance.

No vernal Bloom their torpid Rocks display
But Winter lingering chills the Lap of May

Our Journey was as curious as Ourselves but
we did not feel the tiresomeness of it till we got
into the County Galway where the bad Roads
and parched fields only bounded by loose stone
Walls for many Miles, gave us at once a hearty
surfeit of it—We travel'd a good many Miles
out of our Way to see an old family Seat of the
Eyres then the property of Giles Eyre but long
Deserted—We spent a Day planning the
Alterations that might be made in it could Ned
accomplish his scheme and put me in possession,
no Easy task as Giles was Head of the Eyre
family there and a Man of large property—To
add to our Hopes an Old Uncle of his came to
Linville who promised Ned all his Influence in
weaning his Nephew from the turf and human-
izing him into a Sedate settled Life with my
Ladyship.

Some Accident happend the Vis a Vis which
forced us to stop a few Days at Oranmore a
Village near Galway—where Sim White fell
desperately in Love with my sister Fanny—
This was a New Subject of Exultation to Ned
Eyre who plumed himself on providing for both
his Cousins before he returned—Captain Eyre
the aforesaid Uncle of Giles came out from Gal-

way to pay his Compliments—He introduced us
at Ardfry a beautiful Place near Oranmore belonging to the Blake family where a large party
of Grandees were assembled on the Marriage
of Mr Blake with Lady Louisa Birmingham
Daughter of Lord Louth and Miss Blake's Marriage with Lord Errol a Scotch peer—Lady
Errol Miss Blake that was was a beautiful Creature then on the point of being Married—Lady
Louisa was also a great Beauty and the Miss
Blakes were Beauties and Wits both—However
we got off pretty well from this formidable Set
with only the Misfortune of Ned Eyres Dog
Lady Dapper dirtying the Room and Lord
Louths blindly stepping into it—We were
press'd to Dine there by Mrs Blake but we made
our appology—She assured My Mother they
seldom or ever sat down to a Meal with less than
a hundred in family.

We proceeded on to Galway and had all the
Bells in the Town ringing for our Arrival as
Ned Eyre was proprietor of great part of the
Town—The first thing he did was to Order his
family Vault to be opened Where he descended
and spent his first morning in paying his Duty
to the remains of his great grand Aunt whose
carcase he inspected and brought away some of
the Sacred Ashes till a Mob began to gather
loudly murmuring at the prophanation and Ned
Eyre with difficulty escaped—His Next amusement was treating all the Beggars of Galway to
Hot Toast, Tea, and Chocolate—and we had a

Publick Breakfast at the Door every Morning
where Myriads attended—None were sent
empty away and Ned put a Shilling on every
Saucer he sent down.

But his general amusement was painting and
dressing up one of his Hands as an Infant, and
dandling it in the presence of a Nurse and new
born Heir that lived Opposite—The fine folks
of the Town soon heard of our doings and came
in a Body one Sunday to stare and to gaze—But
Ned Eyre threw up the Sash and thrusting himself half way out of the Window put out his
Tongue at them All on which they retired from
the opposite Windows and never after Molested
us.

Loughrea Races (CHAPTER 58TH)   A Galway Ball
                                   A Proposal

And Loves, and Friendships finely pointed Dart
Fall blunted from each Indurated Heart

We Now set out for the Races at Loughrea in
great Stile with four Horses to Each Glass Carriage and Suitable Appendages—On getting to
the Race Course, Ned Eyre sent a polite Message to his Cousin Giles requesting his presence
and protection—But Giles was too busy with
his Horses to think of any thing Else and contented himself with sending his brother John
Eyre to us—Ned Eyre freely told him that he
wanted the Estated Man for one of the Girls

and As he was only a Younger Brother he might
go about his business—We had a dreadful
fracas at the Course and on our return along the
Road with one Mrs Kelly who made her Servant jostle us in our Glass Vehicles because they
eclipsed her New Equipage, for which Ned
Eyre gave her a hearty set down from His Carriage—we returned quite disappointed in our
Designs on Giles Eyre—However Ned Dress'd
us out for the Assembly that Evening (which
was transferrd to Galway) and got Captain Eyre
to escort us to it—But the renownd Giles did
not make his appearance—We however danced
away all Night and considering the Mode of
Dancing there used we escaped with few Accidents—We next visitted the Convent and congratulated the Nuns on a late Escape they had
from a Regiment of Soldiers who broke in on
them at Night under a pretence of searching for
Contraband Goods—We then received Visits
from Lady Ann Daly Mr Martin and several
other Head folks—We dined at Captain Eyres
and were asked to Mr Martins and some other
places—Inshort we did many things which I
cannot now recollect—and finally quitted Galway swearing Never to enter it again.

Ned Eyre had his Carriage fill'd with the finest
ripe Peaches and Apricots but he kept them all
for his Dog Lady Dapper and would send us
none but the riff raff which we shared with his
other Dog Miss Kitsy—However Sim White
now and then stole a few good ones for us—

Meanwhile Ned Stuffd our Carriage with Galway fish which soon stank so abominably that there was no bearing it—at last we crossd the Ferry near Mr Yelvertons and got out of the Nasty County Galway—the Rain poured down in Cascades and we were forced to enter a wretched Hovel on the Other side where with difficulty we got a few potatoes and Eggs with Rashers to satisfie our ravenous Stomachs.

Nothing else very material happen'd besides common Accidents till we got home when Sim White now overhead and Ears in Love sent in his Proposals for my Sister Fanny—He was then sent off to ask his Mothers Consent who gave a positive Negative—He wanted to carry on a Correspondence which was negatived at our Side and there the Matter dropd but not without Causing very great Vexation and Commotion amongst us—Sim White was a very interesting looking young Man and could make himself very Agreeable when he pleased—but he was very young and had an Artful Mother so could not be trusted.

Prince William Henry	Chapter 59th	A Curraghmore Ball

*When Nymphs were coy, and Love could not
    prevail*
The Gods disguised were never known to fail

The Next Event I can think of at Carrick of any

importance was the arrival of Prince William
Henry now Duke of Clarence the Kings third
Son—He came to Curraghmore in his Tour and
was Magnificently entertained by Lord Waterford, who gave a grand Ball on the Occasion to
which every one was invited, The Carrick people
of course among the Rest—There was no end to
the preparations on this Occasion as he was the
first of the Brunswick Race who had Visitted our
Isle.

Fanny and I thought we could Never be fine
enough on the Occasion and sent off to Kilkenny for New Hats and Feathers, Chapeaus
being then the Rage—We likewise wrote an Invitation to Araminta Blunden to come for the
Ball, But she would not leave Mrs Matthews
who was then in a promising Way, after burying
her first Child—However she sent us the Hats
and very fine things they were—We next applied to Ned Eyre for a loan of his Paste Buttons
as we thought we could never be courtly Enough
on the Event—He was rejoiced to have his
Buttons exhibitted and we as glad to get them—
This put his Spirits again in Motion after the
Damp Giles Eyre and Sim White threw on them
—Some of our Town friends came up, and display'd all their Taste in trimming our Gowns
which were Gawze over Fanny's blue and My
pink silk Linings—They were trimmed all over
with black Velvet Biasses to show off the double
Paste Buttons, and no Eastern Queens ever cut
such a dazzling Appearance—Poor Mr Rankin

who was a good deal here was quite shocked at
our Extravagance in sending for Hats to Kilkenny and warmly remonstrated with us—He
however came up in the Evening to see us
dress'd, and how the Ladies looked, particularly
Miss Faneny as he call'd her she being his
favourite—But when we burst forth on him like
two resplendent Suns Glittering with Diamonds
words cannot express his astonishment, and I
don't think he was ever the same thing to us After
—Our Dresses were much stared at and Much
Admired, but Nothing like them was seen in the
Ball Room—We went peppering to Curraghmore and found all the Rooms full—After Tea
the Dancing began to a very fine Band and other
Music—The Prince danced with most of the
prettiest Females—Fanny Jephson in particular
he admired—Indeed she was that kind of
Beauty that could not pass unnoticed any where
—They were quite proud of the Honour—We
had a most superb Supper in the large Room
newly painted by Head Masters—The Ceiling
and Pannels exhibitting various emblematic and
Mythological Pieces painted with the utmost
skill of the Artist—The Tables were adorned
with every Embellishment Money could Procure—Every thing looked like Enchantment
and the Prince thanked Lord Waterford for
his elegant Entertainment the beauty and
Sumptuousness of which could not well be
described.

After Supper the Ladies first broke up for

the Dancing Room and His Royal Highness
honour'd each one of them with a Kiss as they
passd, guarding the Door that None should pass
out unblest, which affronted some very much
whilst others thought it a high Honour and
various were the Debates it Occasioned—the
Propriety of it became the Subject of all the
newspapers — He played off many Tricks
amongst the Irish Ladies whilst in the Kingdom
and met with some smart Retaliations from the
fair Hibernians and their Spouses—The Day
after the Ball displayed a curious Scene—The
ground was cover'd with snow which fell in
flakes during the Night—Some Carriages going
had stuck in the woods all Night and their
owners were obliged to remain in that Mortifying Situation, without any Prospect of getting
out of it—Of those who were returning from
the Ball some lost their shoes, some their Caps,
and Not a few their Hearts.

| An Odd family party | CHAPTER 60TH | A projected play |

But our vile Tastes her lawful Charms refuse
And painted Arts depraved Allurements use

We spent the ensuing Week with Ned Eyre
amusing him with Anecdotes about Prince
Henry—Our Recluse seldom went to those
places unless some particular Whim occurred to
him as once at Cork when he promised to paint

the Cheeks of a very pale Lady for an assembly
—When she came down dressd to the Parlour,
He at one side and Mrs White at the other
scrubb'd her Cheeks—one with the deepest
Crimson the other with plain Wool, and then
hurried her off without letting her go to the
Glass—For fear the Joke should light all on
their pale friend, and her odd Cheeks of Various
Hue—The Brother and Sister carried Jalap in
their pockets which they secretly mixd with the
Tea and Coffee—So that the Ladies and Gentlemen of the Ball Room soon found something
else to think of besides laughing at Ned Eyre's
pale protegée—The worthy Pair locked the
Ball Room Door and a General Confusion
ensued—Some were fainting Some weeping
whilst their wicked Physicians escaped and
drove home.

At the Age of fourteen Mrs White then Miss
Eyre was devoutly carried to a Confirmation,
but was so vex'd at being forced to take all her
Sins on herself that She stuck her Head full of
Iron Pins with the Points up to annoy the Bishop
who was terribly Scratched and torn when he
laid his hands on his Contumelious Disciple—
Were I to recount all the Feats of those two
Worthies I should fill a volume.

Linville soon became a gay scene, The 17th
Dragoons were quarter'd in Carrick and then
order'd to Clonmell—Mrs Crofton wife to
Captn Crofton a beautiful little Woman dropt
her Mother Mrs Bradshaw at Linville—Captain

Crofton was related to my Mother and his Wife
to Ned Eyre who was delighted to have his Old
Crony Mrs Bradshaw to make one at the Loo
Table and bear his Jokes—A Mrs Mullins also
came there a fine dashing London Lady parted
from her Husband—The Whites, Maunsels
and his Brother Mr Hedges were often off and
on there—and when he was perfectly settled his
Mother came there to live with him—My Aunt
Eyre was even at that Age a beautiful looking
Woman, she was of the largest size and had an
Air of Majesty about her that struck every one
—she had all the Pleasing Manners of My
Father except his Meekness and Patience, for
when rouzed she was very fiery and passionate
—and being a great family Woman nothing
provoked her so much as Ned Eyres taking up
the Almanack and pointing out where his Cousin
the Haberdasher and his Relation the Shoemaker lived in Dublin—She Always stood up
with her Hands clench'd telling the puppy He
was the only Blot in the family from the time
they came over with William the Conqueror
and that his Ancestors were the lineal Descendants of Charlemagne and Pepin Kings of france
—She was so like my Father in every thing but
her hastiness, that we loved her greatly and her
warm temper made her equally fond of her dear
and now only Brother and his family—Ned who
always reflected her Sentiments treated us with
the greatest Defference, And let who would be
there they were obliged to Make Room for us—

Even the fine Mrs Mullins was forced to sleep
on a Pallet whenever we went out.

Mrs Mullinses Theatrical Appearance now set
him Agog to Act a Play—He was to perform
the Part of Jessamy in Lionel and Clarissa—
His Brother Hedges he intended should be his
Harman to Her Diana—she being an Old flirt
of Mr Hedges—but my Aunt perswaded him
not to let the play go on.

Writing of Plays I shall mention one we acted
when Mrs Cooke was here which I forgot to
mention in its right place—The Old Garret the
scene of most of our childish Pranks was our
theatre—The Fair Penitent the play we chose—
I had at once the laborious Tasks of painting
the Scenes and fitting Myself for the formidable
part of Calista—Otway acted Altamont—
George Carshore Lothario—Miss Carshore
Lavinia—and Tom the brave Horatio—We
made the Children act as Snobs, Stage Sweepers
Guards Musicians and waiting Maids—All the
Money we could rap or run was expended in
Canvas, Whiting, Gambouge, Stone Blue and
Oil for the Painter—and many a time the poor
Boys denied themselves a halfpennyworth of
Elecampane or Gingerbread to devote their
little pocket Money to the Theatre—We got a
friend to dig up a Skull in the Church Yard and
ransacked every place for Relicks to make the
last Scene as dismal as possible—My Fathers
old black Cassocks served for hangings, and
his Wig converted Altamont into a venerable

Sciolto—We had the whole Stage decorated with Pictures, flower pots Ribbons Shells Moss and Lobster Claws—Calista was dress'd in Virgin White with her beautiful golden Locks hanging in loose Ringlets and festoon'd with penny Rings and two penny Beads &c—Lavinia was dress'd in a Salmon Colour Stuff ornamented with Natural flowers—Great Interest was made by Captains Curtis and Perceval to be admitted as Snobs, but we limitted our Audience to the Carshores, Jephsons, Mr Rankin and some Others—Many were our failures and Mischances—Our Prompter not yet out of his spelling Book miscalled his Words or lost his place—The gallant gay Lothario grew sulky and refused to act his Part when the brave Horatio tilted him too roughly—The venerable Sciolto burst out laughing just in the Act of introducing the lost Calista to the dead Body of her Lover—Calista and Lavinia fought desperately behind the scenes about change of Dresses —and finally the Candle snuffers set the Stage on fire.

To our great disappointment the Linville Play was suppress'd which no doubt would have been as curious in its way as our former Essay.

In real Life we had now a new Theatre opening before us, as my Father was compelld to lay out a thousand pounds on building a new Glebe House at Knockgrafton within five miles of Cashel and twenty miles from Carrick, which being now just compleated the ABishop com-

pelled him to reside there three months in
every Year.

A Squandering Heir	Chapter 61	A Smart little Lover

*"Love like a cautious fearful Bird ne'er builds
But where the place Silence and Calmness yields*

Whilst we were busy preparing to leave our
truly charming little Place near Carrick for the
barren Wilds and parched Glebe of Knockgrafton Ned Eyre was busy in setling Leases of
his Estates to his different friends—My Father
got Leases to hold for my two Brothers—But
Ned Eyre gave the greatest part for little or
nothing to his favourite Servants John Crowley
and William Wiltshire and both proved un-
thankful and unworthy and forsook him when
they had well wrung him.

One of the Head Attorneys in Dublin Mr
Cooper Crawford now came down to my Father
with a Bill of Costs for Law Business—He was
a smart little Batchelor between thirty and forty
and was introduced by Mr Harden Bradshaw
my Fathers Law Agent—He hinted that it
would be Odd if in bringing in a Bill of Costs
he should stumble on a Wife, and it was notified
to Me that Mr Crawford quite charmed with
my Conversation and Musical Talents was to
dine here the following Sunday in Company
with Mr H. Bradshaw—Meanwhile a Letter

arrived from Sim White to his Grandmother which mentioned that he was doing all he could with his Mother for leave to come here, and as she seem'd wavering, he hoped soon to ask pardon for his Past remissness—Mr Maunsel my Aunts son in law was then at Linville—He was a clergyman, and married to her youngest Daughter—My Aunt and My Mother to be sure laid their Heads together, and were never at rest till they hawked in Old Mrs Bradshaw and Mr Maunsel to their Consultations—Mrs Bradshaw who was really a goodnatured woman fell a crying with Joy at hearing of the Matches in Contemplation and My Aunt and Mother were equally soften'd—Of Sim Whites Match there could be no doubt respecting its Eligibility, and Mr Maunsel who knew Mr Crawford well declared that he was *a very honest worthy little Man*—of good personal property, and one of the first people in his professional Line in Dublin—That he was a Man of very good Family and Connections, and finally that he was every Day rising to a Rapid Fortune—This Account set the Ladies quite up and Mr Maunsel was invited to meet his friend Mr Crawford—When the important Day arrived we musterd up all our Elegance on the Occasion and my Maid Ann Dowling dress'd me up as neat as Hands and Pins could make Me.

{ 1789 }

A Queer
Courtship

CHAPTER 62

Youthful
Awkardness

"Like one that holds a Nobler Chace
"You try the tender loss to bear

At sweet Eighteen I enterd the Drawing Room
of Mrs Herbert to make a full conquest of Mr
Crawford——The Hours passd on before Dinner
rather formally, with only a Sly Hint from Mr
Maunsell——I began to despair as the Jephsons
were asked for the Evening with many other
Confidential friends who though I knew they
wished me well would cool my Courage as I
dreaded their Raillery——The Evening came and
Mr Crawford and I were jostled together to the
Settee——with our friend H Bradshaw to preside
over our Flirtation and see fair play done——We
talkd of the Election, of the Regency, of the
Dublin Amusements, and finally we were very
smart upon the Quakers——Fanny Jephson could
now no longer contain her laughter, She longed
for a Bit of Mischief and gave me so sly a Look
that I crawl'd off the Settee, and hid Myself
amongst the young Ladies at the Window——My
Beau who had disregarded all the Beauties in
the Room for me was all astonishment at my
abrupt Departure——And Harden Bradshaw sat
fiddling with his Watch chain quite disconcerted——The Girls pounded and bruised me all
over to drive me back but they had done their
Job, and the World would not have driven me

back to the Settee and Mr Crawford—We at
length adjourned to the Harpsichord in the next
Parlour—I playd off my own Push about the
Jorum for him and set him bravoing and encor-
ing like a Madman—He had now many Opportunities of moving my Hand when I went
wrong and so forth—He was quite enraptured
with my Musical Performance—The Jephsons
play'd but he disregarded them—when this was
over we all sat in a Circle round the fire which
he pierced and planted himself by Me—but the
Charm was broke, the Jephsons up at My Elbow
and the Devil a Word could I say.

He soon after went off with Harden Bradshaw
who threw an angry look at me as he departed
with My Beau—After twice playing the Garron
so egregiously I expected to hear no more of Mr
Crawford—but Next Morning—Mr Bradshaw
came up and after hinting that he was sorry I
had broke off every Conversation so Abruptly
he said that Mr Crawford went away quite in
Raptures with my Music and thought my Playing
much preferable to the Jephsons, That He was
just Setting off for Dublin where he intended to
inspect his Rent Rolls and to lay them before
Mr Bradshaw or bring them down the Next
Vacation—I never heard more of my little Beau
but that he gave Mr Bradshaw a good Dinner
and made a wonderful display of fine plate—
Whatever pass'd I was not let into the Baby
House, and as nothing was said to Me on the
Subject I concluded contrary to the general

Rule that Silence denoted a Dissent—I there-
fore asked no further Questions till a Lady told
Me she heard a Parcel of Gentlemen at Table
condemn me for refusing Mr Crawford which
I can verily attest he never to my knowledge
Left in my Power.

My Brother Tom had for some time been at the
Temple—We heard often from him but miss'd
Him more than it is possible to conceive—This
Year the Troubles began in France in disputes
between the French King and his Parliament—
England also was unsettled by the Regency
business and Ireland by the Right Boys and
General Election.

Amongst the present Inmates at Linville was
my old Friend Mrs Fleming who had quitted
my Aunt Cuffe on Lady Maxwells Marriage
and now came to live with my Aunt Eyre but
quarreld and Left her some time After.

I may Now I think Shift the Scene from Carrick
and Linville to Knockgrafton—Where we were
from henceforth to reside three Months in
every Year.

END OF BOOK THE THIRD

| A New Glebe | CHAPTER 63D | New Neighbours |

There, where a few torn Shrubs the place disclose
The Village Preachers modest Mansion rose

In the Centre of a New Glebe situated indeed in
a fine wholesome country but with scarce a Tree
or even a Bush to embellish it—stood the New
Parsonage House of Knockgrafton—It was
situated adjacent to the new Church and Village
of Knockgrafton which formed a pretty Coup
D'Œuil suspended on an Eminence at the head
of the glebe, so that our House seemd to form a
part of the Village which had altogether the Appearance of a Neat English One being mostly
newly rebuilt—To this Place we went about the
28th of May 1789.
It was a startling Change from our beautiful
wooded Country to this barren Plain—The
House itself was exceedingly Neat and Com-
pact but except some Articles of furniture
bought at an Auction we had little but our Beds
and the bare Walls—The Country was so very
Open that we could plainly see a small Mole on

one of the Hills over Carrick though at twenty
miles distance, and six miles of the Clonmell
Road which bounded the Glebe Land on one
Side whilst a transverse high road from Cashel
to Caher met at the New Inn in the Centre of
the Village, and bounded our territories in that
line—This was a most convenient Circumstance
especially as the latter was a Mail Coach road
and Military Way—so that we had the pleasing
sight of the Army in perpetual Movement in
that remote Village—and also the advantage of
Conveyance.

As we were Strangers there the Society of Mr
Hares and Mr Clarkes families were our most
pleasing Prospect—them we knew and My
Brothers Otway and Nicholas were still with
them the former as a Boarder reading for Orders,
the latter at Mr Clarke's School—Before we
left Carrick we received Cards for an Officers
Ball in Clonmell from the 13th Dragoons and
were to go to it from our New Residence and
the Moment we arrived My Brother Otway
came out and brought all his Cashel Friends to
visit us—amongst the Rest was Miss Sally
Hemphill an old flirt of his whom he entreated
My Mother to Matronize to the Officers Ball—
she accordingly spent the Interval with us at
Parsonage—Her Brother was Fellow Student
with my Brother Tom in the Temple where
they lived in the same Appartments together so
that we heard constantly of him through that
Channel as well as by his own letters to us—The

Hares and Clarkes came out the first Sunday to
Dinner—Mr Clarke asked Me how I liked
Knockgrafton?—I Inveighed against its lonesome Situation and barren appearance, but he
beggd I would suspend my Judgement till I
became acquainted with the Neighbourhood
which he enumerated, and particularly praised
Mr Roe's family who lived at Rockwell a beautiful Place one Mile from Parsonage.

The Day for the Clonmell Ball arriving we set
out from Parsonage after Dinner, which was
order'd Early, as we had eight long Miles to go
—We drank Tea with Mrs Crofton, Wife to
Captain Crofton of the 13th and Daughter to
Mrs Bradshaw Ned Eyres Visitant — The
Rooms were as full as possible, and decorated in
the most beautiful Stile with a large folding
Door thrown open—The first Person we were
introduced to was young Lady Blunden who
came with Araminta B and some other Company
—She appear'd to me to be very Pretty but
rouged very high, and seem'd quite the Woman
of fashion—She wore a Profusion of Diamonds
and seemd of remarkable Haut ton and Elegance—After the Introduction she turned from
us, I thought rather in an abrupt and negligent
Manner, Nor had Araminta so much of the
warm affectionate Manner usual to her—However towards the End of the Evening they
joined our Party, and fascinately strove to make
up for their first coldness—Araminta seemed
much alterd, and lookd dispirited, but we found

love to be the Cause, for she was on the Eve of
resigning her Name and freedom to Mr Waring
Cousin German to Mr Matthews—We saw
there that night Mrs Elliot, Daughter to our
new Neighbour Mr Roe—a very plain woman
but they said very Amiable—I forget the Incidents of this Ball but I know there was a most
brilliant Assemblage from all parts, And the
Decorations and Supper were uncommonly
beautiful and Superb—We did not get to Parsonage till Eight oclock next morning, and lay
in Bed all that Day till Dinner time.

In the Evening Miss Hemphil proposed a stroll
towards Rockwell to see the place, and ferret out
Young Andrew Roe as a Beau, he being the
only one of the family then at home—We had
our Walk for Nothing, as he did not appear, or
leap from a grove as we hoped—We therefore
sat down disconsolately under a Hedge, where
she gave us a History of all our Neighbours—
Mr Roe was then parted from his wife who
went to live in Clonmell on their quarrelling—
He was a man of very Violent Passions, and
married Mrs Roe for love having carried her off
from a Boarding School, but after living together forty Years they parted—No one could
conjecture the Cause of this Seperation as Mrs
Roe was all Meekness—Their two sons, and
eldest daughter (Miss Roe) lived with their
Father at Rockwell, only paying their Mother
occasional Visits, though they all sided with her
—Miss Roe was a Pattern of Prudence and Duti-

fulness—she managed All Matters at Rockwell
in her Mothers absence—Mr John Roe was
mostly with his Mother, and Andrew had the
Care of his fathers farming to Mind—Their
Place was very handsome, and quite their
Hobby Horse—John Roe was enlarging a fine
lake which so engross'd him, that few ever saw
him—He had a very mechanical turn; Miss
Roe was a perfect Mistress of Music, and Mrs
Elliot her younger sister got her Husband by
her fine Dancing—They lived very secluded in
General.

Mr and Mrs Carew of Woodenstown lived within another short walk of Parsonage, They were
of good families, she was cousin to young Lady
Blunden—She was a pretty, good humourd
woman, and he a real good kind of Man.

The Doghertys of Outrath were a large family
too numerous to mention—The Father was a
Jolly foxhunting Gentleman who kept his
family in good Order—He was fond of good
Living, and generally laid up with the Gout—
His wife was a quiet, good Woman—His sons
Gentlemen Farmers, and his Daughters Country
Beauties and Wits—Mrs Lionel Dogherty
lived in a Cottage opposite our Glebe, with a
Husband who broke her Heart between the
Turf and the Bottle—She was a good Woman,
gave us a Hot Cake Party, Drank Tea with us
once, but We had no further Acquaintance ex-
cept a Salute on the Road every Evening.

The Dexters were a family thirteen or fourteen

in Number, all great Beauties—They lived in a
Farm House on the Rockwell Estate—He was
a great English Farmer, famous for a Breed of
Sheep well known in Ireland by the name of
Dexter Sheep—She a Notable, Bustling Woman,
and a Bit of an Oddity—We had there home
kill'd in Perfection and all the Rarities that a
good Mother could give to set off her Children,
as Cakes, Syllabubs, Tarts, Pies Hams &c.
After trapesing the Road every Day for seven
Days without meeting young Andrew Roe—
Miss Hemphill and we sat down in Melancholy
Retirement at the Parsonage—After which she
grew tired of being alone with her old Cecisbœ
my Brother Otway and his Sisters—So they
both rode off to Cashel leaving us quite
Desolate.

A Cashel
Syllabub   CHAPTER 64TH   A Smart Beau

Union the Bond of all things, and of Man

An Invitation at length came from our good
Brother to us, to meet all Cashel at a Syllabub
and dance he was to give in Mr Hare's Deer
Park, a beautiful Farm, embellish'd with
flowers and shrubs Wherein was an Excavated
Arbour of Wondrous Beauty adorned with
curious Plants and flowers—The same Post
brought us an Invitation to dine at Mr Hares
the Day of this Fete Champetre.

We went, and met all the Cashel folks assembled, and amongst other Introductions young Andrew Roe made his first Bow to us—He was fully prepared to meet us graciously, and to shew all possible Politeness to his New Neighbours—We flirted, danced, ogled, talked Nonsense, and Moralized all at once—The uncertainty of the weather made us confine our Excursion to a green Lane, just outside the Town, where we drank our Syllabub and Danced—Our New Beau was my partner, and was so obsequious the whole evening that my friends congratulated me on my Conquest—The Evening ended with a general scamper to town from an Evening Shower—From that time young Andrew Roe was our daily visiter—He came after Breakfast each Day, and staid till near Dinner time but was too formal to dine with us except on particular Days—He prided himself much on having the honour of introducing us first to his family, who were daily expected.

Mr and Miss Roe at length arrived and paid a Visit in form in their old Family Coach—they were introduced by our little Beau, but John the most formidable of all had not yet appear'd—Little Andy soon grew so fond of us that his Father could get no good of him, and came every Morning to drag him home, but the Sage gentleman soon lost his Prudence as well as his Son, and was so fascinated with our Society that nothing could drive him away till four Oclock, when the Rector and He closed the Back-

gammon Table—Meanwhile his truant Boy
and We were eating Cold Meat behind Backs,
and laughing at Mr Roes prudential Visits—I
was often call'd to try his Skill at Backgammon
—and he grew so fond of me that he called me
nothing but his Dear little Dora, and made such
a fuss about me whenever we met that every
one laugh'd at our friendly Pother—Mr Roe
and My Father were two of the best bred Men
in the World and Perfect Models of Ancient
Good Manners—Our Other daily Visiters
were a Mr Anderson, uncle to Mr Carew—
young Dogherty, and Father Becket the Parish
Priest—The Ladies only paid us state visits.
Otway was too full of his Cashel Amusements
to be much with us and Nick could only leave
School on Sundays—On which Day the Clarkes
and he always came out—Mr Clarke to officiate
as Curate, and his Wife to get rid of her Cashel
gossip—The Hares also generally paid a Sunday Visit, so that we had Always a grand Levee
that Idle Day—Little Andy still continued his
Assiduities with the Politeness of an Old Beau
thrice his Age—He and Mrs Clarke had generally a fight for My arm on our return from
Church, and the common People used to tell me
bluntly that they wished Mr John Roe was as
Polite to Me as Mr Andy, Though in the Mean
he was a good young Man but very Passionate
—John was a universal Favourite with Rich and
Poor—Mr and Miss Roe asked us to Tea, but
said they would not ask us to Dinner till John

returned, who was commission'd to forage the Country, that Mr Roe might entertain his old Rector with Proper Solemnity.

A human phœnix	CHAPTER 65TH	A Church Fracas

"This bright unknown, this all accomplished Youth
"Who charms——Too much——

At length the formidable John Roe returned—— I heard of him every where, and whenever I ventured an Encomium on the rest of the Family, I was desired to wait till I saw John——One Morning two Horsemen gallop'd down——One I knew to be Andrew Roe, and supposed the other to be the Hero in question——When Ann ran up in a great flurry, and lugged out all my Morning finery from my Drawers begging I would dress myself as Mr John Roe was below ——After dressing in a violent hurry for this Strange Beau, I descended to the Parlour, where sat the redoubted Hero, and his Brother Andrew——I was immediately struck with his interesting Appearance, as he had something of a Melancholy Cast about him——His Features were very intelligent His Eyes pierced the Soul ——His Person was much taller than his Brother's ——He was certainly infinitely handsomer, but seemed very silent, distant, and reserved—— Altogether at the End of the visit I liked Andrew much better, who rattled away, and

crackd his Jokes as usual, with encreased
Alacrity.

We were now asked to dine at Rockwell in
form, but some thing intervening prevented us
—However they attended our Levee every Sunday after Church—I thought John Roe improved greatly on Acquaintance, but between
his Mother and his Lake, he was never to be
seen but Once a Week—when I could hardly
form any Judgement of his Character.

An Event now happened that terrified us all
greatly—After My Mother had remained some
Weeks in quiet Possession of the head Pew at
Church, which Mr Roe as Church Warden consigned to her—The Honourable Mrs Robins,
Daughter to Lord Massy, entered with a large
party of Gentlemen one Sunday, and demanded
her seat—Young Andrew Roe, who was the
only one of the family at Church, stoutly maintained our Right to it in the Name of his Father,
and insisted that we should not be disturbed in
our Possession—Mrs Robbins in a great Passion went into another Pew—After Church
there was a Horsewhipping Bout amongst the
Gentlemen—Otway of Course sided with
Andrew Roe—The Shrieks of the Ladies, and
the Interference of the Populace prevented
further Mischief, and we brought off our little
Champion safe—After sitting some time with
us, he went home, but he found a hot House
before him for Mrs Robbins had powder'd off
to Rockwell accompanied by Miss Emma

Massy her Sister, an old reputed Flame of little Andy's—They lodged a most bitter complaint of him before Miss Roe, who fired at their own story, took her Brothers Part, and pronounced that my Mother had an indubitable Right to the seat as Rectors Lady—Mrs Robbins alledged her being a Peers Daughter—Miss Roe sneered at such a Claim of Priviledge in Church, but that no doubt should remain she showed her in Lodges Peerage, that Lord Desart was a much older Peer than Lord Massy, which at once struck her Dumb—In the midst of the Dispute in bolted Andrew Roe, He was instantly the Object of Attack, and the two Honourable Sisters went off, vowing that Mr Robbins should revenge the Insult.

We thought every thing was blown over, when one Evening Otway and I were walking the Road after Nightfall, and met John Roe, who told Otway he was going to Caher for Pistols, and that there was to be a General Duel between the Gentlemen of Rockwell, and the Gentlemen of Hymenstown.

Otway powder'd off for Mr Clarke, and insisted that if any one fought he must, not being yet in Orders—This the Roes would not consent to—Our Gentlemen then strove to mediate, Andrew seemed relenting, but Miss Roe declared he must fight, or be for ever trampled on—She Good Soul, spent the Night in Prayer and fasting, whilst she acted amongst them the Heroine —Mrs Robbins finding matters had gone so far,

was greatly terrified at the Mischief she had
made—She wept, tore Her hair, And soften'd
her Husbands Seconds and Advisers, till they
engaged him to make a publick Appology in the
Church Yard where the fracas had happen'd—
This affair made of course great Noise—The
Roes perfectly satisfied, received their Submission, And from thenceforward Mrs Robbins
left the Church to ourselves.

| An old friend | CHAPTER 66TH | A charming fellow |

" . . . *Methought the shrill tongued Thrush*
" *Mended his Song of Love; The sooty Blackbird*
" *Mellow'd his Pipe, and softend every Note—*
" *The Eglantine smell'd sweeter, and the Rose*
" *Assume'd a Dye more deep!*

Mr Dan Cuffe now paid us a Visit, and brought
us all the News from Carrick—All there were
well, but nothing new stirring Except continual
Alarms about the Right Boys—In the Evening
we all walked to Rockwell, and found the Whole
family at home, and in great Glee about their
late Triumph—We chatted very agreeably till
Night fall, and were Escorted home by the
Roes—Mr Roe relinquish'd my Mothers Arm
to Andrew that he might walk (he said) with his
Dora, and point out to Me the Beauties of Rockwell, as he knew Mrs Herbert thought more of
his fine Cows (of which Andrew could give her

a full description) than of the winding Avenue,
the Shrubberies, or Green House—He soon
complaind I walked too fast for him, and put
Me under the Care of John Roe and his Sister,
whilst he rejoin'd My Mother—John Roe was
all Vivacity, All Animation! We expatiated
eloquently on the Charms of the Rural Scene
around us, and laughd and prattled on divers
Subjects, till Miss Roe also declared herself unable to keep pace with us, and drop'd off to the
Rest—Andrew now made an Effort to join us,
but was not allowed to do so—Behold Me then
left solely to the Care of the all accomplishd, all
seducing John Roe!—Never were sentiment,
and Animation so sweetly blended in One person—The fire of his Eye, his expressive Countenance, the bewitching Sound of his Voice, im-
passiond the Heart, and forced the Mind to
Admiration—Nature had molded him as if she
meant to give a Perfect Model of Elegance and
Perfection, but the Character of Goodness in his
Countenance was his most prominent Charm,
Whether Grave or Gay every turn of his features
bore the Stamp of Amiability—and indeed it
was hard to say which Gravity or Gaiety most
became him—I was surprized at the Unaffected Chearfulness of his Manner, so different
from the reservedness I had imputed to him,
and his Animated Communicativeness inspired
Me with equal freedom—Our walk was delightful, and our Conversation uninterrupted till we
reached Parsonage—The next time I saw Mr

Clarke I frankly acknowledged the Superiority
of his taste, for indeed there was no Comparison
between the two Brothers—He exulted in my
Retracted opinions, and launched into fresh
Encomiums on his favourite friend—From that
time we saw John Roe as often as could be ex-
pected from one of his retired Manner of Life—
Every Sunday the whole family appear'd at
Church, and Never miss'd Our Levee after it—
The Affair about the Robinses had retarded the
Dinner they were going to give us, but we met
almost daily.

The visitation Now came on, and we were asked
to breakfast and dine at Mr Hares on that Day
—Though Mr Hare and my Father always
dined with the Arch Bishop, Mrs Hare had
generally a large Company—Mrs Clarke and I
usually contrived to slip away, that we might
have a comfortable dish of Chat on Old Times
—She enquired very minutely how I liked John
Roe? and on my confessing My Admiration of
him she congratulated Me on the Recovery of
my Senses, as She thought I had lost them when
I preferr'd his Brother—The Roes were at Mr
Hares before us (that is the young Men), for
Mr Roe and Mr Hare were not on speaking
Terms—They were again all vivacity—And
before Dinner escorted us to the Church to take
a nearer View of every thing worth seeing—
John Clarke (Mrs Clarkes Second Son) then a
child, took it into his head to be very much in
Love with Miss Dolly Herbert, as I was his

Godmother, and petted him—He followed me
so about the Church that it afforded the party
great Amusement, an Event that Caused Me
infinite Confusion some days after, as I shall
relate in its place—We pass'd the Evening very
pleasantly in a large Circle, asked to stare and
gaze at us—Mrs Clarke thought she could
never shew us off sufficiently, and though She
could not Puff us off as great Beauties, she
Blazond us every where for our other Ex-
cellencies.

The Hares also were always remarkably
Friendly, and the Roes now seemd determined
to outdo them all in paying us every Mark of
Attention—John Roe sat by Me the whole
Evening, laughing at Andrews Vexation who
did not seem at all pleased at my preferring his
more charming Brother, who at length quitted
his seat for a Moment—Andrew then seized the
Opportunity of whispering in My Ear many
reproachful Hints—He said Miss Herbert was
grown so nice in her Company, that a plain
honest Farmer could not get near Her or speak
to Her—and many other things to that Purport, till John returned, and whisked him out of
his Chair—John now again replaced himself
near Me, and entertained me the rest of the
Evening, to the no small Mortification of Andy
who made many attempts to join our Coterie,
but in vain—The Roes rode home with us as
far as Rockwell, and Next Day the long pro-
tracted Invitation arrived and with it a huge

Bundle of flowers, a Joint of Meat, a Cream Cheese, a Cartload of New Potatoes, and Vegetables in Abundance, with many other Articles as presents from Mr and Miss Roe—as Mrs Clarke had come out with us the Night before, she was included in our Invitation Cards—She was to spend the Whole Vacation with us, and we expected to be very Pleasant and happy.

| A Dinner Party | CHAPTER 67TH | an Awkward Blunder |

" *Down stubborn Heart and learn Dissimulation* . . .

We met at Rockwell all the Gentlemen who had been their friends in the late expected Duel— Mr Carew, Mr McCreath, Mr Clarke and Many Others—The Drawing Room was quite full, and the Company sat, or stood Round in a formal Circle—Conversation seemd Stagnant, when a laugh from the Window attracted every ones Attention — It was produced by Mrs Clarkes telling my Mother and John Roe various Stories about her little Son's John Clarkes predilection for his Godmother Miss Dolly Herbert—They all laughd loudly at her ludicrous description of this Amour, when my Mother most unhappily blunder'd out, Yes John Roe is deeply in love with My Daughter—Instantly the Eyes of the whole Company Crushed on Me —I sat Aghast, quite thunderstruck at her

Speech, and everyone round seemd to pity me; their grave perplexity encreased My Confusion —I looked at John Roe and saw him shrink up to the Corner of the Window seat as if to hide himself from general Observation, He was fiddling with his Watch Chain to hide his Embarrassment, but could Not suppress a Rising titter, whilst Mrs Clarke, My Mother, and Mr Roe had all the Appearance of Culprits—The Company were still Silent as the Grave—I groan'd internally, and for Relief turned to Fanny who sat next Me, but seeing her Face like a Coal of fire, Mine caught the Infection—Instantly I felt all the Blood fly up into my face, and from a death like paleness I turned as red as scarlet.

Mr Roe was the first who broke this awkward Silence with some Observations about the Weather—To do the Company justice, they all seemed feelingly Concerned for Me, though there were some Dashers amongst them—This Incident damp'd Me entirely, till Dinner was announced, which relieved Me from my conspicuous Situation, for to make the Matter worse, I was enthroned alone on a Sopha in the front Centre of the Room.

Every one was so attentive at Dinner time to Me, that I felt quite reassured—I was respectfully asked by most of the Gentlemen to take Wine, and never was a Cordial more needful to drooping Spirits—When we left them, the Jolly Set sat till twelve at Night over the Bottle—But

John, and Andrew Roe gave them the Slip, and
joined us at Tea time—As I was posted as joint
Mistress of the Ceremonies with Miss Roe,
Andrew wanted to sit near me as an Assistant,
but his Brother drove him away, and seized the
Place, so that Andrew could only obtain the
favour of handing the Teakettle—Charmingly
did the Evening pass away—More engaging
than the fairest Sylphs, was the Attention, and
Conversation of the too lovely John Roe—He
never left my Side till the Gentlemen came out
at twelve oclock, and the Carriages being then
Announced, he seized my hand, and with sweet
delay led me to Our Vehicle.

It was now our turn to give a Dinner, which we
did in great Stile as we brought Mrs Wharton
with us to Parsonage, and her Confectionary
was allowed by everyone to be super Excellent
at all times—The Carews, Dohertys, Hares,
Clarkes were all invited with the Roes, and all
came—It was a State Dinner, therefore trouble-
some to Us, but our Guests all seem'd pleased
with their Entertainment—Mr Roe was so Attentive to Me at Dinner particularizing Me
across the Table, that he brought on me the full
stare of the Company—His Sons again stole
away from the Gentlemen, and Joined us almost
as Soon as the Ladies left the Eating Parlour,
and had Again a Contest for the Seat next Me—
but John always triumph'd, as if my secret
Prayers and wishes were heard by ruling
fate.

From that time forward, They were with us every Day—John came generally Alone on one Pretence or Other—We met them at various Parties, and scarce an hour pass'd without Notes, billets, Presents &c—Various Reports soon went about, but this did Not prevent the Roes from continuing the Most Marked Attention to us.

| Carrick
Madcaps | CHAPTER 68TH | Romping
Parties |

Oh Days of Youth! Oh Careless Days!! Untaught To Weep, if Love Shed not the pleasing Tear—

Before we left Carrick, we invited the Jephsons to our Pastoral House warming—Mrs Jephson and her two fair Daughters now came, and the Girls swore they would Cock their Caps at John Roe, and never rest till they carried him Off— Already this threat made Me feel an Electric Shock, for besides the Vanity of the Matter, John Roe's absence two or three Wet Mornings convinced me that he conferrd both health and happiness—for lonesome and vapouring was each Morning Unirradiated by his Resplendence—Prudence precluded Love—but his uncommon perfections could not fail to make his Company desireable to all who knew him, and a girl of Eighteen, could hardly wish to decline his Acquaintance.

To say the truth I felt very uneasy lest the Jephsons should enrol him, and carry him off to Cashel in their train of Admirers—He was a most Enviable Feather in Our Caps, and their Extreme Beauty, rendered them formidable Rivals any where—The Sunday after they arrived, they in reality according to their Menace dressd themselves out at all points to meet him at Church—Whether they were incited by the love of Mischief, or provoked by Mrs Clarke Brags of us round Cashel from whence they came, they seem'd determined to rob me of this New Beau, and pinching me black and blue, bid me go back to my little Champion Mr Crawford—To Church we went —they dress'd out as fine as mischief could make them, But however the Deuce it happen'd, John Roe was not at Church, though he was never absent from it one Sunday before since we arrived—And to mend the Matter he left off his Morning Visits on the Arrival of Our Volatile Visitants.

The Jephsons were Mad at this disappointment, and swore I was a Witch that could spirit him up, or not, as I pleased—We sent daily Enquiries and Invitations to Rockwell—The Answer was always that Mr and Miss Roe were Not well enough to Mix in Company, but would see us when we were disengaged from other Society—The Jephsons though quite provoked, consoled themselves with leaping the Hedges— Running Races on the Cross Roads, and Plaguing the astonishd Villagers—One Day Salisbury

Jephson got a dreadful fall at our usual Circus, (namely) the Centre of the Village opposite the Inn, where the Cross Roads met—In this toss she sprained her Ancle, and was laid up for a week after—Our only Amusement then was playing Cards, eating from Morning to Night, and making Gooseberry Fool of the Rockwell Gooseberries, for we had still a car sent from thence every Saturday Night, laden with all sorts of Provisions, and loads of the Choicest flowers for the Miss Herberts, which the Miss Jephsons seized on as their Property.

Mr Maunsel now came from Linville to spy out the Land of Starvation (as he called it)— What was his Astonishment to see us sit down Morning, Noon, and Night, to the finest Beef in Christendom (for we always bought a Quarter whenever Mr Roe killed one of his remarkable Cows)—We had besides every kind of Fruit and Vegetable from Rockwell—The finest young sucking Pigs from Mrs Dexter—The finest fat Geese from Mrs Dogherty, with quantities of Eggs, butter, Cream Cheeses, and Oaten Cakes —all Gratis, except the 200 lb weight of Beef which we paid for—We had besides a Constant Supply of the rarest fish which we stop'd on the Road between the Markets of Caher and Cashel —Crabs, Lobsters, Shrimps, Mackrel, Haddock, in short almost every kind as fresh as possible —And Rockwell supplied us with Salmon trout tench, Eels &c—In reality, whilst our Guests staid we did nothing but Eat and drink from

Morning till Night—The Jephsons brought
from Carrick a huge Barn Brack, thinking it a
wonderful fine thing in a barren Desert to a set
of half famishd wretches as they supposed us to
be—How were they ashamed of their clumsy
Present in the Land of Elegance and Plenty!
—besides other good things we had remarkable
Chocolate, as Cashel was famous for it.

Nocturnal Revels	CHAPTER 69TH	a boisterous Visit

"Oh Silent Troy!—
"Whose Streets have often Echoed with our Song!

One Night after the Seniors went to Bed we sat
up till two Oclock at a Supper of Cold Meat,
sallad, Gooseberry Fool, and Crabs of our Own
Dressing—Not forgetting our Old Jug of
Punch after it—when Otway and Fanny Jephson became so riotous, and roared so in laughing
that they brought down the whole party above,
some in their Shifts, some more in their Shirts—
The Revd Mr Maunsel stood before us Aghast
in his Shirt, Drawers, and Night Cap like the
poor lean Pilgrim in the Duenna, who when
admitted to Penance before the Jolly fat Friars
found them all feasting on Champaign and
Turtle—Just as astonish'd stood Mr Maunsel
—Mrs Jephson appeard Opposite, exactly as
she started out of Bed in agreeable Nudity—
My Father and Mother crept down after them

in the same trim—When Fanny Jephson and Otway saw their plight, Nothing on earth could equal their merriment, and Not till Mrs Jephson had given her three or four Shakes could we get our Volatile Companion into any decent Composure.

Salisbury Jephson now recoverd the use of her Limbs, and they resolved to make one more Effort to hook in the Rockwell Beaux—We accordingly sallied forth on Horseback, and rode by the Back of Rockwell to surprize them, and cut off All Retreat—We saw Miss Roe running away from us, but this did not discourage the Jephsons from boldly rapping at the Door—I kept aloof, fearful that they would play off some hazardous Airs on People whose touchiness they little regarded—John Roe appear'd at the Door, and asked them in very politely, but Salisbury Jephson could not alight, and their Beau did not pass over the threshold—they pressed him to escort them home, but in Vain, and thus disappointed they returned to me behind the Grove, venting all the Abuse they could bestow on Rockwell and its Inhabitants—They soon after left us, and went to Cashel to their Uncle Judkins—we often saw them and dined one Day at Mr Judkins, where we generally eat a Melancholy feast once a Year when we visitted Cashel—Mr and Mrs Judkins being an Old Couple immensely rich without children—They had a very fine House and garden but none dared make free in them.

{ 1789 }

A Tipsy
Beau

CHAPTER 70TH

A Country
Wedding

Bid her Adieu the Venal Fair

No sooner had the Jephsons left us, than the
Roes again visitted us every Day as usual, with
encreased kindness if possible—which continued
till Mr Roe and John went to Dublin, where
they were summon'd on Business of Importance
—Andrew now left to himself, resolved to make
himself a Man of Consequence—He was so full
of his Farmers Business that he could seldom
find time to come near us—If we met him by
Chance, he took a hasty leave and went Off—
Fanny and I however one Evening met him on
the Road, when he leap'd from behind a Hedge
with Father Becket the Parish Priest—Andrew
Roe was very Tipsy, and would not leave us,
though Father Becket cursed and swore that
they would be too late for a Wedding they were
going to, which it seems was a great Country
One, where Andy was to be Bridesman—In
vain Father Becket swore—In vain we urged—
Andrew fell on his knees to us in the Middle of
the Road, imploring us Not to dismiss him—
He then Set his Horse adrift with a Crack of his
Whip, and again fell on his knees, kissing our
Trains, and weeping over them—Father Becket
finding him incorrigible left us and after much
beseeching we prevaild with Andrew not to dis-
appoint the Wedding folks—At our Entreaties

he followd the Priest, but it was quite dark when he left us—The Next Day he came to tell us how fatal our Charms had proved to the whole Party—Whilst waiting for the Priest and Andrew, the Bride picked up another flirtation —went off—and was married to a Second Lover before Morning—Father Becket lost his Collection, and Andrew his way home.

Miss Roe now seperated from her father, grew more frisky than had been remember'd a long time—She thought it incumbent on her to do the honours of the Place, and was continually with us, or we with her—She was a very plain young Woman on the Wrong Side of thirty— The family were all Plain except Mrs Roe, who had been a Beauty, and her Son John who was charming beyond description—Some would have thought him not handsome, but he had that Je ne scais quoi that rendered him irresistible —Goodness, and Sweetness—Life, and animation beamd in every feature, and captivated beyond any regular Beauty—With all his gentleness John Roe could be very Satyrical, but so skilful was he in the Management of Wit, that it never wounded or offended, and his Shyness only added to his Numberless Perfections—I know Not how it was, but we were often jostled together in Conversation—I was often told that he and I were very like each other and would make a very happy Pair—This was remarkd to me before ever I saw him—As for Mrs Clarke, whenever I said any thing that pleased her, She

always exclaim'd Well! That is so like John
Roe! Oh! My Dear Dolly! You must have been
formed for Each Other, and I shall cry my
Eyes out if it is not a Match!—We used to laugh
then, but laughter does not always forebode
Happiness.

I shall now give a short description of Rockwell,
where I spent the happiest and most miserable
Hours of My Life—The House had once been
intended for an office, when Mr Roe had a
quantity of hewn Stone on the Spot for building
a handsome New dwelling House, but on Mrs
Roe's leaving the Place, he would not suffer the
Work to go on—In the Old House there was a
small odd shaped Room below, which served as
a dining Parlour, Inside of which was John
Roe's Study and turning Shop—Another Room
above served as a drawing Room, besides which
there was a range of tolerable Bedchambers—
Altogether it was quite in the Stile of a Head
Farmers House, like most of the Houses in that
country—The lake which spread behind the
Scite of the New House was very beautiful and
pretty Extensive, for John Roe was yearly enlarging it—It had a handsome Island in the
Midst, with an elegant Cottage, and library,
with Music and other appropriate amusements
—The Avenue was likewise very beautiful,
winding down a long way to the House, with
a handsome Iron Gate—The trees were all em-
bellishd with Climbing Woodbine &c and the
green Slope on each Side adorn'd with flowers

—before the Door was a small Lawn enclosed with a Honeysuckle Hedge, and a Handsome Border of flowers, particularly Clumps of Red and White Rockets mix'd which had an Elegant Appearance—At the Head of the Lawn was Miss Roes Green House—at the back of the House was a beautiful small Grove and Shrubbery, which with the Trees round the House was adorned with Woodbine and other flowery Shrubs to their very Tops—The New Gardens were very fine and Extensive, and the Grounds remarkably rich and well improved.

Vernal beauties	CHAPTER 71ST	A dreadful Fever

"Dear Regions of Silence and Shade,
"Soft Scenes of Contentment and Ease
"Where I could have pleasingly Stray'd
"If Aught in his Absence could please

About May we made a short trip to Carrick, and found our little Eden blooming with all the vernal Beauty of that delightful Season—We spent some Days at Linville, and engaged my Aunt, Ned Eyre, and Mrs Bradshaw to come to us at the time of the Cashel Races, which were shortly to take place—We returned to Parsonage the 28th of May.

About this time a dreadful Fever raged all over the World (I may say) and carried off Millions in every quarter of the Globe—Scarce a family was there but felt its Effects——Mr Hare lost his third son Robert, and Mrs Cox of Castletown her fourth Son William——both died in the West Indies——Mr Wilson of Carrick our Attorney died of it in Dublin, and left a large family—— inshort the Victims within our small Acquaintance were too numerous to reckon.

I had now another Brother almost out of School (Nicholas)——He was quite Mad with Spirits, and broke his Nose leaping when young——however it did Not much disfigure him though he lost his delicate beauty——He often came out to Parsonage, and was so much beloved at Rockwell that they could not live without him—— Otway however was the general Pet there—— Indeed Mr Roe petted us all from his old friend the Rector, down to his youngest friend Nicholas.

Happy hours   CHAPTER 72D   A Present

" *There was a time, I will indulge the thought*
" *When everlasting transport tuned our Souls*
" *When join'd to vernal Life, the Spring of Love*
" *Around us gaily Blowd, And Heaven and Earth,*
" *All smiling Nature look'd delighted on——*

Mr Roe and his amiable Son now returned from Dublin, where they had triumph'd in a great Lawsuit many years pending——I expected to find them both cooler about us after their Jaunt,

but they had not been an Hour returned when
a Summons was dispatch'd for us to drink Tea
there—More warm and friendly than ever was
Mr Roe, More charming and animated his peer-
less son—Mr Roe's usual Routine after the
first Compliments of the Meeting were over,
was to lead his Dora to the large Sopha which
he appropriated entirely to Me—He then always sat by me a quarter of an Hour and none
durst approach the Sopha unless as a very particular Favour he invited some third person to
join us—when our Half hours Conversation
was over, he regularly call'd his son John over,
and after speeching away about young Ladies
liking young Gentlemen, better than Old Ones,
he formally consigned Me and his Seat on the
Sopha, to his Eldest son (as he said)—John
seem'd always to seize the Boon with animated
Pleasure—and seemd entirely to devote himself to me for the length of each Evening, whilst
Andrew contented himself humbly to hand the
Kettle—As I still presided at the Tea Table
jointly with Miss Roe.

If I might credit my Glass, I never looked so
well as that Night—I felt a flush of Joy when
their summons came, and having taken particular Care to make my Muslin Bonnet trimm'd
with Lilac as becoming as possible, I set out
quite pleased with My Success.

Mr Roe conversed with me that night longer
than usual, giving me an account of the Amusements and fashions of the Metropolis, whilst

John Roe plainly indicated his impatience to get
his Seat by twirling the Next chair, and other
broad hints which however Mr Roe would Not
take till his Budget was unfolded—He told me
my Bonnet was quite Outré, and said he had
brought down a fine New one to his Daughter
Betty, but she thought it too small, and he requested my Acceptance of it—He then sent
Miss Roe for the Bonnet, and a Bundle of Shoes
he brought down—Miss Roe returned heavy
Laden, and Mr Roe would not rest till I had
tried on the Bonnet, and led me to the Pier
Glass for the purpose—I felt very Awkard on
many Accounts, as Mr Clarke and the young
Men were all tittering, and making their Remarks on us—besides, I was so contented with
my own that I fear'd to spoil my present Beauty,
by wearing a new one, till I had given it a becoming touch—lastly, I saw that John Roe was
still waiting for me at the Sopha, and feard he
would grow tired, and I should lose him for the
Evening—I could not refuse Mr Roe to try on
my Bonnet so set about my Work—but nothing
then would serve him but to act as my Abigail
in putting it on, and we made such bungling
Work of it between us, that they were all in fits
of Laughter, as Mr Roe stood behind me with
all the methodical fuss of a Fille de Chambre—
Otway to vex him swore I lookd uglier than ever
—Andrew crow'd in disdain—John Roe said it
did not become me half as well as my own, and
Mr Clarke begg'd Mr Roe would let Miss Her-

bert put it on her own Way—Inshort they
worried us so that Mr Roe in a great passion
called John over, and made him Assist at my
Toilette—He then insisted on his recanting his
Censure on the Bonnet, and John was forced to
admit I look'd killingly in it—This Over, the
Shoes were still to be tried on, and my two
Helpers gallantly set about the Operation, but
at the first Essai it was proved that they were
quite too large for Me—and Miss Roe had
them all to herself—Once more Mr Roe re-
seated himself by Me on the Sopha, to admire
me in my elegant Blue Tiffany Bonnet—But he
soon dragg'd his son John over, and placing
him by me with the air of a Master of the Ceremonies, left us together saying "God bless You
both.
Never did the Dear John Roe look half so
charming as that Night—His face dress'd in the
sweetest smiles, The fire of his Eye, the Vivacity
of his Manners, The varied Animations of his
Looks, renderd him compleatly irresistible, And
if I might credit the Language of his Eyes I
appeard not displeasing to him—He gazed un-
dissemblingly at me, and seem'd to think my
Bonnet vastly becoming—Indeed I seem'd to
engross his whole, and most Earnest Attention
—His looks penetrated my inmost Soul, and
their Intelligence betrayd Complacency and Delight—Even Mr Clarke (in whose Conversation he usually most delighted) was neglected
totally for my Society—In vain the good Lads

round the Room strove to rally him away from me—He only answer'd their Railleries by paying me greater Attention—

"From Lips like his what Precept faild to move
"Too soon they taught me 'twas no Sin to Love.

He recited to me all the Events of their Dublin Jaunt, with various droll remarks, and in Return I gave him an Account of our Galway Trip which excited in him equal laughter—Our Eyes only told more interesting tales than our tongues dared to utter—My God what a happy Evening did I spend! So happy! So bewitching! few Evenings have I passd like it, and these only could be spent in the Company of John Roe, the dear beloved object of my Delight and transport, but Equally the Author of my Misery and Woe! I was now fully convinced that my Heart was gone irretrievably for Ever; The exquisite pain I felt at parting him, though but for an Evening, convinced me he was become the Sole Arbiter of My Fate—A fearful Discovery to One who still doubted!

A Mental Conflict	CHAPTER 73D	Sad forebodings

Eer such a Soul regains its peaceful State
How often must it Love! How often Hate!
How often hope, despair, resent, regret
Conceal, disdain,—Do all things but forget!

When I was seated in the Carriage my thoughts took a very different Turn—The very great uncertainty of my Destiny, struck me with freezing Horror—John Roes Image rush'd full on my Mind—His Looks, His Gaze, His Voice, His Smiles seemd pictured before as if necessary all to my very Existence, I felt that I could not live without him, or at least that the Loss of him would be worse than Annihilation—My Situation terrified me, but was so precious that I would not have exchanged it for the Universe —My Hopes were precarious, but so dear that I gaspd at the thoughts of losing them—

"*Dim and remote the Joys of Saints I see*
"*Nor envy them that Heaven I lose for thee*—

But injurious indeed would it be to judge of what my young Heart then felt by any description I can give in the present Mutilated state of my Senses and Affections—Surely there is in Love a Mysterious Law that chains the Soul to silent Endurance, and baffles even the Immagination of those who have felt the full Rigour of that fixt and terrible Passion—Yet delightful as it is terrible! The most luxuriant Mind can give no account of what perforce it feels, And sinks resistless under Sensations it can never satisfactorily define.

INDEX

INDEX

212

INDEX

INDEX

214

INDEX

INDEX

Retrospections
of
DOROTHEA
HERBERT

The first volume of the Retrospections, *covering the years 1770–1789, was chiefly concerned with the authoress's childhood, upbringing, and visits to various relations— Herberts, Eyres, Blennerhassets on her father's side, Cuffes and Blundens on her mother's.*

Dorothea's father, the Revd Nicholas Herbert, who resided at Carrick-on-Suir, was also Rector of the parish of Knockgrafton, near Cashel (twenty-two miles from Carrick), and at the Archbishop's insistence had now to spend at least three months of the year there. In this vicinity the family made new friends, chief amongst whom were their nearest neighbours, the Roes of Rockwell—the father, two sons, John and Andrew, and an unmarried daughter. Mrs Roe had for some time been living apart from her husband in the town of Clonmell, fourteen miles away. The concluding chapters shewed the authoress falling in love with John Roe, whilst he, for his part, seemed also to have taken a great fancy to her.

This second book describes the course of her love affair, to which the first was only the prelude. Dorothea's brothers, Otway, Tom and Nick, and her sisters, Fanny, Matty, Lucy and Sophy, all appear in these pages. Dorothea is the eldest of the family. Otway, who comes next, is about eighteen years old and is reading for Orders ; Tom is in the Temple ; Nick, the youngest of the family, is thirteen years old and is at school at Cashel. The Herbert family are still in the middle of their first year's residence at Knockgrafton. The Hares (Vicar-General's family) and their daughter, Mrs Clarke (the

v

schoolmaster's wife), are their chief friends in the Cashel district. The Jephsons, her chief friends in the Carrick district, have followed her in visiting Cashel. Nearly all the other characters are explained by the authoress at her first mention of them.

G. F. M.

January 1930

CONTENTS

City, Country, all,
Is in a gay triumphant Tempest tost

The Cashel Races now began, and interupted our domestic pleasures with more Noisy delights—Till then our intercourse with our Rockwell Neighbours continued unvariably delightful, but the Hurry and Bustle of the pageant Scene dispersed our more rational Joys —My Aunt Eyre, Ned, Mrs Bradshaw, Lady Dapper, Miss Kitsy* and our Girls, all now arrived at Parsonage to beat up our Quarters for the Races, which were expected to be remarkably brilliant—Previous to their Commencement we introduced our Linville friends to the Roes, who treated them with all possible Civility and Hospitality.

We went to the Course in the Greatest Stile in our New Coach, and four of the handsomest young Bay Horses in the Kingdom—The Coach just come down from Dublin was bespoken by poor Otway, and was really a Most beautiful Vehicle, Bottle Green adorned with a Quantity of Silver Plate, and the harnesses equally enrich'd with Silver—He then went to Limerick for the Horses, and contrived that all should make their first Debut at the Cashel Races—Ned Eyre dash'd away in his Glass

* Mr Eyres two pet Dogs.

Vis a Vis, and inshort we were the Gaze and
Astonishment of the Whole Race Course.

The Roes came every Moment up to the Carriages and remained mostly by us, except in the
hurry of the Running—They let us into the
history of every Strange Carriage that Enter'd,
and supplied us Constantly with Oranges,
Cakes, Comfits, so that we were famously
entertain'd.

We had also another trusty Beau all Day acting
as our Sylph—This was Mr Gwyn, who though
now a Married Man came from Feathard to
Parsonage for the Race—He expressd the
Greatest joy at our Meeting, and hoverd round
us all day, but went away in the Evening
—I felt rather Awkard at first, as it was our
first Rencontre since the Letter business, however we soon were very good friends, and as
free as if nothing had happen'd—He was a
good deal alterd, and not half so agreeable and
Alert as when a Batchelor.

The Morning pass'd away delightfully—there
was a most brilliant Meeting, and very fine
running—We did not return till late to Parsonage, where we had to dine, dress, and go five
Miles to the Cashel Assembly the same Evening.
Fanny and I wore pink Lutestrings (a Present
from Ned Eyre) with thin muslin trains, and
Black silk Bodices, all handsomely trimmed
with black lace and green ribbon with white
plumes and other ornaments in our Heads—
My Aunt Eyre, my Mother, and Mrs Brad-

shaw were all as fine as Hands and Pins could make them—Ned Eyre was one blaze of Brilliants from Top to Toe and cut a most curious figure in a pink Lutestring suit, adorned with quantities of Double Paste Buttons—with Buckles and knee Bucles to match—Thus caparisond we set out at Nine oclock for Cashel with throbbing Expectation.

| An interesting Assembly | CHAPTER 75 | An irrestible Swain |

" *Alas from the Day that we Met*
    " *What hope of an end to my Woes*
" *When I cannot endure to forget*
        " *The Glance that undid my Repose*

We were to drink Tea at Mrs Hares, where we met the Roes before us waiting to escort us to the Assembly—They immediately engaged Fanny and I for the first Sets, and we all proceeded together to the Assembly Room—We found a most brilliant Assemblage before us, amongst whom were the Jephsons in high Beauty, who instantly came up to us—My old Foe Fanny Jephson seeing John Roe at my Elbow acting as my Cecisbeo, mischievously brush'd up to us, and play'd off all her Airs and Graces with many hints that she wanted a Partner—He smiled, but did not take her at her word, and after some smart brusqueries between them he gaily led me off to dance—

Fanny Jephson threw a wicked look at me and went off another way to seek out her Partner— Had I been less interested I should have found the dance pleasanter but I felt too much emotion to dance or Chat with Ease, however we bustled through an amazingly crouded Set with much chearfulness and not a little fun, as my Partner was very Sly, though not illnatured in his Remarks—and to me he behaved with all possible Attention and Gallantry.

The next Set we changed Partners—John Roe asked Fanny—and I danced with Andrew according to our previous Arrangement at Mr Hares—After much jostling for Places, Andrew with great fuss placed me and himself third Couple, and then went off for some lemonade charging me to keep my place—But alas! I found this an arduous task, and soon got into a high Altercation with Miss Dogherty who very rudely push'd me down, seeing me without a Champion—She was very tart and uncivil for I plainly told her I could not relinquish my right, as Mr Andrew Roe had got it for me with much trouble—She turned up her nose saying, Really Miss Herbert, I see no reason why Mr Roe should give you my place, though you and his family are so very Neighbourly, that your horses cannot even pass their Gate without turning down to Rockwell, Whilst you cannot find time to return a Civil Visit any where else—Her abrupt accusation struck me all of a heap, as it was partly true, for in reality

our young Horses could never be got to pass
Rockwell Gate without turning down the
Avenue, as if they meant to confer a favour on
me who always equally longed to turn down—
Miss Dogherty had by chance pass'd by in her
Carriage that Morning, and witnessed their
Obstreperous Good Neighbourhood, which
caused her present ill humour and Rage against
them and me—Andrew Roe at length returning
with the Lemonade had some very high Words
with her Partner, but the Gentlemen near us interfered, and adjudged the place to be ours—so
Miss Dogherty went off in high Dudgeons, and
never afterwards would visit at Parsonage.

When we sat down, the Roes went round the
Benches to recognize their Acquaintances—
My Eyes of course travel'd with them—I saw
the Ladies every where tapping John Roe with
their Fans, whilst he with arch gaiety parried
their Railleries—In the Height of their merriment a long Bench of them gave way, and the
whole Row came tumbling to the ground, in
every ridiculous attitude it was possible to
Conceive—for the first time I rejoiced I was
not amongst them—The Gentlemen now all
flew divers ways, some to assist the prostrate
fair Ones, and others to procure Smelling
Bottles, Wine, Lemonade &c to restore their
Spirits—I saw John Roe disappear amongst
the rest, and gave him up for that Night, as
he was enlisted amongst the most brilliant
Belles of the Ball Room, Lady Massy, the

handsome Miss Pallisers, Miss Mansergh, Miss Lane, and many other head Beauties, whose present awkard situation engrossed all his Knight Errantry—Indeed I thought he had already shewn us as much Attention as was reasonable to expect at such a place, so resignd myself to live without him the Rest of the Evening.

They now began to replace the broken Bench which drew the whole Company to that Side— I was sitting solitarily when Mrs M. a Carrick acquaintance came up, and saluted me—She sat down by me, and after some Circumlocutory Compliments and Discourse, she with much Mystery in her looks asked, how I liked the Roes?—After much humming and hawing, she enquired further, whether I was not going to be married to John Roe? or which of the Brothers was to be my future Spouse? I was quite dumb founder'd at her abrupt Interogatory, and in much confusion told her, I believed neither had any such Intentions—Mrs M. however insisted that from their continual Attention to me, one or other of the Brothers must have Matrimonial Designs on me and that it was universally said I was to be married to John Roe, and that Andrew too was deeply in love with me—She wished me then much Happiness, and launched into high Encomiums of John, who she was certain was my Real Intended—I attempted honestly to undeceive her, but at that moment an Orange was thrown into my Lap, and I felt

my Shoulder tapp'd, I turnd about and beheld
John Roe all smiling! lovely! animated! One
would think he had heard me Exclaim in the
Words of Thompson—

Oh come! sweet, smiling, tender, Come!

A dish of Chit Chat	CHAPTER 76	A pleasing interruption

Those smiling Eyes attemp'ring every Ray
Shone sweetly lambent with celestial Day

John Roes Smiles were never forced or unnatural—His Wit was fine, delicate, and redun-
dant—his sentiments natural, and his Benevolence unaffected—Every Emotion sprang from
the Heart—nothing forced or affected—Love,
Joy, Sensibility, play'd in each beauteous feature.
He approached me with a gay, tender feeling,
and I could not help thinking it somewhat particular that he should search me out whilst the
whole Room was in Confusion replacing the
Benches—He had not been more than a quarter
of an Hour absent from me and now left the busy
Croud to single me out—What could I infer—
Love, Desire, I may say adoration beam'd in his
face, as he gaily addressed me with affectionate
Freedom—He now sat down near me, and
enter'd into Chat—Mrs M. grew silent on his
Approach and contented herself with making
her Observations—I felt rather Awkard, and
John Roe seem'd to wish us out of her Neigh-

bourhood—He proposed that we should retire to a snug Nook that formed a kind of Recess in the Room, to which I acceded, and we left Mrs M. to make her Comments alone—In our new station we were quite separated from the Company, but had a full View of them under us, and could make our Remarks without being observed—here we conversed the rest of the Evening—John Roe was all gaiety and Wit—The word Love never enterd our Vocabulary, but if ever Mans Eyes spoke its Language his did that night, and I swear mine could not have appeard Stoical or Insensible.

We remained as happy as possible tete a tete in our Recess the rest of the Evening—John Roe declined dancing on my account, and never stirrd from my side but once to obtain for me a fresh supply of Lemonade and China Oranges—and even then precipitately returnd as if he thought every moment of absence a Century—Our Attention was now excited by the numerous Tassels that hung suspended from the Silk Robe of Miss S. who sat on a Bench just under us, this brought on a Dissertation on Female Dress and Fantasies—John Roe was pretty smart in his Strictures, and I laughingly reproved him—Our evening pass'd in a pleasing Delirium—I never saw him in such a flow of Spirits as he was in that Night, and I of course was exhilerated—We stuck close to our assylum till the Carriages were announced, which aroused us from our delightful Trance—He then eagerly seized my

Hand, almost smotherd me with Handkerchiefs
and led me through the Croud to the Carriage—
The Roes rode by us as far as Rockwell, and by
Day break we reach'd Parsonage, and retired to
Bed.

| Race Course | CHAPTER 77TH | Ancient good Breeding |

Love has seized me, Tyrant Love
Inthrals my soul! I am undone by Love!

The next morn Mr and Miss Roe accompanied
us in our Carriage to the Race Course—My
Mother thank'd the former for his sons attention
to us at the Assembly—I would knock them
down if they were not obliging to you, was his
answer—He then told us he had given them
strict orders not to leave us, and to watch that
we met with no Insult or Incivility—I was somewhat damp'd by his accounting for their Attention but when I recollected the whole aspect and
Demeanor of John Roe, I could not think that
his Lover like behaviour proceeded merely from
a dutiful Obedience to his Fathers Commands—
No! He was all that Female Heart could wish in
its Fondest Excess!

Mr and Miss Roe dined that day with us at Parsonage, as the young men gave a great Entertainment at Rockwell to their Turf acquaintances, and Mr Roe was glad to get out of the
way—My Aunt Eyre and he were quite smitten

with each other—indeed no two could be better associated—The same Hauteur, and Enthusiasm for Liberty—The same Politeness and ancient good Breeding were conspicuous in both —Ned Eyre would have it that they had kicked up a flirtation which afforded him a large field of amusing nonsense—We went to one more Assembly which was merely a Repetition of the former, and frequented the course the whole week—at length the Races ended to our great grief—Saturday Night we finish'd our weeks dissipation by drinking Tea at Rockwell, with only the addition of Doctor Hemphill to our party—John Roe and I sat together again the whole Evening in a retired corner of the Parlour —We made ourselves very Merry on the Events of the week, and Ned Eyres odd Drolleries furnish'd us with a fresh subject for Mirth—Mr Roe presented me that Night with three pots of Curious Amaranthuses, which I carefully nursed for the sake of my Rockwell friend, and afterwards carried them to Carrick as Souvenirs— Inshort his Dora (as he called me) was the whole Object of his Care and thoughts always, and every where.

| A Morning Levee | CHAPTER 78TH | A delicious Evening |

I have for Love a thousand thousand Reasons
Dear to the Heart and potent to the Soul

My every thought, reflection, Mem'ry, All
Are a perpetual Spring of Tenderness—

On Sunday morning we had a full Levee after
Church to visit my Aunt Eyre and Ned—Mrs
Clarke came out—The Roes as usual attended
it—but all went away after the usual sitting
except John, who lingered an hour after them,
as He, Mrs Clarke, and I were too merry to
part—We had her between us, and roasted her
well about a story of Otways that she weighed
eighteen stone—John Roe staid so long that
my Mother askd him to Dinner which Invitation he accepted, and then took leave, saying, he
must take a gallop to Rockwell, but would be
back presently—When he made his Exit Mrs
Clarke had her full Retaliation on me—She
declared she never saw Miss Herbert look so
killingly vivacious, and that either she, or Mr
John Roe, must have inspired me with an uncommon fund of Wit and Spirits—This observation made me blush consciously, and Mrs
Clarkes arch enquiring Eye was well calculated
to encrease my Confusion—My Aunt Eyre
next attacked me, and calling me over to them
said, God bless you my Dora—I never saw you
look half so pretty or so animated as this Morning—You should always keep up your flow of
Spirits for Spirits become you more than any
one I ever saw and turning to Mrs Clarke she
bid her observe what a beautiful complexion I
had got—Mrs Clarke full of Roguery answerd

Yes and I protest Miss Herberts Eyes too look
uncommonly brilliant surely she has found
some new charm in my society that makes her
all Life and Animation—They then without
giving me time to recover myself poured out a
volley of Encomiums on John Roe and declared
he also had caught the Infection for they never
saw him appear so Charmingly Brilliant before
—Inshort their Eyes and Tongues ran on so
that I was forced to run out of the Room to avoid
their Inquisatorial Researches—As this took
place before Ned Eyre I was terrified lest his
Mischief Making mind should urge him to his
usual pranks before John Roe.

The Dear Swain now returned to Dinner—We
had hardly reached the Drawing Room after it
—when he broke loose from the gentlemen and
took shelter under my Wings—Mr Clarke and
Otway follow'd him and strove to drag the
Deserter back but he clung to my Chair and
they were forced to return without him—We
sat together all the Evening apart, for Mrs
Clarke contrary to her usual custom, avoided
me, and left us Tete a tete together—Amongst
other Chat he gave me that night a full description of the New Canal and its Machinery—He
was a great Mechanic himself and finding I
readily comprehended him he promised to con-
sult me next Day on a Model of a new Bridge
he was to build over his lake and to shew me the
whole mechanism of his Undertaking promising
me a great boating party when it was finish'd—

Mrs Hare also dined with us and was all astonishment at his very particular Attention to me—She declared if any one had sworn to her that John Roe would attach himself so totally to any girl in the whole World, she could not have believed it as he was always remarkably shy of our sex and carefully avoided a partial devotion to any Female—She could not suppose but he had serious Thoughts of me—Though we were in the family way, the party did not break up till twelve at Night—John Roe then returnd home not having once quitted me the whole Evening from the time we left the dining Room—All this was very remarkable from so Isolated a person as he was—But Alas! all this time the Words, I love! never passd his Lips though we often touch'd on the sweet passion in general conversation, but ever in a laughing rallying Manner.

We spent the next Evening at Rockwell—John Roe still hoverd about me but I perceived that Night an uncommon diffidence and confusion in his address that I could not account for—He brought out the paper model of his Bridge and after explaining asked my advice whether he should make such and such Alterations—He blush'd stammerd and hesitated extremely whilst he consulted me—His Eyes were cast down as if fearful of every word he utterd—In vain I racked my Brain to account for this odd and sudden Change—I could not fathom it— He then renew'd his promise of giving me an

Entertainment on the Lake, and afterwards our
Conversation turnd on a great Horse Race he
and Andrew were to have—He pumped me on
which side I should bet, as it was quite a party
affair—I frankly acknowledged I should feel
more Interested for his Horse than Andrews,
whose brags and taunts were loudly provoking
on the Occasion—We again sat till late, and
parted with Mutual Regret as it seem'd.
The Linville family now return'd home, and
took off some of the girls—Whilst they staid
we were obliged to have a regular Dinner every
day at one Oclock for Lady Dapper and Miss
Kitsy, either a fat Duck hot from the Spit, or a
tender Chicken with Sippets, for Ned though
very plain in his own meat would not allow his
Dogs to feed on coarse Viands—unluckily he
one day caught Mrs Bradshaw stealing the leg
of a Duck from Lady Dapper, which bred a
Mortal Quarrel between them—Another droll
Circumstance happen'd one Day while they
were with us—The Clarkes and Roes dined
with us—It was a shocking wet Day and Mr
Roe sat bemoaning his Harvest which was all
cut down My Corn! My Corn! was his whole
subject at Dinner—Mrs Bradshaw partly over-
heard him and assured him wet weather was the
fittest for the operation, and he need not be
afraid at its bleeding which was the best sign
in the world—Mr Roe stared and begged leave
to differ from her in every assertion—But she
maintain'd her Dogmas so stubbornly that she

set him in a Violent Passion whilst the whole
Company were forced to pour down Bumpers
to hide their Laughter——An Explanation at last
took place——It appear'd that Mr Roe was
talking of his wheat and oats——and Mrs Bradshaw thought he meant the Corn on his Toe.

A Breaking up	CHAPTER 79TH	A dreadful Hurricane

Follows the loosen'd aggravated Roar
Enlarging, deepening, mingling,——peal on peal
Crushd horrible, convulsing Heaven and Earth

The Linville family and most of the girls now
left us——The Night they went one of the most
dreadful Hurricanes happend that ever was
known in Ireland——About 12 or one oclock we
were awoke by the violent bursting in of all the
Windows and Doors——The family in every
Room started from their Beds and ran down
half naked to avoid the showers of crashing glass
flying about us——Whilst like Milton's fallen
Angels " With horrible Combustion down we
fell " beneath the pelting Storm——We groped
and wept in " darkness visible " till we formed
a miserable groupe below but there it was
equally affrighting and a hideous Crash from
above stairs convinced us the Roof had fallen
in——We screamd not knowing who was safe or
who lost, till another furious Blast shook the
parlours so about us that we ran down to the

Kitchen which was under ground, but we were
there told that was the most unsafe place of all,
and that our only Chance was to escape to the
Open Fields—Frantic, we open'd the Area
Door, when such a Hurricane blew in that
Every Man in the House was employ'd to shut
it again, for it was quite impossible to stand out
and we were forced to await inactive our Fate—
Meanwhile all was hideous Uproar above—
We now missd John Roberts an Apprentice Boy
and an Old Man who both lay in the garrets—
The storm abating my Mother took a fearful
peep up stairs—And finding that the House
was still whole she crept on until she saw the
Roof which was also standing but with many
Chasms—this encouraged us further till we
founded the great noise proceeded chiefly from
the falling of slates on the Leads—We now
musterd what Spirituous Cordials we had, and
having well dosed ourselves went to Bed about
four or five Oclock, having first secured every
thing as well as possible, and on our Knees
recommended our Souls to the protection of
Providence—The next Day all was pretty calm
but we found the massive Iron Door of the
Leads carried three fields off by the Storm which
had been equally dreadful to all our Neighbours
—and was not only felt all over Europe but we
afterward found the same tempest had desolated
the West Indies and other parts with unprecedented Horrors.

And still new Needs new helps new Habits rise
That graft Benevolence on Charities.

After dispatching our kind Enquiries round
the Vicinage we sat down to Breakfast which
was scarcely over when the Door opend and
Mr Roe stood before us much like the man
that drew Priams Curtain in the Dead of Night
pale and portentous—After begging we would
not be alarmd he told us his friend Nicholas
who almost lived at Rockwell had been taken
suddenly ill in the night, that they had sent off
for Doctor Hemphill who pronounced his complaint a Pleurisy and orderd him to be blister'd
instantaneously from head to foot—It seems
Nick and the two Roes went out in the Height
of the Storm to see if the Stable and Horses
were safe, and was suddenly taken ill as above
mentioned—Great was our consternation at this
Intelligence—My Father and Mother rode off
with Mr Roe to Rockwell quite distracted for
our Coachman having got drunk the Race week,
was turnd off—We remain'd at home in the
greatest anxiety till a Note came from my
Mother to inform us Nick was much better
and Mr Roe sent his Coach to take us to
Rockwell.

We found Miss Roe in her Bedgown having
sat up all Night with a Maid Servant, attending

233

Nick, who was now a good deal better, but very
weak, and Enfeebled by pain—We spent a
melancholy day in his Room, only leaving him,
to eat a hasty Dinner of Beefsteaks below, and
then returnd to our Nursetending—The Young
Men had been out all Day looking for Trout
for him—When they returnd they looked in
now and then, but Miss Roe would not let
them stay in the Room for fear of their catching
the Disorder—She told us she had reared
Andrew in Cotton, and was in perpetual Alarm
about him—Towards Evening however they
insisted on coming to Nick's Bedside to know
from himself how he was, finding him in a dose
they went off for fear of disturbing him.

A week pass'd in this manner—part of it very
gloomily, as he grew very bad and had a most
allarming Crisis—Doctor H. pronounced him
in imminent Danger and we were all distracted
—Fanny and I were sent home every night in
Mr Roe's Coach and went back every morning
with two fresh Maid Servants—My Mother
Miss Roe and the Servants of both Houses
being quite fagged with sitting up and attendance on him.

At the end of a fortnight Doctor Hemphill gave
it as his Opinion that his patient might get up—
Mr and Miss Roe were out of their wits for Joy
for they had all along conceald the worst from
us—Great preparations were made for the Invalids Reception in the Drawing Room—My
usual seat the Sopha was laid out with pillows

Bolsters &c but he was not able to stay above a
quarter of an Hour—However Doctor Hemphill insisted he would be quite well in two or
three Days and so it happen'd—As for me I was
not at all comme il faut—Nicks Illness had
given me a great fright and lower'd my Spirits,
and now that he was recovered, I had another
grief that secretly preyd like a Worm on my
Damask Cheek—My Mother fixed the period
of his Amendment and going to School for our
Return to Carrick—I cannot pourtray my secret
feelings on this Occasion—A thousand Daggers
could not wound me more deeply—The Idea of
losing the Opportunity of seeing John Roe
daily, and hourly hearing of him was too much
for my shattered senses to bear—I felt as if soul
and Body were seperating and my alterd Looks
soon indicated my Inward Torment—I could
not help thinking that John Roe too had lost
his usual Spirits—His Manners became em-
barassed and his speaking Eyes were now ever
gloomily cast down—He was naturally reserved
and shy and I found it impossible to fathom his
present Sentiments—I had heard that in a great
dispute after the Races about beauty he had
declared I was the prettiest girl at the Assembly
and that he preferr'd me even to the beautiful
Jephsons in opposition to the whole Company—
God knows how matters really stood—Mr Roe
and my Father still continued their Back gammon with intemperate avidity as they were so
shortly to seperate and it was universally re-

solved that the two families should not miss
being a Day together during our short stay—
We accordingly spent every intermediate day
at Rockwell or Parsonage together, and never
broke up till near Morning.

I spent every solitary moment of Interval Weeping, to ease my burden'd Heart—I quite lost
my rest and found a horror in Concealment
that was insupportable, but Alas! in Concealment only could I vent my Sorrows.

| Inuendoes | CHAPTER 81ST | Unexpected Ill Humour |

" *A Sickly Langour veils mine Eyes*
" *And fast my waning Vigour flies*

One Evening we were seated at Tea at Rockwell
before the Gentlemen joined us—Miss Roe
seem'd more inclined to be free and communica-
tive than ever I had seen her—She gave us
many hints about her father and Mothers
Quarrel and the Situation of the family and
expressed many wishes that her Brothers were
happily settled that she might have a female
Companion in her Solitude—With many things
to that purpose—The Kettle was now Brought
in and we all gatherd round the Tea Table—I
was seated just opposite Miss Roe and the
Evening Sun glared full on my Face—she was
unusually busy in arranging the China and
looked big with some important Budget still

undisclosed—At length she broke silence with
a most pathetic Lamentation on the loss she
would have in our Society and complain'd so
bitterly of not having any female Companion
that my Mother to comfort her said Oh you
won't be so bad—You will still have Mrs Clarke
and Mrs Carew and if your Brother John should
marry you will have his Wife—Miss Roe
quickly and sternly replied, No Madam! My
Brother John intends Never to Marry—The
pointed keeness of this Speech—her Eye glan-
cing hastily by me aided by the reflection of the
sun on my face threw me into such Confusion
that the China rattled in my hand so violently
that all the girls made an involuntary Spring
to save it but in vain for my Cup Saucer and
their Contents all fell from my trembling Hands
—I remained rooted to my Seat perfectly in-
animate, but as red as Scarlet whilst they picked
up the scatterd Fragments—Miss Roe herself,
thrown off her guard stared full at me, and lost
her usual precaution—As not one of us had
presence of Mind to turn it off—we all remain
in Silent Embarassment till the Entrance of the
gentlemen relieved us from our awkard perplexity.

The Moment they came they heap'd down
piles of wood on the fire and when they had
made a sufficient Blaze they dragg'd me over
but not having spirits to bear a Mauling—I
crept back to my old Seat on the Sopha—
Andrew follow'd and for the first time he had

approached me a long while strove to wedge
himself in along with me—The Tea Table and
Chairs were before us—John vaulted over
both, kicked down the China and seizing
Andrews collar he heartily shook and pitched
him to a proper Distance—He then shook his
head in triumph and seated himself near me—
Miss Roe was inclined to be very angry both
for her China and her Brother Andrew—but
Mr Roe interfered and rebuked Andrew for
his forwardness in seizing a Seat he had always
allotted to John—John Roe and I remain in
quiet possession the rest of the Evening but
I saw that Miss Roe and Andrew looked dreadfully Sulky—As for John he parried them off
by tormenting Andrew about Miss Emma
Massy a woman he detested above all others.
The Day following they dined with us—We
play'd Cards all the Evening to humour Nick—
and gave Miss Roe a head ach with our squabbles
at Pope Joan—We left off at 12 Oclock but
my Father Mother and Mr Roe were so deeply
engaged at Backgammon that they did not
break up till One—Meanwhile John Roe sat
down vis a vis to me and leaning his head on
the Card table affected drowsiness—He held
his hand to his face but I could perceive I had
prevail'd over Morpheus for his Eyes were
intently employ'd in surveying me from Top
to Toe as I was standing up near him—In these
Attitudes we both remaind till One when Mr
Roe broke up the Meeting.

238

The next Evening we drank Tea at Rockwell—
We played small plays all Night and were as
riotous as possible—I believe Miss Roe never
saw such a Scene at Rockwell before—Amongst
other tricks Nick blackend all our faces with
the Candle Snuff—John Roe bore it all very
patiently till he saw me transmogrified, he was
then very angry and sent Miss Roe for soap
and hot water whilst they scrubbed at each
side of me—But in vain they strove to restore
my Beauty for the black grease stuck like pitch
and not till I went home could it be rubbed off—
The word pitch puts me in mind of Mr Roe's
doseing us all with Tar water to make us wholesome—Our Ratio was two Quarts a day and
neither his own Children or we durst appear before him till we had drank our full Beverage.
The following Day was to be our last at Knockgrafton and it was agreed that we should breakfast at Rockwell where we were to join the family
in a party to Dundrum the Seat of Lord de
Montalt then absent in England—After viewing the place we were to return to Dinner at
Rockwell and there to End our Knockgrafton
Carreer.

| A Morning Excursion | CHAPTER 82D | Provoking fickleness |

Oh save me from the Tumult of the Soul!
From the Wilds Beasts within!

Mr Cowpers family then lived at Dundrum he
being agent to Lord De Montalt—They consisted of Mr and Mrs Cowper their Daughter
and two Nieces—Fanny Butlar Mrs Cowpers
niece was a beautiful Orphan whom they reared
—Her situation and Beauty gained her universal pity—She somewhat resembled Fanny
Jephson to whom she was related—by some
she was thought handsomer, others thought
not but she was certainly a most interesting
object—She was just fifteen—with an air of
Naiveté and Youthful Innocence.
We all set out from Rockwell for Dundrum
after Breakfast—Mr Roe and my father and
Mother went in his Coach, Miss Roe the girls
and I in ours—The two Roes and Mr Carew
followed on Horseback—We drove on with
little remarkable but Andrew's continually
popping his Nose to the Window of our Carriage and I could not help feeling vex'd that
his Brother did not do so likewise—When we
arrived Mrs Cowper had a cold Collation for
us—When we had regaled and rested ourselves
we proceeded to examine the House Garden
and Improvements—John Roe escorted us
through each chamber but left us to patroll
the Improvements alone whilst he enter'd into
a deep flirtation with the beautiful Fanny Butlar
who acted as Bar Maid—When I found there
was no chance of their following us in our walk,
my spirits sank entirely and I strolled about
the place quite insensible to its Beauties—

" *Then the Lilies no longer were White*
" *Then the Rose was deprived of its Bloom.*

I at length rejoined the walkers—and on our entering a broad winding Alley, we heard a wonderful Clatter of voices, and amazing loud female Laughs—The next turn displayd Fanny Butlar and the other Young Lady with John Roe at the side of the former and Andrew escorting her friend—We had some way to get up to them—and they put a sudden and affected stop to their Merriment when they beheld us—I was ready to burst out Crying at this capricious Conduct in John Roe, and the Constraint I laid on myself made me Worse —They stop'd to speak to our party, I could no longer command my Tears which ran copiously down my Cheeks and were too perceivable to all present though my Mother and the girls strove to screen me—Andrew gave me a most insulting look the young Ladies stared John Roe look'd down condemnd, and they walked proudly on whilst the Ladies burst into another Horse laugh after they passd us— We soon heard a different key and on turning about to know the Occasion we saw John Roe struggling to get away from the fair ones who laid violent hands on him, he at length broke from them and ran after us—placing himself by my side when he got up to us—The party he quitted were palpably provoked, and sending a most murderous look after us walked off— He and I strolled on Tete a tete for some

minutes in profound silence—I had lost my
usual freedom with him and he seem'd to catch
my Awkardness till it began to rain—He then
begged I would let him shelter me with his
Surtout—As I was still weeping I suffer'd him
to do as he pleased—The violence of the Shower
now made us run hard towards the House—
finding he still held his Coat over me I slackend
my pace but I felt too much hurt to say a Word
—we at length reached the Salloon, and I sunk
into the first Chair in Strong Hystericks.

My Hero stood vis a vis to me and looked like
a Condemn'd Criminal—He made some attempts to succour me but finding he only made
me worse he slunk to the Wall at my Elbow
awkard perplex'd and not knowing what to do
with me—The arrival of the rest of the Company relieved him from his responsibility—
They made many Enquiries to none of which
he could make any satisfactory answer—My
Mother appologized by saying I was subject
to fits of Low Spirits—This encreased John
Roes Confusion and he leand over me without
uttering a Syllable—The young ladies and
Andrew now came in with a Titter but stop'd
short on seeing my Situation—They then all
dispersed for Salts hartshorn Water et cætera—
John Roe alone remained in Statuquo near me.
The Carriages were now announced and in the
midst of the rain we set out on our Return to
Rockwell.

Rack'd by a thousand mingling Passions, Fear,
Hope, Jealousy, disdain, submission, grief,
Anxiety, and Love in every Shape.

It now turned out one of the wettest Days that
ever was seen—Andrew staid by the Carriages
and was up at the Coach Window until he got
such a drenching that he was forced to take
shelter behind with John and Mr Carew—They
soon turned off across the fields and left him to
escort us alone—When we got back to Rockwell
we found them both dress'd and powder'd out to
the Life—They shouted at Andrews crest fallen
appearance and set him in a violent passion
—Miss Roe now took me up to her Dressing
Room to spruce myself, for she said John and
Mr Carew were great observers, and smiling
said with particular Emphasis I must not let her
Brother John see me in that trim—She then
went off to borrow his Rack and other dressing
Apparatus—I beggd she would not trouble
him and she told him I was in the greatest
pucker at her going into his Room for them—
On emerging from my Toilette I saw John
standing with his back to an amazing wood fire
in the drawing Room highly amused at my
prudery—We now all assembled there and
walked about by firelight to stretch our legs—
I saw him several times take up the Back-

gammon Box and then lay it down as if irre-
solute—He at last in a hesitating Voice asked
if I would do him the honour to play with him—
I agreed and he seemd quite happy at my Consenting—I saw he had mischief in his Countenance but sat down with him—Mr Carew came
over and asked what we play'd for—John Roe
said Kisses to be sure—I beggd he would name
a Sum or otherwise I should be always on the
wrong side of the Question whether I won or
lost—as I could not ask him to pay me if I came
off victorious—He laughingly assured me I
should be paid the Debt with double Interest—
Mr Carew shouted at our bargaining so
methodically—We playd on and both fell into
such Reveries that neither minded the game but
left our Umpire to rectifye our moves—I won
by Chance the two first Gammons—This
rouzed John Roe from his Trance and he loudly
calld on Mr Carew to help him vowing he would
not lose his Right either to kiss or pardon me—
He now cheated so Abominably that I complain'd he was taking an unfair advantage of me
—He suppress'd a laugh and looked very sly
and Mr Carew with as arch a look said Madam
I should be sorry my friend took an Unfair
Advantage of any young Lady but particularly
of my friend Miss Herbert—John Roe now by
gross cheating won so rapidly and exulted so in
it that I was quite in Stew as he vow'd he would
shew me no Mercy but exact rigid payment—
However he let me off after a polite offer of taking

244

payment—Mr Roe then sent him to call for
Dinner as it was past six Oclock—He returned
with the melancholy news that the Round of
Beef Et Cætera had been render'd uneatable
by the Soot falling from the Chimney—This
made us all quite Cross as our Jaunt had given
us appetites, but we were forced to wait until
Eight Oclock for another Dinner.

Animadversions on Beauty	CHAPTER 83D	Unexpected Ill temper

Nor Peace nor Ease the Heart can know
Which like the Needle true
Turns at the touch of Joy or Woe
But turning, trembles too

When Dinner was served I was about to take
my seat at the lower End of the Table but was
universally call'd on to go up and sit near John
who sat at the Head to Carve—After my
Mother was help'd he in a jesting manner picked
out all the nice bits for me—He asked me carelessly how I liked Fanny Butlar—I was glad
to hear him talk in so easy a manner about her
for so interesting an Orphan was an enticing
Neighbour to a young man of his turn—I however felt very awkard on the subject after my
mornings Exposure but spoke the truth that I
thought her a very beautifull girl, indeed taking
a peep in a pier glass at Dundrum did not add
to my spirits or Self Vanity in her presence—

John Roe smiled at my Encomiums—he acknowledged them to be just but said she would make a very gross Woman, that she had likewise bad Teeth and should never open her mouth as her voice was coarse and masculine which in his mind would spoil the Effects of the most beautiful face—I looked at him as if I thought his Strictures pretty severe but with a good natured smile he assured me it was because Miss Butlar was a great pet of his and he would not give her any merit she did not deserve and he took great pains to convince me he did not mean to be ill natured—He was so gay all the time at Dinner that both Mr Roe and Mr Carew remarkd it and the former said —Come! John is in such good spirits this Evening that I think we must ask him for a Song— After a good deal of pressing he sang a ludicrous song on the Misses—Every Chorus Ended with a Miss Dolly as Rhyme for Madam Polly— which excited general laughter at my expence— as for him he was quite choking with laughter —I at length declared (as the Song grew more and more ridiculous) that I could sit it out no longer, and to make me amends he began one of a more sentimental turn—He had a very good voice and sang with great humour or pathos as the subject required, indeed he did every thing gracefully—I was now tormented to sing but my spirits were not up to it—and Mr Roe finding that my voice trembled excused me saying I had not yet recoverd my mornings

Indisposition—When we left the Room they
came up very soon after us and John as usual
seized the next seat to me on the Sofa—Never
did I see him in such spirits—he was all Life,
Love, and Animation—Cupid God of Love
never appeard half so charming as John Roe,
nor ever knew so well how to manage the " belle
passion "—He attacked Andrew about Miss
Emma Massy and to his great Mortification
gave me in his hearing a full account of his
Brother's Courtship with Miss Massy who was
plain, Odd, Elderly, and his mortal Aversion—
He however drew near us on hearing his name
mention'd—John Roe was my prompter to say
so and so to him, and we worked him up into
a most violent Fury—In the midst of our merriment large packets were brought in from the
post and Mr Roe went down to the parlour to
read them, Shortly after John and Miss Roe
were summon'd to attend him—They staid
some time below and I impatiently waited for
their Return—John at length came up, and my
Eyes flew to welcome him—but I was quite
thunder struck to see him look dark, gloomy
and offended—Instead of bounding to me as
usual—he stopp'd at the Door and enter'd into
a Trivial Conversation with Mr Carew—He
at length strolld towards the Sopha, and though
I made Room for him according to Custom he
rudely brush'd by me with Looks of Sullen
Anger and Disdainful Negligence.

But Cooly thus!——How could'st thou be so cruel
Thus to revive my hopes, to soothe my Love
And call forth all its tenderness——then sink me
In black Despair!

His cruel glance en passant had its full Effect
and was doubly felt after his previous smiles——
Deceitful harbingers of my Sorrow!——I now
was fully convinced that something in the
Letters had Ruffled him thus——and strove to
catch his Eyes but in vain——He obstinately
averted them and avoided me——Mr and Miss
Roe now came up——the latter seem'd full of
important intelligence but only informed us
That she had received amazing long Letters
from her Mother and her Sister Elliot——She
then called for Cards and with unusual alacrity
arranged our Pope Joan party——We all sat
down to play——but though I kept the next
chair vacant for him he deignd not to accept it
but after I had offer'd it sat down vis a vis to
me at the other Extremity of the Table——He
was cursedly out of Temper, and sat either
sullenly silent, or growling at every one round
the Table——all my Efforts could not induce
him to lift up his Eyes from his Cards——I
attempted to laugh and Chat with him across
the Table, but he only answered me by crossly
drawing my Sister Lucy's Chair close to his

with an evident design to vex me—I felt extremely awkard at having kept a vacant Chair for him—I hoped that Andrew would seize it and relieve me by his Rattle from Observation —but Andrew had perceived Johns coldness to me and avoided me in the Hour of Distress— Meanwhile John looked as black as the Mischief and obstinately persisted either in a gloomy Silence or in an affected Squabble with Lucy about the Cards—I felt choaking with Tears that I durst not shed and their Suffocation gave me a pain about the Heart that was quite intolerable—My Countenance fell and trembling, distracted, I could hardly keep my Head from falling on the Table—I can compare my Situation to nothing but that of a person suddenly blasted by a Stroke of Lighting, and I sat as pale and aghast as if such a thing had happend.

At length John Roe in a sulky manner looked towards me—he perceived the plight I was in— But How shall I describe his Looks at that Moment—They conveyd a thousand meanings equally severe and terrible—He seemd convulsed with inward passion and his Visage darkend as if he too had felt the same thunder-stroke that convey'd Stagnation through my Veins—But "his was a grief of Fury not Despair"—He seemd to say, " I love you past utterance I feel a shock of the passion beyond any thing I ever felt before beyond any Conception I had formed of it—But I am resolved

to tear it from my Heart, and discard you as
artful and dangerous—as a Viper inimical to
my Happiness!—Resolving henceforth to become a Villain sooner than risque the Calamities
you would bring upon me "—Oh John Roe!
Too adorable Man! These were the very Sentiments your looks expressd at that Moment—I
could not be mistaken—Love helpd me to read
your inmost Thoughts—Unkind John Roe!
My Passion and Despair at that moment should
have bound you to me for Ever! A poor timid
Creature was I! Inexperienced in Worldly
Craft, and bound down to Silence by Fear,
Modesty, and Education! Alas I had then no
Weapon, no Defence—Doom'd to suffer like
a poor Dumb Brute whatever my severe Tyrant
inflicted! He had me taken in inextricable
snares! Nor had I yet learnd to Shun them or
defend Myself—Ungratefull John Roe!—How
terrible was the moment that joined us! and
how terrible were we both to each Other at that
black Instant when you Infamously resolved to
forsake me and I as desperately Abandon'd
Myself to Despair! I swear by the great God
of Heaven I think that Hour united us in Bonds
that were indissoluble—In an Eternal Union
sacred and sure—That Bolt of Heaven or Hell
struck him a determined Villain but all its
Terrors lighted on me and left me as a stiffend
Corpse—Blasted!—Undone for Ever!
Sure No Woman had ever such strong Claims
to any Man's Love as I had to John Roe's for

No Woman was ever so wrap'd up in One Man or so ruin'd by him.

Well might I that Night have cried to my Destroyer, How art thou fallen! Oh Lucifer! Son of the Morning!—No other Idea could be so applicable to his Conduct and Phisiognomy at that decissive Moment.

| A Passionate Effusion | CHAPTER 85 | A Cruel Parting |

Long loved, Adored Ideas All Adieu

It was Easy to see that John was provoked with his Brother for having observed us—Andrew and Miss Roe fond of the Mischief, were unusually facetious and Andrew being very noisy, John vented his ill humour by repeatedly threatening to Horsewhip him—Which he at length attempted, starting up, and collaring him for the purpose—I had never before that Night seen him the least way out of Temper— He now stood before me wild and furious his face black again with passion—Grief and Astonishment had kept me all night in a deadly Stupor but Terror now rouzed me, and with the Rest I shriekd aloud—Miss Roe with Difficulty parted her two Brothers by throwing herself between them—Our screams made Mr Roe call over from the Back gammon Table What's all that Work there—John Roe now sat down with the Fury of Hell pictured on his Counten-

ance—His Eyes and Mine met once more, I
was in a beseeching Attitude but he turned
away with as black a look as if I was a Serpent
and I again relapsed into a heavy hopeless
Stupor—We playd on in profound silence for
a Time—The Boys and Girls began to cheat
by way of restoring good humour—but in vain
—John Roe wrangled surlily with every one
round the Table—and when twelve Oclock
Struck he huddled up the Counters and broke
up the Party.
The Back gammon Table closed soon after and
I heard the Coach call'd for with much the same
feelings that a Criminal has on hearing a summons for the Cart to carry him to Execution—
The Coachman being out of the way we sat in
melancholy Grandeur round the Room—John
always closed the Evening at my Side, but this
Evening he chatted with my Mother—We sat
about an Hour waiting for the Coach—I defye
any Pen or Tongue to describe the Various
Agonies of my Mind in that short Interval—
His Nonchalant Air in conversing with my
mother seemd a sarcastic Ratification of his Cruel
Behaviour at the Card Table—Throughout the
whole Day his temper had been so variable that
I was bewilderd and lost in horrible Doubt and
Surmize which I had now no chance of seeing
cleard—We were to set out early the next Day
for Carrick—Parting him was enough to over-
whelm me but parting him in this Manner was
insupportable—I was inwardly all Horror and

Despair—with difficulty I sat out the Hour
suffocating with Grief and every Moment certain I should faint away—Not one Chearing
look did He vouchsafe me but studied palpably
to be as cruel as possible.

Andrew seeing me a forsaken Damsel throughout the Evening came up and with affected goodnature but a cursed Sneer strove to entertain me
—John Roe was no longer my Champion
against his Brothers impertinent Officiousness
—He seemd in a few hours compleatly to have
resign'd me to Woe and the malice of my Ill
wishers—My Heart was so sunk I could not
speak and I suffered Andrew to vent his spiteful
Nonsense unanswer'd—At length the dreadful
Words The Carriage is ready sounded in my
Ears like the Knell of all my Earthly Happiness
—I arose half Dead at the Summons—Andrew
seized my Hand to lead me down which de-
spondently I sufferd.

At the Head of the Stairs however John darted
forward and giving his Brother a push, dragg'd
my Hand from him and led me down but with a
profound Silence—The Action however was so
unexpected at the time that it acted on my heart
as a Magnetic Charm—I would have given the
Universe to stay one Hour longer, and thought
if I had that one Hour's Reprieve I could do
Wonders—A Confused Idea that I could summon Resolution to say or do any thing, left me
full of Self Condemnation for the many precious
moments I had sacrificed to Timidity—I now

saw that my desperate Case needed a desperate
Remedy—John Roe maintained a studied Silence all the way down, but Stopp'd me at the
landing Place to tie my Handkerchief about my
Neck—It was pitch dark, and he put, or rather
pushed me into the Carriage, without once bidding me Good bye—When we drove from the
Door I threw myself back in the Carriage and
gave full vent to the Tears that had been choaking me all the Evening—Oh! What a Relief
was it! I stuff'd my mouth that my Sobs should
not be heard—The Darkness hid me—and my
sorrowful journey pass'd in a Real Luxury of
Tears, the only Solace left me.

| Mental sufferings | CHAPTER 86TH | A sorrowful Journey |

" *No More those Scenes my Meditation Aid*
" *Or lull to rest, the Visionary Maid*

When I got home I flew to my Apartment and
there wept aloud in all the Agony of despairing
Love—Lucy who slept with me at length came
up to Bed, and I was forced to Undress in
Silence—I was the whole Night in a high Delirium—and my Head grew quite distracted
with weeping and Sobbing—Every five Minutes
I started out of Bed and walked barefooted about
the Room to cool the Fever that oppress'd me—
Then as distractedly lay down again without
once closing my Eyes till Morning—I at length

disturbed Lucy who supplicated to know what ailed me—Her stupidity in not guessing the Cause of my Sorrow provoked me and I begg'd she would not pester me.

The next Morning I bade a Melancholy Farewell to every Object about Parsonage—My Walks, my Seats, were all washed with my Tears —Even my Chest of Drawers where I used to sit at Work or settling my Cloaths was kissd a thousand times—There I brooded over some happy Occurence or pleasing Expectation— There I pourtray'd in my Mind every smiling look, every winning grace of my adored John Roe.

We at length set off—I wept as I pass'd the Church and Village, but spoke not a word till we reach'd Clonmell—My Mute Grief was beyond the Agonies of the Inquisitors Rack—At the other side of Clonmell my Mother began to plan out how we should entertain the Roes, for they all promised solemnly to visit us—This Topic rouzed me a little but the great uncertainty of the Event kept me silent—I foresaw that Mr Roe would not be suffer'd to fulfill his Engagement as Miss Roe ruled all his Motions, and I could not build much on his Promise to spend great part of the Winter with his Old Rector, though Miss Roe made the same promise and John and Andrew set to it their Seals.

END OF BOOK THE FOURTH

> " *Now I know What it is to have strove*
>   *With Torture of Doubt and Desire:*
> *What 'tis to admire and to love,*
>   *And to leave him we love and Admire.*

Once more we were quietly seated down at
Carrick for the Winter—But Oh! How different the Circumstances—No longer was I the
gay I may say Childish Creature I was—A fixt
and ungovernable passion ruled over me, and
Colour'd every Event—I saw that I was now
doom'd to be compleatly miserable or happy,
and the Chances Alas! were very much against
me—I now began to dislike and shun all
Society, my only Companion was a large Spaniel
that John Roe gave my Brother Otway—I often
fed the pet at Rockwell—Here he followd me
like my Shadow and was my greatest Consolation—I had also Mr Roe's three flower pots,
and the blue Tiffany Bonnet he gave me, and
over these Relicks I continually pored and wept
—A visiter from the neighbourhood of Knockgrafton was a treasure to me and the sound of

257   s

John Roes Name was the sweetest Music I
could hear—Even Andrew would have been
here an incalculable Favourite

    —Whilst busy Meddling Memory
  In barbarous succession musterd up
  The past Endearment of our happier Hours.

We stop'd at Linville on our way home and
met Edward White there—He was Brother to
Sim White and was just setting off for the East
Indies—He was a beautiful Young Man about
the age of Eighteen—but was doom'd never
more to return for soon after his arrival there,
he was kill'd in a Duel by a Brother Officer—
He was youngest son to Mrs White Ned Eyres
Sister.

My friends were very uneasy they said to hear
Numberless Rumours flying about John Roe's
attention which it was thought prevented Mr
Crawford from making the serious Application
he once intended—The Affair had been dis-
cussed in a large Party at Linville two days
before and Mr Bradshaw expressd much anger
at the flying Reports—As for me, my Heart
was now gone and I thought no more of any
living Mortal but John Roe—All my Enquiries
now turned on Mrs Roe who I was told lived a
very secluded Life in Clonmell with Mrs Walsh
another Grass Widow—that she was a Charming Woman but very distant and reserved and
that John Roe was entirely led by her and his
Sister Elliot in all his movements—A Junta of

Females are seldom friendly where there is no fortune to biass them and I began to trace my Misfortunes from that source, trembling at the Precipice I stood on.

Fanny was somewhat in a similar Situation all this time as Sim White was still off and on whilst his Mothers Sway over him foreboded no good Consequences—He however had Explicitly declared his Love, a Satisfaction my Adorable had never given me—And I would have given the World to be in Fannys Situation —Indeed Edward White when at Linville said he was sure his Brother Sim and She would be Man and Wife before he returned.

Whilst we were at Knockgrafton we lost an old Neighbour here Mr Cox of Castletown who died of a Fever in Dublin—He was much respected in Carrick—Mrs Cox sometime after married Major Lloyd of the 17th Dragoons, then a Lieutenant in it.

| Unfounded Greetings | CHAPTER 88TH | an agreeable Surprize |

" *Oh Name for Ever Sad, for Ever dear*
" *Still breathed in Sighs still usher'd with a Tear*

At my first Walk into Carrick I was saluted by a general Volley from all my friends who every where wished me joy of my supposed Nuptials with John Roe—and they stared disappointedly when I flatly denied its Certainty—The Jeph-

sons had heard the same in Cashel, and san-
guinely commented on every Circumstance—
They spent a whole Evening here in deep
Counsel on the subject and made me produce
Mr Roe's presents—giving me every Encour-
agement from the News they had Collected—
Poor Mrs Dobbyn brought me out a Curious
foreign Smelling Bottle wishing me Every
Happiness as Bride Elect—I could in no wise
account for this general Certainty but by supposing that the Servants had spread the Report
and gave Ann Dowling a great Lecture about
it but she flatly denied it for herself and Fellow
Servants—Indeed if appearances were to be
credited the very particular Attention of the
Roes might well cause such a Report.

A Gentleman at this time lent me Xenophon's
Life of Socrates—The Arguments for Resigna-
tion were so strong and Convincing that I resolved to make it my future Companion and
fence against rising Misfortunes—foolishly
resolved for Alas I found no reasoning can cure
the pangs of Love—However with my Book I
wanderd in the most deserted Paths continually
brooding over the one Subject—continually
weeping and deploring my Fate—Mrs Ryan
the Clergyman's Wife and her Daughter came
here for a night—She was so full of John Roe
that she could talk of nothing Else—I know not
whether my Family designd it or no but of
late they never mention'd him and the Monosyllables dropping constantly from Mrs Ryan

made me quite in Love with her Conversation—
I had still hopes of their promised Visit and as
far as I could set about rectifying every thing
disorderly about the Place—I also got the
Harpsichord put in order and we sent to Water-
ford for a new Backgammon Box—These
Avocations amused my Mind and warded off
Despair.

When all was prepared for their Reception—
we wrote to remind them of their promise—
Mr Roe wrote a long and affectionate Letter
appointing a Day for our meeting them in
Clonmell that they might send their own Coach
back to Rockwell as they purposed spending
most of the Winter with us—but the next Post
brought us a Letter from Miss Roe and the
Hand writing made me forebode the Contents—
It was a put off on account of ill Health.

Heavens! What a transition from happiness
to Misery did this Letter cause in my Mind—
I now gave up all Hopes and expected never to
see or hear more of them, indeed I did not think
I could outlive the disappointment—I moped
about in a state of Stupor and totally lost my
spirits, rest and Appetite—One Day as I was
sauntering about the fields very melancholy, I
thought I saw some one pass the turn of the
Road very like Andrew Roe—I ran down to
our House in hopes I might catch another view
of him before he passd the lower Gate—I met
Ann searching for me who told me Mr Andrew
Roe was in the Parlour and very anxious to see

me—I ran in to tighten myself—but he did not
stay five minutes and went off to Waterford—
I was most terribly disappointed but on entering
the Parlour was told he set off Express after his
Brother John who went on before to see their
Uncle Harry Couglan then at the point of
Death.

CHAPTER 89TH

Oh thou hast Soothed my Passions into Peace

The Roes were to come in for Equal Shares of
their Uncles Property but did not expect to
meet him Alive—Andrew said they both intended calling on us on their way back—Accordingly two nights after as we were sitting at
tea—on a very wet night, a Rap came to the
Door and in came John and Andrew Roe—I
musterd all the dissimulation I was mistress of
to hide my Emotion and succeeded tolerably
well—We chatted away pretty freely—They
were both dress'd in deep Mourning as their
Uncles Heirs but Neither affected to be very
sorry for him—After they enter'd we were
forced to leave them the fire to dry themselves
a most lucky Circumstance for me or I should
have egregiously exposed myself as it was impossible to express the variety of my tumultuous
feelings—Once more I was under the same
Roof with my Dear John Roe! Once more I

could Contemplate his features and his Voice!
What Happiness!

Towards Supper time he told me he had seen
a Harpsichord in the other Room and begd I
would let him hear me play—I playd my best
for him, but was so flutter'd that I could not get
through it to please myself—However they
both praised my Performance—We supp'd but
he did not sit near me though he made some
attempt of the kind but my Mother I think kept
him near the fire—They told us they were
under the most urgent Necessity of leaving us
next Day but promised to strain every Nerve
to bring their Father and Sister to us—and
they of Course would Accompany them.

Next Day they breakfasted with us—How
lovely did John Roe look in his Mourning—
Indeed I was in such Goodhumour that I could
have hugged even Andrew himself, and was
very grateful for the Joy the poor little fellow
testified at seeing us and the more so as he
behaved quite prudently—John Roe was in
high Spirits and seem'd to me All Perfection—
After breakfast I was by chance left Alone with
the two Brothers—and Andrew began to be
very Obsequious—John did not forget his old
trick—for he jostled Andrew compleatly from
my Side—Andrew strove to get to the other
Side of me but his Brother took up a Chair and
kept him off—Poor Andrew was quite mortified
and did not relish the Joke—John and I then
enter'd into Conversation, and his Eyes seemd

to say that he did not forget the many happy
hours we spent together at Rockwell and
Parsonage—He was all fire, all Animation, all
Smiles and Charming Joy—Paddy Pup now
came to fawn on his old Master and me—John
Roe patted him and with a penetrating Gaze at
me observed how fat he was grown and that
he saw he was very well fed—I could not help
blushing for I often fed him by Stealth—The
Horses were at length announced—Andrew
shewd evident marks of Sorrow at removing
but John more cautious laughd it off though it
seem'd as if he tore himself away rather than
left us Voluntarily—however he carried it off
better than Andrew, and Jestingly as he was
setting off promised to send me an Account how
Andrew went on with Miss Emma Massy.
Delighted and grieved together I went up stairs
and threw myself on the Bed overcome by my
feelings—I could scarce credit the Reality of
this short Apparition after all I had sufferd by
the Idea of John Roes last leave taking, to see
him restored to me again the same Charming
Good John Roe as ever—This was so unexpected
a Happiness that short as their visit was I lay
an Hour ruminating in delightful Delirium not
daring to stir for fear of spoiling my present
Happiness—He had fervently shaken Hands
with me at parting and tore himself away with
a Reluctance he hardly attempted to conceal—
His intelligent Eyes spoke ten thousand things
which I was too apt [to] construe favourably—

I now with more Spirit and better Hopes, prepared every thing in case they should prevail
on their Father and Sister to come here.

" *To Dream once More I close my willing Eyes*
 Ye soft Illusions! Dear Deceits! Arise——

CHAPTER 90TH

Is there kind Heavn no Constancy in Man
No steadfast Truth no generous fixd Affection
That can bear up against a Selfish World

The Winter pass'd on and no chance of the
Roes coming though we repeatedly wrote to
Miss Roe who as often wrote back some Excuse
or Other—I therefore again set to my Xenophon
in hope of acquiring some Fortitude—One very
wet Night at tea time a Message was brought
that Mrs Elliot and Mr John Roe were at the
Hotel, that as Mrs Elliot was an Invalid he
could not leave her but would have the pleasure
of calling as they passd by, being obliged to go
on to Clonmell that night and they requested
my Brother would go down to them—It was
then eight Oclock and I waited with a palpitating Heart till I heard the Rap at the Door—
Away flew Xenophon and all my stock of philo-
sophy—Trembling with Delight I mixd in the
crowd and ran to meet them—we went out to
the gate but Mrs Elliot would not alight—
John Roe however came in, but it seemd more

265

a visit of Ceremony than any thing Else—He
was quite absorbed in thought all the time he
staid, he kept his Eyes fix'd on the fire—One
Yes, or No, were the only Words my Mother
could squeeze out of him—As for me, he hardly
saluted me and when I ventured to ask him a
Question he scarce deign'd to answer me even
in those short Monosyllables and with evident
Design averted his Eyes whilst he employd
himself in fiddling with his Watch Chain—
Again I sat petrified unable to account for this
odd variableness of Temper—He gave us no
hopes of seeing the Family, and after a Quarter
of an hour he took leave in the same manner he
enterd, and joind Mrs Elliot.

He indeed did not seem to be well, he was
pensive and melancholy and seemd to have some
Chilly Complaint over him but this did not
account for his frigid stiffness to all, and his
pointed coldness to me in particular—When
he was gone I felt I should never be happy—A
deadly Weight of Woe overpowerd me and
Despondency crept through Every Sense—I
took up Xenophon with a desperate Resolution
to read away every feeling, but the disgust I felt
at its philosophic Comforts convinced me I was
ruind for Ever—After some minutes reading
I burst into a flood of Tears which relieved my
poor heart from its Mortal Oppression, and
when able to stand up I crept to Bed and instantly fell asleep through downright Despondency—Even when John Roe paid a markd

Attention, the fear of some fatal Change kept
me miserable—but now that it really began,
my heart entirely sunk, and I gave up all hopes
of a Man who had so often changed his appearance with one who had never Offended him—
It was impossible but he must have known my
desperate Passion for him—every blundering
attempt to conceal it only developed it more
glaringly—Indeed I often saw him laugh at my
awkard dissimulation though he said nothing
but seemd inwardly to Enjoy my Confusion
and Blushes—God knows how madly I Idolized
him.

CHAPTER 91ST

Oh blindness to the future kindly Given
That Each should fill the Circle Mark'd by Heaven

" Hope springs Eternal in the human Breast "
(says Pope) and I do suppose it crept imper-
ceivably into mine or disappointment would
have killd me—I must now leave the most
interesting of all Subjects, to recite the intermediate incidents that happend in the Circles I
frequented.

About this Time Mr Hamilton Cuffe my
Mothers second Brother living paid us a Visit
and on the 27th of March 1790 my Mother
went with him to Desart to try and accomodate
the incessant Disputes about Money Matters
that had for some Years alienated the two

Brothers; but her Efforts had not the desired
Success.

Ned Eyre had now changed his Abode—He
gave up Linville and took Pill for the sake of
being near us in Winter—Pill was a melancholy
old House in the Green of Carrick with a field
and garden annex'd—we had only to cross the
Green to be with them so were there Morning
Noon and Night—But my poor Aunt was mostly
Bedridden, and Ned kept his Room—Our usual
Society there was Captain Jephson related to our
Jephsons and Mr Lloyd a Welshman both in
the 17th Dragoons—Mrs Cox of Castletown
took a fancy to Lloyd who had nothing then but
his Lieutenantcy and she generously bestow'd
on him her Hand and by her Influence and a
jointure of 800 a Year she got him made a
Colonel—Captain Jephson was very Satyrical
but a friendly little Man which he evinced by
pursuing a handsome Clergyman who had stolen
a young Lady's Heart and bringing him from
Cashel where [he had] fled to evade his Engagement, to be married here by my Father—as his
fair one took shelter with us from the Rage of
her Family I stood Bridesmaid and Captain
Jephson Bridesman—They were married at Ten
Oclock and by previous Agreement were restored to Mr Ryans family as Mr and Mrs
Smyth—The Roman Catholics made a great
sputter about it but Every impartial Person
thought her a lucky Woman to get him.

Mr Kenny a Clergyman related to us now spent

some time with us—He was a fine Sensible
Young Man, and flirted so with my sister Matty
that I thought he had a Mind to propose for her
but some time after he married Fanny Herbert
—one of his and our Muckrus Cousins—his
Brother also another Young Clergyman came
here but he had volunteerd to fight the Rebels
and went off in a Day.

CHAPTER 92D

*Dreadful Zeal fierce and intolerant of all Religion
that differs from their own is the black soul of
that infernal State*

Lady Dowager Blunden and her Family spent
some time with us now—for the Gentlemen
being all Volunteerd to fight, the Ladies could
only assemble to keep up each others Spirits—
The Rebels were now shewing themselves every
where to the great Terror of all honest people
but we had a more domestic cause of alarm—My
sister Sophy was seized with the same fever that
carried off such numbers all over the World the
preceding Year—It was highly infectious and
none of our friends would venture near the
House—The Servant Boy took it and we were in
hourly dread of it spreading through the Family
—however it went no further though Sophy was
totally given over I hardly ever saw anyone
worse—She lay some weeks at the Jaws of Death
and her sufferings from a pain in her Bones were

dreadful—My Aunt Blunden fled at its first
appearance and we were a long time shut up on
Quarantine—However both patients recover'd.
About this time a terrible Fracas happen'd between this family and the Carrick Yeomanry—
Matty heard that a meeting of the Rebels had
taken place near Bonmahon—She heedlessly
mention'd the fact and that some of the Yeomen
were amongst them—for which the Yeomanry
deputed some of their Corps to bring her to an
Account for spreading such a Report and they
decreed if she was found guilty she was to be
posted at the Drum head—Matty met them on
the Occasion and pleaded guilty of having mention'd the Affair—A terrible paragraph appear'd
against her in the next Newspaper—which paragraph she answerd through the same Channel
with such a superiority of Wit and reasoning—
They deputed their Captain Mr Jephson to
write to her in very unneighbourly Terms which
he very foolishly complied with and a terrible
Paper War ensued—on which a Boxing bout
took place on a Sunday in the open street between my Brother Tom and Mr W.S.—The
horsewhip being used a Duel was the proposed
Consequence—The Blundens and Mr Matthews
were sent for and three Brace of the best pistols
procured—God only knows what we suffer'd for
four Days whilst the Magistrates and a Gentlemans Jury assembled in the Parlour to strike out
methods to prevent so horrible an Affair.
Gentlemen who never before visitted here came

to offer their Services amongst whom was Mr
J. Congreve a relation of Mr Jephson but quite
inimical to his proceedings in this Affair—The
Upshot was that Mr W. Smyth was condemnd
by all the gentlemen round the Country to make
a publick appology to Tom in the open Street
and to offer him a Horsewhip for Retaliation or
to do as he pleased—Mr Smyth being laid up
with a black Eye he received from Tom, a Depu-
tation waited on him but only met with Abuse
and Insult—Mr Smyths nephew challenged Mr
Matthews—Mr F. Smyth his brother challenged
Otway—and Mr W. Ryan challenged Nick so
that we had now four Duels on hands instead of
one—However the Country Party prevail'd and
our Gentlemens four Antagonists were forced
by the public to make a public Appology—Thus
ended this horrid Affair which brought us
females almost to Deaths Door during the four
Days the Gentlemen were in the House for none
of them would leave it till the Affair came to an
Issue—Indeed nothing could be more shocking
than our Situation—Listening at every Door and
fainting at Every Rap—But our three Darlings
got off safe with universal Applause—The Yeomanry in a Body begg'd Matty's pardon and Mr
Congreve effected a reconciliation between Mr
Jephson and our Family.

CHAPTER 93D

For long the furious God of War
Has crush'd us with his Iron Car

Mr Jephson soon after this went to England
and was laid up for fifteen months on the broad
of his back in the Gout and given over by all
his Physicians—This made the Reconciliation
more moving for though a very Young Man
he was all muffled in Flannels and could not
stir a limb—Sometime before this Counsellor
Lee a gentleman of large property, admired and
proposed for the beautiful Fanny Jephson—
The affair soon got abroad and we got a hint
that he was accepted.

The Rebellion now began to assume a most
allarming Appearance—Not a night pass'd without Nocturnal Meetings and Depradations and
the public places were full of their threats and
proclamations—In many places Open War was
declared, in many more began—all Ranks and
Ages were enrolled on one Side or the Other—

" *Rage, blood, and Flames, and shrieks of Murder*
round us."

We had now a new Old Neighbour here Mrs
Wall of Coolnamuck—After living all the time
of her childrens Education in England she came
over to settle at Coolnamuck just at the commencement of the Rebellion—And a greater
Coward never faced the Rebels—Her very

great Terrors made her at first lead a wandering Life between England and Ireland—She
had some little meddling about the Yeomanry
Business, and not behaving as staunch as might
be expected from a Relation, friend, and Neighbour, a coolness took place between her and
this family—However she strove to exculpate
herself, and every allowance was to be made
for a Woman's and a Stranger's Fears—To
make Amends for her own fault, she sent her
two young men to support us when our Boys
were challenged—William and Daniel Wall were
very fine Young Men—and Miss Wall a fine
Girl very good but not handsome—They were
all highly polish'd by [?] and Education and
the Incessant pains of their Mother and Grandfather Mr Dan Cuffe both quite capable of the
Task—Mrs Wall was a Grass Widow as her
Husband had been for many Years out of his
Reason and was kept in England under proper
Guardians—When they first came over they
came to us Coolnamuck not being ready for
their Reception, and a great friendship took
place amongst the Young People as formerly
amongst their Parents—My sister Matty recommended her friend Eliza Butlar to William
Wall as a Wife—He paid a visit to Lowesgreen
—admired the young Lady—And she soon
after became Mrs Wall—Matty of course was
Bridesmaid and from thenceforward was everything at Lowesgreen and Coolnamuck—We
at that time lost very amiable Neighbours in

Mr Mansfield's family who rented Coolnamuck
—Mrs Mansfield formerly Miss Woolfe died
a young woman—Mr Mansfield some time
after quitted the neighbourhood that had been
so fatal to him—Besides the Walls we had
another family of English Neighbours in that
direction Mr and Mrs Disney—They were
very genteel people of good families—She was
Daughter to an English Admiral—She being
an English Woman they soon grew tired of
Ireland and went back again not without having
undergone various Terrors from the Rebel
Teagues.

But the Neighbour who was fated to be most
interesting to us was Captain Russel, just returned from the East Indies—He was a friend
of the old Widow English and now occupied
her house in Carrick—At a future period I
shall give an account of my brother Otways
attachment to his only Daughter and his consequent Marriage with sweet Nanno Russel—
but at this time she was in a Convent at Cork—
and Otway pursuing a boyish attachment with
Miss H. a beautiful Carrick girl but not in our
line of domestic Connextion—My brother Tom
was now obliged to go back to his Studies in the
Temple—We parted him with heavy hearts
and were the more uneasy after he went as his
fellow Mr Hemphill died in the general Fever
in the same appartments Tom occupied.

I shall now take leave of my Carrick Friends
for a time to relate what happend in a Second

Years Trip to Knockgrafton—But before we left Carrick an Event happen'd that gave us all the deepest Concern—This was the Death of my Mothers youngest brother Major William Cuffe of the 18th Dragoons who died of the Fever at Athlone universally and most deservedly lamented—He was indeed a charming pleasant man—My Mother was in the deepest Woe for his loss—and her friends hoped the Change of Scene, and Knockgrafton Air would restore her—Indeed the variety of Alarms, disasters, and frettings we had latterly undergone between the Fever, the Rebels, the Yeomanry business and this last sad Event renderd us all Invalids, worn down with fatigue and constant fretting, and the plague of the Heart in addition rendered *me* not the least miserable Object amongst them.

CHAPTER 94TH

Where are the Joys by flattering hope supplied
Dear distant Dreams of yet unknown Delight

We set out for Parsonage and "Hope ever springing in the human Breast" made the Journey salubrious—The Sight of the Rock of Cashel made my heart bound with Transport as its Abbey towerd in the Horizon over the interesting Plain so dear to my Soul—On our arrival once more at Parsonage I ran about every Place with Joy unutterable and haild my old Chest of Drawers as if I had met an old and

valued Friend—Love endears the commonest
Scenes and creates an Eden round.

We always slipp'd on our Bedgowns the moment
we got there and three Days were occupied in
arranging ourselves and the Parsonage—It
was a charming light airy House with a bound-
less Expanse of open fields behind it, always
freshend with sweetest Zephyrs and harmonized
by the Song of the Lark—Everything about it
produced in me the Vernal Delight which Mr
Addison in the Spectator so beautifully describes and attributes to the Influence of the
new born Spring—Mrs Hare the Clerk's wife
drank Tea with us and told us all the News of
the Place—Doctor and Mrs Hemphil came to
Rockwell on the Death of their Son and the
Roes saw no Company on their Account—
John Roe was mostly at Sir William Parsons—
and Andrew so busy building a new House on a
new Farm that no one ever saw him—The rest
of the Neighbourhood were in Statu quo.

We sent a Complimentary Message to Mr and
Miss Roe and they sent us Word they would
see us next morning—They came accordingly—
Miss Roe was dress'd out to the Life, but Mr
Roe was the same as ever, friendly, and Affectionate—My Nerves were so shatter'd with
Illness and continual fretting, that I trembled
all over when summon'd to the Parlour—They
met me with great Warmth but scarce was I
seated, when Mr Roe in a very pitying Tone
asked what had made such a terrible Change

in his little Doro? for he never saw any one
grow so thin and pale in so short a time, but
said he, my Doro must throw off her Mourning
for it makes her look ill—Miss Roe answer'd
I thought rather tartly that in her opinion I was
as fat and as well as Ever—My Mother I
thought seem'd provoked at her unfeeling
Drawl and told them I had been very ill—Mr
Roe expressd great Concern, but Miss Roe's
stiffness was very perceivable—She was dress'd
unusually fine with white crossings before
picqued down in the extremity of the fashion
and pinned with exact nicety—They expressd
their sorrow that they could not see us at Rockwell while Doctor and Mrs Hemphill were in
such grief for their son, and after some more
Commonplace Chat took leave.

Our other Neighbours soon visitted us and made
the same observation about my terrible Looks
that Mr Roe had done—Mrs Dexter was for
sending me off to Bath, but I preferr'd drinking
Goats Whey at Knockgrafton which was luckily
to be had just opposite, where an old blind piper
kept two pet Milch Goats.

Mrs Dogherty was in such trouble about her
eldest Daughter who married and died in Childbed, that she could not visit us, this was the
Young Lady who attack'd me at the last Races.

CHAPTER 95TH

Alas in vain I try within
To brighten the dejected Scene

Sunday morning I dress'd myself for Church as usual and expected to see the Roes there, but when I contemplated in the glass my own sunken appearance and my Eyes hollow'd by continual weeping, I despair'd of pleasing the Object of my Heart and foresaw that unless Pity sway'd him Nothing Else would fix him my Constant Swain—In vain my aching Eyes watch'd for him, none of the Roes appeard at Church—but Mrs Carew came with a large company from Woodenstown and blazed forth like a Star of the first Magnitude attended by two Satelites the Miss Atkinsons—These three Ladies with very Smart Persons added all the advantages of knowing how to set them off by the strictest attention to dress and fashion, and I was heartily glad that my long Veil hid me from Observation as I really did nothing but weep during Church time—I could not help drawing Comparisons between that and the former Year when my beating heart flew to meet its Conqueror with Joy and Delight— Divested of the Melancholy that now destroyd me I then flutterd away with the gayest, and had every Sunday the pleasure of meeting the Object of my Affections, seemingly as devoted to me, as I was in reality to him—Weeks

278

passd away in this manner, without my seeing
him.

Meanwhile the Visitation came on, and of
course we spent that Day with Mrs Hare and
Mrs Clarke——I was not at all in Conceit with
myself and every one I met seem'd bent on
making me worse by Observations on my ill
looks a grievous Theme when so near the
Object I most wished to please——My Mourning
had also this disadvantage that it made me look
less than Ever——Mr Hare who delighted in
large persons was continually thwarting me
about my size and thinness, and always drew up
his six fair Daughters in a Row to illustrate his
Constant Position that fat people were better
than lean, tall people superior to low——however
John Roe was not yet in the Country to witness
my daily Mortifications——He was still at Sir
William Parsons, but great was my terror when
I heard that there was a Match on the Tapis
between him and Sir William Parsons Niece
who lived at her Uncles.

I moped about the Glebe like a Ghost, and grew
quite Stupid with Grief——I went no where, and
would see no One——One Day that I had walked
and pined myself sick, I was descending the
Area Steps without minding——when my foot
slippd, and I tumbled headlong into the passage
down the whole flight of Steps——My Leg
turnd quite under me, and I could only groan
out my Despair——my Thoughts in descending
were occupied on my miserable Prospects, and

the dreadful Agony I was in from the fall,
joined to the wretched state of my Mind, quite
overpower'd me, and I was taken in fainting
and senseless—My leg was dreadfully sprain'd
and I was miserably bruised—Mrs Wharton
dressd my Wounds but I was laid up for
a long time undergoing all the Misery that
Pain, impatience, and a Wounded Spirit could
inflict.

Mr Roe came once or twice to see me, and
Miss Roe sent a bag of flax seed for my Leg,
but this was all we heard of the family who had
quite Cloister'd themselves with the Hemphills
—Mrs Clarke now came out with her two little
Boys to spend the Vacation with us—I sunk
more and more every Day though she exerted
all her charming Spirits to amuse me—I grew
quite heavy and was continually on the bed
sometimes Absolutely Raving—She always sat
by me Crying—One Day I caught myself
raving about John Roe and was frantic to find
her at my Bedside—I used every Art to draw
from her what I had said, but though she wept
plentifully she would never tell me what droppd
from me—She was not well herself having a
sore Jaw that gave her continual uneasiness—
I used to dress it, and every morning, when she
shewed me her Jaw after rubbing it with Blue-
stone I had a trick of saying it looked beautiful
that Day, which always made her laugh heartily
under her Misfortunes—This dear friend and
I mutually comforted each other and I believe

her coming out to Parsonage that time saved
my Life.
We sent every Day for some time to know if our
Rockwell friends wished for our Company, but
the answer was always a put off on account of
the Hemphills being there—We therefore desisted from further Intrusion though Mrs
Clarke was quite mad at the Airs they put
on.

CHAPTER 96TH

*Friendship that every veering Gale could move
And tantalizing Hope, and faithless Love*

Mrs Clarke now returnd to Cashel on the
Vacations ending and the second sister, Ellen
Hare came out to Parsonage—She was a wild
young Girl mad with spirits and cared not what
she did—She swore she would storm Rockwell
for us and force the Roes from their Retirement
—One Morning she pulld and drag'd me till
she made me dress to go there and bully them
from their Churlish Solitude—We found Miss
Roe sitting with Mrs Hemphill, and as busy as
possible making up laced Aprons and other
finery so superb that we were quite at a loss to
know where she meant to display them but
could never find out—Mr Roe was not at home,
but to our great astonishment the Door opend
and in walked John Roe—I thought he was
pursuing his Courtship at Sir William Parsons,

and his sudden appearance threw me into dreadful Confusion—Ellen Hare perceiving it asked
for some Broth for me saying I had been very
ill—John Roe at first looked somewhat disconcerted and sat gravely silent with his Eyes
fix'd on the fire and his hands enployd in
fiddling with his Watch Chain his usual trick
when he had a mind to play off his distant Airs
—however he soon got into better temper, and
was again the gay and fascinating John Roe—
He walked with us a good part of the way home,
though Miss Roe ran after him and pulld him
by the Coat to keep him—When he quitted us
on the Road Ellen Hare was in Raptures at our
Victory over Miss Roe and God bless you
Dolly said the goodnatured Girl—for I never
saw [you] look so well as you did all the time
you were conversing with John Roe for you got
the most beautiful blush in your cheek and your
black dress made you look as fair as a lilly—I
thought she was bantering me but on turning
about saw the tears running down her Cheek
and she pulld out her pocket glass to shew that
she had not been flattering me—In fact my
Walk and Commotion had given me a most
dazzling Contrast of Bloom.
Ellen Hare was in a Roar of Laughter all Day
at our triumph over Miss Roe, who was every
where blamed for smuggling her brothers—We
were now forced to go to Carrick on some
urgent Business—John Hare and Ellen went
with us, and Mrs Hare and Mrs Clarke were

to come for them to Carrick——We found all the Carrickonians well except my Aunt Eyre who was a constant Invalid——The Jephsons were wholly engaged about Mrs Lee's Match——I could now compleatly turn the Tables on Fanny Jephson who was so rallied and plagued on her approaching Nuptials that she grew as Cross as the Mischief——We did all we could to make the place pleasant to John and Ellen Hare, but they were so accustomed to a Cashel Society that they grew tired of Rural Seclusion and soon summond their Mother to come for them—— Mrs Hare and Mrs Clarke spent some time here driving about and viewing the different places round us——They then all took leave and went back to Cashel.

CHAPTER 97TH

" ——But from my Soul to banish
" While weeping Memory there retains her Seat
" Thoughts which the purest Bosom might have
   cherish'd
" Once my Delight now even in Anguish Charm-
   ing——

We returned to Knockgrafton the 9th of July for the Races of Cashel——They were far from equal to the former being very thin and dull—— We met the Roes at the Race Course every Morning but they seldom came to our Carriage and when they did they appeard cold and formal,

nor did they this Year appear at the Assemblies
—We went to One which was as stupid as possible very few being at it and those that were not
of the first Class—I was not asked to dance so
sat down all Night pining over the Melancholy
Comparisons I drew between that Years Races
and the former—The Girls all came to us from
Carrick, and with them a Mr Bushe of the Co
Kilkenny an Admirer of my sister Sophys who
proposed for her in our absence from Carrick
on a short acquaintance and they now came to
dash away at Races and lay the Matter before
my Father—However they could not agree in
terms so the Match went off and saved us all
from dancing in our Vamps she being the
youngest of us—She look'd beautiful after her
Recovery from the fever and I thought her by
far the prettiest Girl that Year at the Cashel
Assemblies—We went with the Hares and
Clarkes to one play to see the Miss Ryders and
had all the Roscommon Militia Beaus in our
Party—The Roes were expected to join us but
did not come, perhaps luckily for them for there
was a most alarming fracas amongst all the
Gentlemen there—When I found they were
not to be there, I sat very quietly the rest of the
night between Mr and Mrs Clarke who did all
they could to amuse me—Amongst other incidents that Night there was a general Clapping
for the Miss Herberts—which surprized me
in a town where we were almost Strangers—
some parties in the lower Rows opposed but

were forced to join by the Clamour of the
Multitude.

August the fourth we went to Carrick to pay a
Bridal visit to the lovely Mrs Lee once Fanny
Jephson——Otway who had just been ordaind
married the Happy Couple but was so agitated
at parting his old wild Playmate and Companion
that he could not go through the Ceremony
which was one of the first he performed after
he got into Orders——The Jephsons on their
parts were deeply affected and this parting of
Young friends made the Wedding very gloomy
——We arrived the Day after——and after the
usual Visits and Dinners we returned to Knockgrafton to compleat our three Months Residence.

CHAPTER 98TH

———But in my Breast
Some busy thought some Secret eating Pang
Still restless throbs

The Yeomanry business was still the common
topic of Cashel——The Newspapers and Letters
were handed about and excited much Curiosity
but all opinions favourd our family.

About this time the Hemphills left Rockwell——
The young Men were both return'd to it and
Miss Roe had no longer an Excuse for not
giving us a Dinner——At long last an Invitation
came but she resolved it should be as general

a One as possible, and asked the Carews and
L'Estranges with their long Suites and every
other acquaintance they could pick up.

We went and spent the Interval before Dinner
in staring at each other—And after Dinner
the Misses being very stiff and formal we did
nothing but yawn at each other—Miss Roe
gave the youngest Miss Atkinson my old important Post of filling out the Coffee and second
Teapot—However my Successor did not enjoy
the perquisites, for John Roe when he came up
transferrd his flirtation from the Tea table to
the Circle where I sat—This struck me as
particular, as I never knew him to leave the
Tea table all the time I presided there—We
had a good deal of laughing and chatting together though somewhat seperated—he seem'd
as gay and complaisant to me as the vast Ceremony of the Coterie permitted, but still this
was not the Year 89—or like it.

Immediately after this Dinner he and his
Brother went to Lucan and we heard little more
of them or Rockwell though Mr Roe often
came to see my father and was as affectionate
to us all as ever though his Spirits seemd much
broken since last Year—At length the Day was
fix'd for our final Departure from Parsonage
for that year—which was the more annoying
to me as the Roes were just Return'd from
Lucan—The night before we set out Nick
came from Rockwell and told us Mr Roe insisted on our spending that Evening with him—

We were quite surprized as we heard nothing
of them for a long time and we knew Mr Hill
was still laid up in the Gout there which was
the Reason alledged for their not having us more
frequently—My Mother hesitated about going
as our Cloaths were packed up but my Father
and Nick teazed her till she consented to go as
John and Andrew were come home for the
Winter—I like a fool unpacked my Cloaths—
The hurry of unpacking and dressing gave me
a beautiful Bloom and as I spared no toilette
pains I looked that Night remarkably well in
Blacks which as Ellen Hare said set off the
Lilly and Rose of my complection.
As ill luck would have it it poured as if Heaven
and Earth were coming together—It was pitch
Dark when we rapp'd at Rockwell Hall Door
and torrents pouring round us—but in vain we
rapp'd and rappd again—No one answered and
the House seemd quite dark and deserted—At
length a drowsy Servant came half asleep and
told us his Master was not at home—God bless
me said my Mother Not at home! Well wheres
Miss Roe? She's gone to Bed said the Servant—
And the young Gentlemen said My Mother—
They're all gone Out was the answer—At that
moment Mr Roe roar'd from the parlour No
Sirrah we're all here—John and he now made
their Appearance with a light and handed us
from the Carriage—They shew'd us into the
Parlour which was all in a Litter—The punch
spilt about the Table—the Glasses all in dis-

order and Mr Hill and Andrew nodding in
their Chairs quite tipsy—Never shall I forget
Mr Hills appearance—As he was a Patient of
Miss Roe's, he was swathled from Head to foot
in flannels with a huge knit Night Cap on his
head—his Gouty leg as thick as his Body with
flannel Bandages rested on a Stool coverd with
flannel and he lolled in a Huge Arm Chair lined
with flannel—Our entrance startled him from
his Evening Nap and the poor Man made an
Effort to escape but hurting his Gouty Leg he
sunk again in his Chair roaring and bellowing
like a Bull, whilst Andrew at the other side was
venting a thousand Curses on John for awaking
him—Mr Roe himself though much confused
could not help laughing at the Scene, as for the
rest of us we were almost in fits—Mr Roe now
rang to have Miss Roe call'd out of Bed and
Tea brought in saying if he had expected us he
would have been better prepared for us and he
and John goodhumourdly begg'd we'd sit down
and take pot luck at the Bottle—God bless me
said my Mother here is some Mistake—Pray
Mr Roe Did you commission my son Nick to
ask us to tea this Evening?—Oh the little
Rogue! (said Mr Roe)—To tell you the truth
Mrs Herbert I did not but now you are come,
I'm heartily glad to see you, and much obliged
to my friend Nick—John and Andrew crow'd
again at the Joke and even Mr Hill forgot his
Gout whilst his pursy Sides shook with laughter
—Tea and Miss Roe now appeard—John

placed me on a high Mahogany Bench and
coverd my black cloaths whilst the Room was
dusting out and there we sat together for the
rest of the Evening laughing at our nights
Adventures—He would not let me join the
Tea Table party but brought me my Tea himself and on our exalted post we sat and conversed tete a tete the rest of the Evening—he
gave me an Account of his Summers Tour—
Absence had not diminishd the Expression of
his Charming Eyes, at least I fancied him in
unison with every fond feeling of my Heart—
however a few hours seperated us once more
and left me to pine for the slow revolving Year
—Thus ended our second Season at Knockgrafton.

CHAPTER 99TH

But Me not destined such delights to Share
My prime of Life in wandring spent and Care

The next Morning we set off for Carrick where
we were to settle for the Winter—Soon after
our Return my Aunt Eyre and Ned Went to
England—the former for her health, the latter
to avoid his usurious Creditors—Mrs White
and her three Daughters joined them at Pill for
the Excursion, and my Sister Fanny was to be
one of the Party under the protection of my
Aunt who liked her Nursetending better than
her own Daughters or Grandaughters—Fanny

was glad of the Jaunt and more so as Sim
Whites Mother and Sisters were to accompany
them—The Girls were very fond of her but
Mrs White treated her badly and there was no
Prospect of her consenting to her becoming her
Daughter in Law.

We were all in the deepest Woe after them and
felt a Presentiment that we should never meet
again unbroken—Our greatest Comfort was
that Fanny would be a most Acceptable Companion to our dear Tom in London, especially
as he had lost his friend and fellow Templar
Mr Hemphill—We pass'd the rest of the
Winter very gloomily and miss'd them more
than can be conceived though we constantly
received Letters from them.

This Memorable Year the French Constitution
was overthrown under the Democratic Tyranny
of Marat and Robertspierre two Villainous Up-
starts—Louis the sixteenth and most of the
French Royal family were Murderd after a long
and shocking Imprisonment—The greater part
of the French Nobility were masacred and
France was deluged in the blood of its own
Children.

After the Murder of the Royal Bourbon Race
War broke out all over Europe and England
after long Parliamentary Debates agreed to
avenge the Murder'd Monarch—My Design
does not Extend to a Delieration of Publick
Disasters but History will show that these were
times of almost unprecedented Horror and

Misfortune—War, Famine, Pestilence, and intestine Rebellion ravaged all Europe.

CHAPTER 100TH

Take then this treacherous Sense of Mine
That dooms me still to Smart

In the Summer of 1791 we went again to Knockgrafton, to fulfill the Arch Bishops Injunctions of an Annual Residence, and to reap the Benefit of its fine Air, but we pass'd a most melancholy Summer of it—The fearful State of the Country and of the Whole World, made everyone gloomy, and despondent.

John Roe was most dangerously ill all the time we staid with such dreadful Complaints in his Head that his Life was despair'd of—nothing could be more dismal than my Mind during this period of doubt—None gave satisfactory answers to my Enquiries—How I envied Miss Roe her privilege of Nursetending him! I watched the Road incessantly to pick up Intelligence of him, and often after twilight, stole as far as the Wall of dear Rockwell to take a peep at the Mansion that held him—He had been always subject to those Head Achs, but caught his present Illness by attending too closely to the Improvements of the Lake—Indeed, though I watchd his Walls, I was little better myself, from constant fretting and sorrow of Heart—Certain that I should never behold him more, my only Consolation was to treasure up every little Circumstance that reminded me of him " *Ah fled for Ever as they Ne'er had been!*".

We now got a dreadful Shock from some English Letters informing us that Fanny had fallen ill of the Fever in London, and had been for many Weeks at the Point of Death—She had three physicians attending her, was Cupp'd, blister'd, bled, and sufferd a variety of tormenting Remedies—Poor Tom's situation may more easily be imagined than described— He never stirr'd from under her Pillow where he sat night and day, breaking his heart about his poor Sister—Two more pitiable objects can hardly be conceived—As her little Cash was soon Exhausted, the dear fellow spent every farthing he had in paying off her Physicians, which reduced them to absolute Want—When Fanny was somewhat recover'd, the whole party took Shipping for Ireland, but Ned and my Aunt took a Whim to visit France before they returnd, and Bag, and Baggage they changed their Route for Dover—Tom would not let Fanny go without him, so both set out on their Travels almost pennyless—Several times they were near being torn to pieces in Paris, in the dreadful Butcheries of the Revolution, though the worst of it was over before they went—After many Adventures there, Tom was obliged to return to England to pursue his Studies, and would not leave Fanny behind

him—My Aunt Eyre and Ned went off to
Brussels—were there when the French enter'd
it, and after being pillaged, and forced to fly
from place to place, they at length return'd and
settled at Brussells where they experienced
numberless Viscissitudes of Fortune—This was
the State of half the Party that left us—Mrs
White and her Daughters went no farther than
England, and soon returnd to Ireland—I shall
now take leave of the Wanderers for a while to
relate more domestic Occurrences in their
proper periods—We wept incessantly over our
poor Wanderers melancholy Epistles but as
several Letters came at once the same post
abated our Fears.

CHAPTER 101ST

" *And there to listen to the gentle Voice*
" *The sigh of Peace, something, I know not what*
" *That whispers Transport to my Heart*—

We had no races in Cashel that Year on account
of the Rebellion and spent our time I know not
how but certainly not very gaily—Mrs Clarke
came out to us towards the last Month of our
Stay and her Arrival somewhat enlivend us—
One Evening when the Hares were all with us
she seized the opportunity of her Mothers
Jaunting Car to pay a Visit to Rockwell—and
insisted on my accompanying her—We set out
together and such a dreadful Vehicle I believe

never before was invented—We were pounded
to Mummy—We met Andrew Roe on the
Road, and Mrs Clarke out of fun made him
get in along with us—We had him roaring all
the Way and gave him a Compleat Bumping before we set him down at Rockwell as he sat on
the opposite side and had no second Person
to tighten him in.

We found Miss Roe alone, (Mr Roe being from
home—She was quite alert and good humour'd
as usual when she did the Honours of the House
alone—She, Mrs Clarke, Andrew, and I sat
down to Tea—Andrew was all Politeness and
Miss Roe all agreeableness—When we had
almost done Tea, the Door open'd and in came
John Roe, but so alter'd that one would hardly
know him—He had cut off his Hair and wore a
Wig—His face was pale and emaciated and his
whole person worn to a Skeleton—He appear'd
quite languid and dejected and on entering the
Room totter'd to his seat where he sat some
Minutes panting with Weakness before he could
speak—His Eyes alone kept their wonted Expression and fire—He wore a loose Surtout and
a Hair Cap to hide his Wig—Miss Roe utterd
a scream when he enter'd as this was his first
Appearance down stairs—She appear'd greatly
vexd and received him cooly saying she did not
expect to see him down that Evening—She
however calld for the Water and made fresh Tea
of which we partook to keep him in Countenance—Mrs Clarke and I exerted ourselves to

put him in Spirits and he laughd incessantly at
our Anecdotes and Bon Mots—Andrew however seeing his Brother unable to silence him
annoyd us perpetually with his Noisy Rattle—
And sat down by me whilst he hung over me
with cordial Looks enamour'd and seemed resolved to make me flirt with him whether I
would or no—In vain I complaind that he tore
my fine trimming off my Gown and that I was
afraid he would bite off my Ear, he persisted in
haranguing me in a Close Whisper whilst his
Shoes were Entangled in my Glazed Lawn train
—however I had the Satisfaction to see that I
both pleased and amused John by my Efforts to
shake off and silence my assiduous Beau—He
seemd to thank me with his Eyes but sank in
his Chair quite powerless against Andrews bois-
terous Vocifferousness and complaining bitterly
of his head—Miss Roe was now all spirits and
good humour whilst John seemd Grave vexed
and Spiritless at being debarr'd from Retaliation
by Sickness—My Brusqueries however provoked Andrew so much that he left the Room
and John soon reviving we pass'd the rest of the
Evening as agreeably as possible—We were
however forced to break up the Party as Mrs
Hare was to return to Cashel and would be Mad
at our keeping her Jaunting Car—John Roe insisted on seeing us to the Door which caused a
Strong Altercation between him and Miss Roe
who caught hold of his Coat saying he must not
go to the Door for fear of Cold, but finding him

obstinate she button'd him up in his Surtout
and he handed us out.

Andrew just then came to us from the Stable—
Well Andrew said Mrs Clarke, Will you see us
home?—Andrew affectedly said there were two
Words to that Bargain, but if Miss Herbert and
she would give us as many kisses as he pleased
and let him sit between us he would escort us
though he hated a Jaunting Car—We really had
occasion for his protection but rejected the terms
—After much huxtering we compromised to let
him sit between us—Andrew now to make himself of Consequence, calld for his great Coat and
other Muffling but whilst he was buttoning himself up and tying handkerchiefs about his Neck
et cœtera, John seeing us reduced to so many
degrading Terms of Capitulation, suddenly
threw off his Surtout and Sick Cap, put on a
smart Beaver Hat and vaulted in his own charming Manner into the Seat between us prepared
for Andrew.

Andrew roar'd, Miss Roe ran out scolding, we
implored John not to venture out in the Night
Air, but he calld to the driver and bid him drive
off with full Speed—The Boy followd his Direc-
tions and gallopd up the Avenue—The Gate
however stop'd our progress and Andrew came
up puffing and blowing with John's Surtout, a
half a Dozen of Miss Roe's Handkerchiefs—
John kicked him away but told him if he chose
he might sit on the other Side of the Jaunting
Car—Andrew said he would walk by our side

but John swore he should not stay there to listen and bid him either mount or go home—Andrew quite crestfallen mounted the opposite side of the Jaunting Car and well bumpd and mortified sat fretting and fuming in Solitary Sadness.

John now quite forgot his late Indisposition and became as lively and animated as ever I had seen him—Mrs Clarke and he rattled away with Anecdotes that kept them in continual Laughter —The Noise of the Car and my Deafness prevented my hearing them to my great Disconsolation, though John Roe by a sly look peculiar to him invited me to join in their Merriment— He tucked up the lilac streamers of my black gipsy Hat which flutterd in the Gale between him and me and prevented him from seeing me and me from hearing him whilst Mrs Clarke grew out of all patience at my not joining in their Mirth—But all was vain! My Anxiety to hear and speak only made me more deaf and dumb—When we got to the parsonage Mrs Hare gave us a dreadful scolding for keeping her Jaunting Car—We now all sat in a Circle and the Conversation becoming general John Roes spirits flagged and he relapsed into a languid pensiveness—Mrs Clarke and I were peppering about our Invalid and got my Mother to offer him proper Refreshments—The Hares and Mrs Clarke then set off for Cashel but just as they got out of the Gate the Horse plunged, their Legs got entangled in the Gate and had not Andrew Roe leap'd the Hedge and stopp'd the

Horse they would have been torn to Atoms—
They were now led out of the Gate, but the
Horse again took head, ran away, and spilt them
all on the Road overturning the Jaunting Car
and kicking poor Andrew into the next Ditch
—We ran out screaming thinking they were
all killd but providentially they escaped with
a dreadful fright and some slight Bruises—
We soon after left Knockgrafton and finished
our third Years Residence.

<hr>

END OF BOOK THE FIFTH

CHAPTER 102D

" *In confused March forlorn th' adventrous Bands*
" *With shudd'ring Horror Pale, and Eyes Aghast*
" *View'd first their lamentable Lot—*

We remain'd for some time at home in Carrick,
till Otway returning from bathing at Bonmahon,
gave us a most romantic account of his Cottage
there, and proposed that we should all go there
—In enumerating the Company he said John
Roe and Mrs Elliot had taken Lodgings there
and were daily expected—We had never been
to any Sea bathing place and the Girls were all
mad to go and Otways Intelligence made me not
the least anxious amongst [them]—The Road
being then impassible for Carriages we set out
on Common Cars with our Beds and Luggage.
Bonmahon was a small village fourteen Miles
from Carrick in the County Waterford—We
travell'd all Day through tremendous Wilds
over Bogs and Precipices—But we were struck
dumb when we arrived, for instead of elegant
Cottages cover'd with Roses and Jessamine as
Otway described, we found only a set of dirty

Cabbins newly White wash'd indeed, but quite
destitute of Elegance—as they served in the
Winter for Cowhouses and Pig Styes—However as we were there we had only to make the
best of our Right and title to one of the dirtiest
Cabbins in the place whilst Otway wisely
loiter'd behind to lounge sumptuously in Carrick
and laugh at the Exchange—The Scenery of
Bonmahon however was so wild and romantic
and the Strand so beautiful that we grew quite
reconciled to suffer a Variety of personal In-
conveniences—The first Night the Rain pourd
dreadfully into our Beds—and our only Remedy
was a Covering of wooden platters as Resevoirs
—but overturning them at Night it encreased
the Inundation tenfold and our Situation was
truly lamentable—The next Morning brought
fresh Disasters—Amongst the Rest as I was
knocking a Nail in the partition of my Bedchamber to hang up my Wardrobe a most
dreadful clatter of Delft ware convinced me
that the Kitchen Dresser parted my Dormitory
from the Common Refectionary—and on going
out I found the family all aghast over a whole
set of broken Crockery which could by no
means be there replaced.

To enumerate all the Ludicrous Circumstances
of that whimsical place would be impossible
and it would be equally so to tell the number
of our new Acquaintances or to reckon up the
various parties and Entertainments that ensued
—We had many Beaux but the desired one did

not appear and in the end Mrs Elliot and he
wrote to have their Lodgings given up which
caused me the most bitter disappointment—
After staying there till near Winter we purchased a piece of Land half way up the Rock
that overhung the Village—in a beautiful
Scite that commanded the whole vicinage—the
Sea and its rocky Shore and the opposite windings of the River Mahon—We there laid the
foundation of an excellent new House or Cottage
with two Bows—One gabelling towards the
Sea and Strand—The other commanded a full
View of Carrig Castle the Seat of Mr Anthony
whose beautiful Daughter Jane Anthony paid
us a long Visit in Carrick afterwards—The
front of our House commanded the River and
all th' adjacent Country—The Rocky Mountain
rose in its rear and almost blinded up the back
Windows—We had on the first floor a very
large eating parlour Bow windowd and a small
one at the opposite Bow—We had two good
Bedchambers a long Lobby a Kitchen and
Larder—Above stairs were excellent Garrets.
Quite enchanted with our Plan we gave Direc-
tions for building our House and longing for
the next Bathing Season returnd to Carrick.

CHAPTER 103D

" *That awful Gulph no Mortal eer repass'd*
" *To tell what's doing on the Other Side*

All this time Tom and Fanny were in England
—We often heard from them, and also had
constant Letters from my Aunt Eyre and Ned
who still lived at Brussels without any thoughts
of coming Over—But two years after my poor
Aunt worn out with Dangers Fretting and
infirmity died in that strange Place, and Ned
did not outlive her three Years—some say
he was murder'd by his own Servant—Thus
ended my Aunt Eyre and her darling Son
Edward—

" *Lovely in their Lives, and not in death divided*

I cannot describe our Grief at losing them and
the melancholy Circumstance of their dying
banish'd for Debt in a Strange Country added
not a little to our Sorrow—My Aunt was a
most incomparable Woman with all her little
foibles—and her Son was ever our warm and
Steady friend throughout every Scene of his
Variable Life.
This Year we had constant Letters also from
Lady Maxwell and my Aunt Cuffe who with
Lord Maxwell and our Cousin Fanny Herbert
were travelling the Continent and drinking
the German Spa—Fanny Herbert was one of
my Aunt R Herberts three Orphan Daughters
—Two of them lived with Lady Anne Fitzgerald since their Mothers Death—Fanny the
Eldest was a fine Young Woman—Mr Maxwell
Lord Maxwell's Cousin a Man of large pro-
perty met her in Germany took a liking to her

and they married at Bonne on their travels—
but the same Post that brought us tidings of
her Wedding brought also the melancholy
Account of her Husbands death—He died of
Fever a week after their Marriage—She took
the Fever and recover'd but soon after the
party return'd to Ireland she grew deranged
and died—She was but Eighteen when she
married—and not more than twenty when
she departed this Life.

We were now settled at Carrick for the Winter
and were very lonesome as Mrs Jephson was
seldom at home since Mrs Lee's Marriage—
Mrs Hare, Mrs Clarke, and Jane Hare came
for a week but it was to get over a disappointment Jane had lately met from a Gentleman who
was going to be married to her and then went
off therefore it may be supposed they were not
in good Spirits whilst they staid—Miss Anthony
also spent a long time here—She came inclined
to a Consumption, but we sent her home as fat
as a fool—She was a beautiful delicate Girl
then and vere elegant in her Manners—She
therefore left all our Beaux in a dying Condition and Otway amongst the rest—But our
most fix'd Visiter was Major George Herbert
an old whimsical Batchelor Cousin and School-
fellow of my fathers who lived with us for a
twelve month and incessantly plagued us with
his fanciful Complaints, however he was really
paralytic, and meritted Compassion—He was
a hot brained politician and had been an old

Engineer in the East Indies—had we understood half his descriptions they would have
been Amusing.

CHAPTER 104

" *Joy and extatic Wonder held them mute*

One very wet night we were all seated round the
Tea Table when the Door open'd and in walked
Tom and Fanny—As we had no Idea of their
return to Ireland their sudden appearance seemd
a Delusion of the Senses—Surely never was
meeting more Joyful! We embraced, laugh'd,
sobb'd and play'd a hundred antic tricks about
them before we were restored to our Senses—
My poor Father trembled all over and burst into
tears at seeing his two Children safe return'd
after so long an Absence and their providential
Escapes—When we were somewhat composed
we enquired how they came to steal on us in
such a Manner? They told us they had fix'd a
period for surprizing us but their Money fell
short and sooner than wait for fresh Bills on
England they agreed to travel in the cheapest
manner so footed it most of the way from
London except whilst on Shipboard—Sometimes
they were relieved by a charitable set down in an
Idle Carriage and sometimes they mounted a
Waggon—They managed their finances so as to
walk into the paternal Mansion clear of the
World, its Debts, Dues, and Demands though

without a Shoe to their feet——After scolding
them for their hazardous Undertaking we gave
them a Recital of all our Doings here and the
Night passd on in weeping laughing and story
telling.

The whole Country soon rang with the News of
Mr Toms and Miss Fannys arrival and the
whole Country high and low rich and poor
pour'd in to welcome them——Tom had always a
strong tincture of Quixotism and Fanny his
Dulcinea pro tempore gave us a history of his
Benevolent Exploits that would fill a Volume——
Rescued Damsels, and liberated Knights could
testifie to the great outlines of his Character,
Rectitude of Mind, and Goodness of Heart——
Fanny herself was that kind of girl of whom you
might say in the Irish Dialect " The Devil a
better——She had a touch of the Romantic, the
Whimsical, and the Adventurous——But was in
the mean a fine honest hearted girl, a stirring
notable piece and a most facetious agreeable
Companion——What a Treasure must she have
been to Tom and he to her in a strange Land——
He brought her home a fine accomplish'd Damsel A la Mode de Paris and a la Mode de
L'Angleterre.

CHAPTER 105

Now all is Preparation for the Nuptial Celebration

The Summer after their Arrival we had another

305   x

important Event in the Family—This was the
Marriage of my third Sister Lucinda with Mr
Bradshaw an Attorney who lived in Dublin—
His Father was Brother to Mrs Carshore and
being much in favour with Lord Clonmell he
went to reside in Dublin when his patron became
Attorney General—The Bradshaws held many
important posts and when William Bradshaw
proposed for Lucy he had a large official Property, but lost six hundred a Year on the Eve of
his Marriage which help'd to keep him distressd
Ever After—As Lucy's was the first Wedding
in the family it may be supposed that we were
all much agitated about it—Mr Bradshaws
family, ours, and the Jephsons and Captn Russel
were the only Company—She was the third
Sister of us, younger than Fanny or I, older than
Matty or Sophy—She was then very pretty—a
small person—plump Cheeks, a lovely Com-
plextion, and fair skin; pretty soft blue Eyes,
dark brown hair, and a mighty pretty Mouth—
She was altogether a remarkable pretty Bride—
Mr Bradshaw was a very handsome man but
very dark Complextiond with fine Black Eyes—
Mr Smyth the Clergyman married them—We
had some dancing in the Evening, and Fanny
and I danced a Jig in our Vamps—The next
Day we set off for Parsonage that the young
Bride should escape Visits and Entertainments
here—Mr and Mrs Harden-Bradshaw accompanied us as far as Clonmell—Mrs Bradshaw
was sister to Lucy's Husband.

When we arrived at Parsonage the Hares and
Clarkes came to see us and asked us to Dinner—
They were not a little proud to be the first to
give us an Entertainment on the Occasion—Mr
Hare was full of the Brides Beauty and praised
her Cleverness in getting a Husband so soon—
He scolded me greatly for being so much in the
back ground and said I was in imminent Danger
of dying a Maid, indeed I fear'd so myself—
William Bradshaw and we strolld about the
Village and its Environs every Evening—He
singing " How careless with the Village Maids
I stray" for he had a fine Voice and a great taste
for Music, drawing et cætera—He strongly recommended to his Wife and us to copy Fannys
Parisian Air in our Walks saying there was nothing like a french Cut to give Ladies a dashing Air
in Dress and Manners—In such Bagatelles we
passd our time En Badinage all aping the french
Lady and owning her preeminent Graces.
On our Arrival we sent Andrew Roe a Yard of
green Ribbon—for he had just lost an old Flirt
of his the rich and beautiful Miss Lane who
married the same week that Lucy was—Andrew
soon came to wait on us, and being now disengaged he fell desperately in Love with our Parisian Lady who with all the Vivacity of a frenchwoman received his Gallanteries till it ended some
time after in a serio comic though Oblique Proposal from him—Indeed the fuss he kept about
Miss Fanny Herbert in all our Petit Parties was
quite laughable—I was now truly a forsaken

Damsel in a Mortifying Situation between a
young and beautiful Bride and my Lady smoak-
ing hot with fashion and Elegance from Paris—
As Nobody noticed me I quite gave myself up
as a poor broken Spinster—John Roe was not at
home and I mournfully waited the Coup de
grace from him when he returnd.

At this time a new star appear'd in the Irish
fashionable Hemisphere—This was the young
Lady Caher lately Miss Jefferies—The story
of Lord Caher was so remarkable that it made a
Noise every where—His Mother was a poor
Mendicant Woman in the Town of Caher for
many Years and winnowd Corn for her subsistence—When the late Lord Caher died his
Expectants found out that this old Womans
Children were Next Heirs to his Lordship—
they had them kidnapt and Secretly convey'd
to France where they were rear'd in miserable
poverty—Mrs Jefferies Sister to the Chancellor
passing through Caher, heard at the Inn the
History of the old Beggar Woman and her two
Children—She sent for the Woman took Notes
of her Tale which she laid before the Chancellor
Lord FitzGibbon—On further Investigation
the whole was proved a Fact and the Chancellor
procured Warrants for bringing the Children
over—Miss Jefferies was in a Convent in
France—Mrs Jefferies went over for her
Daughter and undertook the Guardianship of
the lost Children—They were found in a miserable Garret all overgrown with Hair—Mrs

Jefferies had them educated and then made up
a Match for her Daughter with the young Lord
Caher—The Chancellor was much enraged at
this Proceeding and threatend to imprison his
Sister and Niece for inveigling the young Heir
but Mrs Jefferies's Cleverness got her over it—
They all came over to Ireland and took the
Dowager Lady Caher from her winnowing Sheet
to enjoy her new Title and live with her Son—
They now settled at Caher and the Butlars of
Lowes Green who were their Relations promised
us an Introduction to the Noble Pair.

But another Affair was then the Subject of
Conversation and was much more interesting
to my Attention—this was a Reconciliation
between Mr and Mrs Roe which was at length
Effected by their mutual friends—And the
whole Country was one Scene of Gaiety and
festivity at this novel Hauling home—We
however quitted Knockgrafton before their
Public Entrée.

The Bradshaws left us on our Return to Carrick
and went to old Mr Bradshaws House in York
Street Dublin—where they were to reside but
some disagreements happening, William Bradshaw and Lucy first went to Lodgings, and then
took a House in Earl Street—It gave us much
concern that they could not agree with his
family as living with them would have saved
them a Vast Expence but there was no help
for [it] and as soon as they were settled Fanny
went to them for the Winter.

309

CHAPTER 106

Immagination fondly Stoops to trace
The Parlour Splendour of that festive Place

We spent a great part of the next Summer at
Bonmahon—for impatient to see our New
Cottage and to shew it to Tom and Fanny we
set out Early in the Spring—and had time to
put the House in perfect Order before any
Company arrived—We were quite enchanted
with our Cottage which was built quite to our
Satisfaction on our own Plan.

But the Year had like to have been very fatal,
for one Day my Father walking the Strand, perceived that Tom had left his Cloaths there
whilst Bathing—My Father amused himself
with gathering Shells till his son returnd—But
a dreadful Storm and Swell of the Sea happening
the Night before poor Tom had been toss'd by
a Violent Tide many Yards beyond the usual
depth—He could no longer command himself,
and roard out to my Father, who thinking he
did it in Sport bade him stay there—Tom was
carried still further and further out, till providentially a turn of the Tide drove him in with
the same Velocity it carried him out—He now
felt something like a Bottom strike his Toe, and
though quite Exhausted made one desperate
Effort to swim and the Buoying Waves helpd
him forward till he got safe to Land—Two
days after Fanny and Matty got into pretty

much the same Situation and were saved the same way by the reflux of the Tide.

The Place now began to fill for at our first going there, there was no family but Mr Blundens with whom we spent most of our time and were most hospitably treated by them——When the Place was full we determined on giving such a Housewarming as was never before known at Bonmahon——We had Miss Bell Blunden and Miss Butlar in the House with us and the Young Blundens were quite at our command—— We set all Hands to work, got our Pastry and Music from Carrick with every Rarity the Season afforded in Meats Fruits or Vegetables ——The two Blundens got us all Manner of fish and wildfowl——Miss Butlar, Miss Blunden and Fanny manufactord the Whips Jellies and Creams and I made a Central Arch of Pasteboard and Wild Heath with various other Ornaments and Devices——Inshort a more flaming affair never was seen on the Banks of the Seine——what then must it have appeard on the Banks of the Mahon——We then asked all our friends from every town within twenty Miles of us and had a most crowded House——I went to Carrick for a week beforehand and as Summer was now in its prime the Sweet Serenity of our rural Abode struck me so much after the Noisy Turbulence of a seafaring Life that my Muse produced my poem calld the Villa which may be seen in my Book of Poems——I went back to Bonmahon——dashed away at our Ball and was

inspired by the Comic Muse to write The Sea
side Ball or Humours of Bonmahon which may
likewise be seen in my Book of Poems (See
1st Vol. of these Works)—I had made several
attempts before and it at length became my
principle Solace and has whiled away many a
long blank melancholy hour of my Life.
But to return to Bonmahons Joyous Scenes—
Our Ball was followd by one from Mrs Hayes
who not being able to outdo us in Elegance
resolved to Eclipse us in the Number of Supper
Dishes—We had Sixty Nine and she had
Seventy—This caused much Comment amongst
the Neighbours—But my famous Arch carried
the Votes and was accounted worth a Shipload
of Common Dainty Dishes—It had for its
Motto two Lines from Goldsmiths Retaliation—

" *Let our Landlord Supply us with Beef and with*
   Fish
" *Let each Guest bring himself and he brings the*
   best Dish

Nothing could equal the Applause we and our
Supper excited.
A general Round of Balls now took place and
we were so Jocund the whole Season that Tears
were on all faces when the place began to clear
—We always spent our Summers pleasantly at
Bonmahon as we could do as we pleased—
There was indeed much fuss in Dress amongst
the Belles there—But the Same Belle might
appear one Hour in Stuff Petticoats, Leather

Brogues, and blue Stockings—And the next Hour glitter in Gold Muslins Spangled Silks, and embroiderd Sattins—Our Parisian Lady's Morning Dress was a green Stuff Petticoat a Crimson Rug Spencer, a Pair of blue Yarn Stockings—and a Pair of strong Irish Brogues —And she was universally allowd to have displayd great taste and to cut a most knowing and appropriate appearance—Here our Romantic geniuses were likewise gratified in living amongst a number of the most beautiful Rocks and Strands that can well be immagined, which was indeed the chief Excellency of the place, for though we gave so flaming a Regale there we were often Days together without a bit of Bread—and many a Time fed on the flesh of an Old Goat in Lieu of Venison—however it was a wholesome Place and a comical Place.

We return'd home as we went on truckles— And after spending some time in Carrick we set off for a fourth Years Pilgrimage at Knockgrafton, quite prepared by our flaming Equipage to meet Lady Caher and the Cashel Races.

CHAPTER 107

Oh Come! Oh teach Me Nature to Subdue
Renounce my Love, my Life, Myself—And you

It was not without a painful degree of Awe, I expected an Introduction to Mrs Roe though I sincerely rejoiced at the Reconciliation that

had taken place and at her restoration to her
family—John's Illness had given them all a
right sense of the impropriety of squandering
away family Happiness in Domestic Quarrels—
I expected with reason that her Return would
blast all my little Hopes there which were now
at a very low Ebb, yet I was disinterested enough
to be pleased at an Event that conferrd happiness
on John Roe and his father.

Mrs Roe was accompanied back to Rockwell
by a Mrs Walsh an old Lady wife to the famous
Davy Welch who lodged in the same House
with her in her Exile—I had always formed a
formidable Idea of those two Ladies both noted
for their Prudence, Virtue, Sense and Sanctitude
—Both parted from their Husbands and Exer-
cising an inflexible Magnanimity more awful
than Encouraging—Mrs Roe soon paid us a
Visit on our Arrival—She had the traces of
being very handsome—Was like John in Person, face and Manners—She had much of his
expressive Sweetness but with a tincture of
Severity in her looks that he had not and that
convinced me I had formed a just Idea of her
Character.

The Races commenced soon after we went and
were very brilliant—Lady Caher and the three
Miss St Legers were the leading Belles—
Before they began Mrs Butler sent Lady Caher
to visit us—We had now a large Acquaintance
and encouraged by our Success at Bonmahon,
we resolved to give a most dashing Entertain-

ment—The whole Regiment of the Roscommon Militia were quarterd in Cashel—their Colonel Sir Edward Crofton was an old friend and Relation of my Mother's—We therefore asked all the officers to Dinner—Besides them we had Lord Cahers family—The Butlars of Lowesgreen, the Roes, Hares, and many others —We got Venison, Grapes and Pine Apples from Curraghmore besides accidental presents from all Quarters and Mrs Butlars Donations alone would have furnishd a Magnificent Feast —Lady Caher rode to our House en Cavaliere —She was dressd in a Scarlet Habit and a Military Cap and Feather—She was a beautiful little Creature, wild with Spirits and very Affable, but she cursed and swore tremendously —In the Metropolis she was chief Leader of Fashion and Ton—Indeed she was worthy of the Distinction for she was an uncommonly elegant little Woman—Mr and Mrs Roe and Andrew came—Miss Roe was an Invalid and staid at home—John Roe was hourly expected —We sat down to Dinner an immense Croud as the Bradshaws and all our family were assembled—We had two very long tables but could hardly cram all our Company round them as the Roscommon Lads alone formed one Score.

I was quite down at the Mouth at John Roes not being there but just as we sat down to Dinner he suddenly enterd in a great Heat having rode Post for our Dinner—They made

Room for him at the first Table but he preferrd Ours—We were not long seated when
the Room grew so intensely hot that Lord
Caher got up to throw open the Windows but
there being no Pullies to them the Sash fell on
his hand and shatterd it to pieces besides making such a dreadful Clatter of broken Glass
that it made the whole Party leap out of their
Skins—Poor Lord Caher was forced to go
home and was laid up for a Month after—
Lady Cahir however behaved like a Heroine
though she was much frighten'd, and the
Butlars perswaded her to stay till Evening.

CHAPTER 108TH

" *Ah Can you bear Contempt?*
" *The Venomd Tongue of those whom Ruin pleases*

We patrolld the Roads in the Evening in the
rural Stile as her Ladyship laid herself out to
be agreeable and acted the Simple Rustic Maid
to Admiration—The Gentlemen about thirty
in Number sat very late at the Bottle but we
had Tea for them when they came out—I
shrunk diminishd amongst so many fine Belles,
wearing the Willow with a broken heart and
faded Person in the presence of the Only Object
I wish'd to please—My Spirits sunk dejected
Nor had I the Art to conceal my Misery—
The Roscommon Lads were drawn up at one
side of the Tea Table under the Command of

Sir Edward Crofton, the rest of the Gentlemen
were posted at the other side under the Tuition
of Richard Butlar-Hamilton Lowe Esqr—I
was conspicuously placed in the Centre to make
Tea for them and Vis a Vis to me sat Lady
Caher Mrs Butlar and Mrs Roe—How I
trembled at Mrs Roes keen Investigation—
This was my first Interview with John Roes
Mother and her looks seemd to research my
Soul—I shrunk abash'd from her Gaze—I no
sooner began to make Tea than I attracted
the Stare of the whole Company, and as Gentlemen are often fonder of spying out Blemishes
than admiring Beauties in our Sex—the Roscommon Lads neglected even the beautiful
Lady Caher to criticize my Dress and Person—
My face was like a Coal of Fire—I did everything awkardly and was so confused that I was
at last forced to resign my Office to one of my
Sisters—I singled out three of the Roscommons
as my principal Foes, Captain Irwin, Mr
Mitchel, and my Mothers old particular friend
and Relation Sir Edward Crofton—The rest
soon followd their Example though none behaved so badly as themselves—I would have
given Millions to be out of the place, and
Millions more for a thicker Handkerchief to
cover my Bosom which was evidently the chief
point of Observation—Mr Butlar though an
old Veteran amongst the Gentlemen and a
most exact and rigid Censor of the Ladies kept
his side of the Table in strict Discipline to the

Rules of politeness—Such of the Roscommons
as feard to offend left their rude Companions
and went round to Mr Butlar's Division—
This Deriliction of their Friends only made
them worse—They Nudged, Whisperd and
tickled each other without ever taking their
odious Eyes from my Bosom, till one of them
(Mr Mitchel) got into Hystericks with Laughter
—I sat " the poor Dumb Image of Despair "—
to be thus singled out for Derision in such a
Company and before John Roe was the most
dreadful thing that could happen me—to get
out of the triple rowd Circle was impossible,
and to stay was insupportable.

I at last took out my Pocket Handkerchief, held
it to my Mouth and let it fall down to hide my
Bosom—whilst my anxious Eyes sought out
John Roe who had left the Tea Table—He was
walking up and down the Room with evident
discomposure and Agony for me whilst he alternately Eyed my Tormentors and me—one time
he paced quick by the Tea Table then stood behind the Screen, then came back in hopes their
illnatured Jest was over, but finding they still
continued it he in visible Confusion Singled out
a Gentleman for Conversation as if to get rid of
his thoughts—My Assailants proved as inde-
fatigable as unmerciful and never desisted from
their cruel Mirth till the Company broke up to
go away—To describe my Sufferings and the
various Revolutions of my Thoughts on this
trying Occasion would be impossible—I felt

sinking to the Earth with Confusion but thought
of no Individual but John Roe—He after walking about in fruitless Expectation of the Scenes
changing left the Company and went home—I
was not released till they all broke up—I then
ran up Stairs—threw myself on the Bed and fell
a Crying—Nay! I roard again with Mental
Agony—Adieu! (thought I) Dear Amiable John
Roe! You cannot—you must not Again take any
Notice of Me, thus publickly Scandalized and
derided!

CHAPTER 109TH

And when we wild resolve to Love no More
Then is the triumph of excessive Love

The Races now began—By force they dragg'd
me from my old Sanctuary the Settle Bed to
figure away in Tears every Day at the Race
Course—John Roe and Andrew came up constantly to our Carriage—Nothing could divest
the former of his natural Politeness—I positively
refused to go to the Assemblies though I had
painted two very pretty trimmings for the Occasion—In the first place I was quite hopeless and
sunk in Spirits—Next I did not like to risque
another Rencontre with the Roscommon Officers,
and lastly I did not wish to lay John Roe under
the painful Alternative of hurting his polite feelings or dancing with One who had lately been
exposed in such an ignominious Manner—for of

319

all Persons I did not wish to trespass too much
on his Good nature—My Friends however
draggd me there in Spite of me.

The first Assembly was a miserably bad One—
It however offered me some Revenge for my
late Disgrace, for Mr Mitchel one of my tormentors a very tall, large young Man, in mount-
ing to the Music Loft threw down the Ladder,
and fell with it many feet from the Ground with
his gigantic figure sprawling at full length—He
lay some time quite stunn'd and Senseless whilst
the terrified Crowd gatherd round him—When
he recoverd he gave them a Sulky Look and
walkd off—seemingly as much mortified by this
public fall, as I was two Nights before by his
rude Mirth—The Roes were expected there but
did not come—I sat all Night as an humble
Wallflower for no one asked me to dance and
as John Roe was not there I did not much care
—Indeed there was not much dancing, and what
there was, was very stupid.

The Girls dragg'd me again to the Second
Assembly—As I had reserved my handsomest
trimming for the last—I equipp'd myself in my
best Robes, but did it very quietly not supposing
the Roes would be there—When we got to Mrs
Hares, Mrs Clarke gave us a great scolding for
staying so late—Said that John and Andrew Roe
had waited there two Hours to Engage us for
the first Sets—and brushing down my dress with
her Gown she very angrily bid me not Stand
there prating but get into the Carriage as the

Roes were mad at being Disappointed—I had
hardly time to comment on this unexpected Good
News, when the Coach stoppd at the Assembly
House—and John Roe appeard at the Door
lovely as possible, and equally Gay and Good
humour'd—After a hasty salute to the Rest he
eagerly stretched out his hand and drew me from
the inner Side of the Carriage—You are not
Engaged I hope said he, and without waiting
for my Answer he wheeld me up Stairs into the
thick of the Dancers—leaving the Coach Party
to bustle after us—We have been waiting for
you these three Hours said he, two at Mr Hares
and one here—I asked if this was the first Set?—
It is my first Set said he with Emphasis—They
have been dancing all Night, but I stood at the
Windows and Door looking out for your Carriage
—You have not danced yet then? (Said I)—Not
a step he replied—Andrew grew impatient, and
joined the Set but I waited for the honour of
Your Hand—In the hurry of entering my Shoe
slippd down behind and I went behind backs
to Mrs Lee (once Fanny Jephson) for Pins to
fasten it—John Roe followd with my fan, which
he tapp'd over my Head as if to secure me from
running away from him—Mrs Lee gave him a
significant look—He laugh'd and returnd it—
She in a scolding manner gave me the Pins and
a Blow on the Shoulders bidding me get back
to my Set—She archly shoved me on John Roes
Arm, and with a gay Air he led me back to Dance
—He was that Night more Charming if possible

than Ever—His Eyes darted the most lively
Expression—his Face was dress'd in Good
humourd Smiles—His Wit and Address uncommonly Animated and Seducing, and if I had
seen him thus with any other Girl I should have
pronounced him her Gallant, bewitching, Captivating Lover—Ah John Roe! Too well did you
know every Passage to my Heart, and too ready
was I to frame Interpretations favourable to my
own Ardent Wishes—His Behaviour the whole
Night kept me in a Delirium of Hope and Happiness—In changing Sets I was involved in a
round of Engagements to dance with the Roscommons and others — Though John Roe
danced with other Partners I engrossd his whole
Attention whenever we met—We suppd there—
John Roe made an Effort to get to our Table,
but the beautiful Mrs Colonel Penefather detain'd him as her Cecisboe at the first Table.
Andrew Roe was all this time making fierce
Love to Fanny which was now become quite a
Serio Comic Medley, for Andrews fits of all kind
were so violent, that his busy bustling Manners
always produced laughter—and Fanny was just
the person to humour the Joke.

CHAPTER 110

Whither? Whither?
Through what Enchanted Wilds have I been
    Wandering?

{ 1793 }

After my various Despondencies, and late mortification—I could hardly believe my Senses that I had once more danced with John Roe and found him more Assiduous, more irresistibly Charming than Ever—He was dressd in a remarkable handsome light mixd Cloth which became him of all things, and he seemd to have bestowd more than common pains that Night on his dress and Appearance—

" *I hear thee, view thee—gaze oer all thy Charms.*"

When I got home I retired to my Bedchamber to meditate deliciously alone on the Events of the Evening—With a Childish folly I amused myself for some time in surveying my pretty Trimming—It was Lilly of the Valley and Roses painted on White Sattin and excited much observation from several People who thought it was a curious Embroidery—I perceived that it often attracted John Roe's Observation though he said Nothing—After this I looked in the Glass, and thought I looked tolerably with the Assistance of a beautiful pink feather I wore in my Head—Considering all I had gone through, and that I was just come from a Blaze of Beautiful Women, on a second peep I thought I looked miraculously well, and went to Bed quite content with John Roe and myself.

After the Races the Dear Inconstant wanderd about with gay indifference, and left me " To

323

think on what was past and sigh alone "—How
often did I invoke Death to rid me mercifully of
a Life which he had renderd insupportable by
Doubt and Passion—but I was doomed to a pro-
longed Existence more cruel far than Death.

Andrew Roe staid at home (whilst John roved
amongst his Acquaintance) to mind his Farm,
make a fortune, and flirt daily and Hourly with
Miss Fanny Herbert—How tantalizing was
this Mockery of Courtship in lieu of the one
that ought to have taken place—How intoler-
ably did it Cauterize my bleeding Sore—After
the Assembly I had this Harangue from my
Lady Sisters—Now Dolly if you would Exert
yourself and keep up your Spirits you would
soon be a New Creature—But my Spirits were
as transient as my Joys and in the End both
faild in toto.

My poems were now carried to Cashel and read
every Morning at Mr Hares to a Levee of
Roscommon Officers and all the Literati of the
Place—Mr Hare was pleased to commend
them and Mrs Agar the Arch Bishops Lady
sent for them—His Grace himself was much
entertain'd with them and some Parts of them
made him laugh heartily—Mrs Walsh got
Andrew Roe to apply to me for a Perusal of
them—I gave them up with a Palpitating
Heart but could never learn what Reception
they met at Rockwell though it may be supposed I was rather curious about it.

Lady Caher now gave us a most flaming Fete

Champêtre at Caher—We dined under Marquees in the Lawn and danced all the Evening —but again I droop'd like a blighted Flower for the Roes were not there and without John Roe the gayest Scene was to me tiresome and disgusting—Lady Caher danced an Irish Jig for us in her Stockings to the Musick of an old blind piper—All was conducted in the Old Irish Stile—Lord Caher and she did every thing to make it agreeable to each individual Guest, and though the throng of fine folks was immense his Lordship did me the Honour to dance with me—We had a superb Supper in the three largest Rooms all crowded as full as they could hold—It was a very gay Scene but Alas! John Roe was not there!—We did not return till Eight Oclock in the Morning so slept all the Next Day—This was follow'd by a Dinner en Famille at Lowesgreen, where we were crammd to the throat with Strawberries, and entertained with the greatest Hospitality.

We were promised a Dinner at Rockwell, but something always happen'd to prevent it, and we left the Country without Mrs Roe's first house warming to us—Much to my Regret did we quit Knockgrafton—Greatly as I loved our Carrick Residence, I never returnd to it without the most poignant Regret for the Scenes I had left behind me.

CHAPTER 111TH

Labour overcometh all things

Our Carrick Residence now underwent a
thorough alteration and Repair—The Windows
were all Enlarged and many Improvements
made—The Superintendance of these prevented the many melancholy thoughts that
preyd on my Mind on quitting Parsonage—I
had always a taste for Improvements and spent
great part of my time in Embellishing the
Garden which I greatly beautified by planta-
tions of Shrubs and flowers and altering the
straight angled Walk into a circular winding
one—These avocations not only pleased my
natural taste, but were endear'd by knowing
that John Roe passd his time the same Way—I
remember Mr Gwynn took great pleasure in
looking at the Moon, supposing that his absent
friends might just then be gazing at the same
Object—such a pleasure did my Improvements
afford me in Absence, nor was I without hope
that I might one time or other point them out
to John Roe.

We spent some time in Carrick and then went
to Bonmahon for the Bathing Season—After
which we sat down for the Christmas in Carrick,
and when its festivities were over we set off for
Dublin to attend Mrs Bradshaw in her first
lying in—Some time after our Arrival she produced a fine Daughter who was christend

Matilda after my Mother—We had fuss enough
about the young Prodigy who came into the
World without much trouble.

In Dublin we met all our friends except my
Aunt Cuffe whose health was rapidly declining
—We dined once at Lord Maxwells—once
at the New Customs House with Mr Beresford and once at old Bradshaws—We went to
Evening Parties at Mrs Brownes, and Lady
Anne Fitzgeralds—Twice to the private
Theatre—which were all my share in the
Amusements going forward—I spent most of
my time in improving myself in Drawing
having got Mr West a head Master to brush
me up—I drew three very strong likenesses of
my Aunt Cuffe, and Lord and Lady Maxwell,
from half length portraits that hung in their
eating Parlour—These with three other Size-
able pieces I left to be handsomely framed for
our large Parlour lately done up—My Mother
bought a beautiful Wilton Carpet and scarlet
marine Curtains and when we went home
Employed a Head painter to paint it green with
a beautiful lilac Cornice and the whole Appartment had an air of grandeur that would not
have disgraced a Nobleman's House and as the
whole Dwelling was correspondently improved
we livd in tiptop alamode Stile—after spending many Years amongst tumbling Walls—
tattered hangings and broken sashes—Still
to surprize John Roe was my Vain delight in
those real Castle Buildings, for he often dropd in,

in the Morning at Carrick, passing to and from
Waterford—but to return from my digression
—we were made the most of by our Dublin
friends but our Chief Morning Visiter was
young Lady Blunden who sat whole Mornings
with my Mother in a very friendly Manner—
Sir John and she never lived much together—
(It was supposed on Account of her ill health)
—My Poems were shewn to all the Circle of
our Friends in Dublin who honourd them with
great Applauses, but I soon grew tired of trite
Eulogiums—We brought the Bradshaws and
their young Heiress down with us, and spent
the rest of the Spring in Carrick.

The Yellow Fever now raged with dreadful
Fury all over the World, and carried off
Millions — every post brought us a list of
Deaths which encreased the Horrors of War
and Rebellion, besides a Threatened Invasion
from the french who menaced our Island continually—so that the Summer passd on gloomily
enough.

About this Time Two of my female Cousins
died Mrs Maxwell and Miss Thomasine
Herbert, The former a Young Widow of 21
whose sad history I have before related—
The similiarity of their Fates were striking—
Mrs Maxwell lost her husband a week after
her Marriage—Miss Herbert lost an amiable
Lover on the Eve of her Espousals—They
both died of Grief in the same year.

A Domestic Accident allarmed us about this

Time—my Brother Otway one night staid out
till ten Oclock and on our sending to Search for
him he was found with his Collar Bone broke
and otherwise much bruised by a fall from
his Horse returning home—the sad forerunner
of a more disastrous Event—but proper care
restored him then to his family.

CHAPTER 112TH

*Heav'n from all Creatures hides the Book of
    fate*
All But the Page prescrib'd their present State

About June we set out again for Knockgrafton
which was now become a Martial Scene by the
continual passing of the Army to and from
the Camp of Ardfinnan a Romantic Village
eleven miles distant from Knockgrafton—We
had this Year the Advantage of a fine Garden
open to us—As Mr Carew and family were
from home they left Orders that we should have
the full use of Woodenstown Garden whilst
we staid—This was a valuable Acquisition to
us, as the Rockwell Car droppd coming from
the time Mrs Roe returnd and our own
Garden was not yet come to any Perfection—
Mrs Bradshaw who was again in a thriving way
felt most the Advantage of our prerogative
and was continually at Woodenstown grazing
on vegetable Thrash—Mrs Hare and Mrs
Clarke were often with us but we saw very

little of the Roes—the young Men were from
home most of the Summer—and Mrs Roe
pleaded the ill Health of her friend Mrs
Walsh as an excuse for her not being a better
Neighbour.

June the 19th, poor Mary Neale our old dry
Nurse died in Carrick—She had lived 40 years
in the family and dry nursed every one of us,
of course we were all in great Affliction—An
Express came off to us immediately with the
sad tidings, and we directly set out for Carrick
to see her interr'd—After paying her Remains
every Duty, we returnd in two days to Knockgrafton with the addition of little Matty Bradshaw to our Society—We expected great fun
that Year with the Vicinage of the Camp so
near us, but it turned out quite the Contrary,
and I never found the time hang so heavily—
the Roes were absent, and nothing seemd gay
or smiling—Mrs Bradshaw at last put forth a
Son who was christend John after old Mr
Bradshaw—This was a Novel Scene at Knockgrafton—We had some Caudle Drinking and
our Carrick friends were induced to partake of
it—After which all things relapsed into the
usual Routine.

Mr Bradshaw having come up to hail his Son
and heir—we made a party to visit the Ardfinnan Camp leaving the Lady in the Straw to
nurse herself and her Bantling—Though we
knew the Officers of many of the Regiments
we declined all Civilities and Invitations till

we reached the Cantoons of the Kerry Regiment
commanded by Lord Glendore and Mr Herbert
of Muckrus my Fathers Nephew—They had
been hospitably Entertaind at Carrick by my
Brothers on their way to the Camp, and seem'd
now desirous of returning the Compliment—
We were shewn to Mr Herberts Marquée
which was reckond the most beautifull in the
Camp and he and Lord Glendore pressd us to
Dinner but we declined the Honour of their
Invitation.

The Races of Cashel at length came on and were
uncommonly crouded because of the Camp—
Lady Caher and Lord Glendore figured there
with a new Set of fine people—and as the
former did not visit us this year our Acquaintance totally droppd—We did not feel spunk
enough to visit Lady Glendore who being
Sister to Mrs Herbert of Muckrus could not
well have declined an Acquaintance had we
solicited it especially as Lord Glendore was
otherwise nearly related to my Father—
Brilliant and Crouded as the Scene was there
was a something in it that struck me as Pro-
phetic of the bloody Years that were to ensue—
A black Cloud seemd hovering over the mimic
Theatre of human Bliss, and blackend all
Enjoyment—We did not go to any of the
Assemblies—As the Roes were from home I
did not much regret it—but the Comparisons
I drew between this and former Years struck
me with dismay—A sad Presentiment of Woe

rose like the Ghost in Hamlet and Even in the
Pageant field I was ready to Shriek out

" *Art thou a Spirit of Hell, or Goblin damn'd?*

Sometime after the Races John and Andrew
Roe returnd home and once more my Droop-
ing Spirit sprang like the Phœnix from its
Ashes.

(CHAPTER 113TH)

But the Divinity that breathes in thee'
Has broke the Charm, and I am in a Desart
Far from the Land of Peace

Mrs Roe had now no pretence for not giving us
a Dinner and we were invited to Rockwell for
the first time since her Arrival—We spent what
is call'd a very comfortable Day, but quite en
famille—Mrs Roe had all the Ease of a Woman
accustom'd to Society, but I thought the Entertainment rather a plain one for the first house
warming—Miss Roe had now resumed her
Music which she had forsaken on her Mothers
leaving Rockwell, though once esteemd the first
Player in the County—She and I playd in turn
after Dinner—John Roe rose from the Table on
my sitting down to the Harpsichord—He stood
opposite me—with what an earnest Gaze it is
impossible to describe!—The Vibrations of my
Music seemd to have its full Effect on him, but
more intently was he employd in surveying the

Effect of harmony on my Too intelligent Countenance—His eyes wanderd from my Face to
my Bosom with Speaking Emotion, whilst I
playd on all fluttering at his Earnest Gaze—But
who could develope John Roe's Heart? Not I
I ll swear—Every speaking feature spoke Love,
Delight, Desire—Every treacherous Action
spoke Apathy, Cruelty, and Guilt—Mysterious
Man! Why rack my unsuspecting Soul?

He came up to Tea Early as in former times, but
by hap hazard was wedged in in the Window Seat
—I was calld on to fill out Coffee, and he made a
great racket to get from his confined Situation to
sit near me—He accordingly devoted himself
to me the rest of the Evening with all the Assiduity of former Years—I however saw him that
Year but Seldom—He was ever on the Wing—
Whilst drooping and mourning I bewaild his
fickleness.

One Sunday we went after Church to pay a
morning Visit at Rockwell—We found the
Ladies in the Parlour just risen from family
Prayers, and John enterd afterwards—but instead of coming over to salute us Spinsters, he
sat down in the Window near his Mother, playing with a huge pet Tabby Cat, and lavishing
all his Caresses on it with the Air of a bashful
Country Booby—Mrs Walshe animadverted
with severity on the Manners of the Age and
said it was a melancholy sight to see a Set of
fine Young Ladies sitting quite dull without a
Gentleman whilst the Young Masters were tied

to their Mother or Sisters Apron Strings or per-
chance squeezed up in a Corner with some dirty
disagreeable animal on whom they lavish'd all
their Caresses—Here John Roe threw the Cat
a Mile off, but the Animal crawl'd up again
familiarly and her Master fought with her to get
her away—Mrs Roe seem'd much disconcerted
and Miss Roe sat in angry fidgets—whilst John
blush'd, look'd down, and twisted his Watch
Chain with conscious Guilt—I would continued
Mrs Walsh have young Gentlemen act like
Young Gentlemen and not stay skulking in dark
Corners or stabling it with their Grooms when
they ought to be figuring in the Drawing Room
or chusing some amiable Partner for Life—
Here she looked over at us who sat drawn up in
a Row—I'm sure said she the Young Ladies are
all of my Opinion if they dared to own it—John
Roe could no longer bear her Sarcasms—and
with a Grace all his own, he darted forward to
me, and addressd me with an elegant Gallantry
—Miss Roe however enviously interrupted our
discourse by bidding me get up to look at some
family Pictures newly finish'd that hung up behind us—We all stood up, and she contrived to
slip between me and her Brother whilst Andrew
secured me on the Other Side—John made
many Efforts to get near me but whichever way
he turn'd they impeded his progress till at length
he wedged himself between me and the Wall
and standing with his back to it smilingly asked
which I preferr'd him or his portrait?—The

334

Question made me blush violently, for what
Artist indeed could paint him so charming as he
at that Moment appear'd to the trembling, lost
Dolly Herbert—Wickedly he threw every Grace
into his inimitable attitude and smiling Features
to accomplish in my heart the Mischievous rav-
age they had already made—Miss Roe strove to
interupt our Badinage by talking louder and
faster than any one—After some further Conversation my Mother broke up the Party and we
returnd to the Parsonage.

CHAPTER 114TH

Oh May the Furies light his Nuptial Torch
Be it accurs'd as mine—for the fair Peace
The tender Joys of hymeneal Love
May Jealousy awaked and fell Remorse
Pour all their fiercest Venom thro' his Breast

Here ended my happy Carreer at Rockwell and
all the halcyon Days of hope and Bliss—We
soon after quitted Knockgrafton for that Year—
and I may say I then bade an Eternal Adieu to
the too lovely faithless John Roe!—Thus ended
an Acquaintance that conferr'd on me as Exquisite a Bliss and as Acute Misery as the human
Soul is capable of feeling—with shuddering
horror I am forced to relate that the perjured
Wretch has since married another—Joined himself in execrable Union with a Common Drab
of the City—a mere street strolling Miss—

Daughter to one Counsellor Sankey of Dublin—
Surely to my beloved she can be no more than
one of those harlots Milton describes whose
Venal smiles

Are loveless, joyless, lifeless, unendear'd.

What could induce the specious Villain to seduce
my Affections, betray me to lingering Torments
and then desert me for Ever, is a Problem I
never could solve—Ah My Poor Heart! What
Cruelties did it suffer in the Days of Doubt and
Incertitude—What more than Hell Born Woe
when the Monster struck his last Blow and left
me for Ever Benighted in intolerable Despair—
Never Never again may so black a Scene be
transacted Never may an innocent unsuspecting,
susceptible Dolly Herbert find a too Attentive—
Too Amiable John Roe!
From that time every Happiness of Life fled
and I became a prey to the Censorious, the Cruel,
the Plundering World—John Roes Desertion
was the signal for my suffering every Abominable Affront Every Attrocious Injury!
The last sad scene of my Tragedy was not however completed till four Years after, and I
quitted Knockgrafton still nourishing the fatal
hope that undid me—too well did my Viperous
Foe wreathe around me his Snaky Torments—
With insiduous treachery he insnared me to my
Doom, and gloated in my Ruin with horrid joy

All that is lovely in the Noxious Snake
Provokes our Fear, and bids us fly the Brake.

CHAPTER 115

Fortune her Gifts may variously dispose
And these be happy calld—Unhappy those

On our Return to Carrick I stood Bridesmaid
to my old Friend Salisbury Jephson who was
happily disposed of to Mr Rothe a very fine
dashing young Man of good property in the
Co Kilkenny—The Wedding was quite a
private one—but we had a flaming Assembly
in Carrick some days after—We had the South
Cork Band and the Presence of Lord Barrymore
their Colonel—We were to have had the young
and beautiful Lady Barrymore but her Lord
had given her a good beating which confined
her at home—Mr James Butlar Lord Ormonds
brother and many other fine Beaux graced the
Assemblage which was very splendid and
numerous—But the most beautiful object in
the Room was Mrs Lee—Never did she appear so lovely—so animated as when dancing
at the Nuptials of her Elder Sister—Every one
remarkd the same—but it was follow'd by the
most fatal Consequences—She was just out of
her Lying in, and threw off her flannel for that
Night—She got a Cough, fell into a Consumption and died three Years after at Bath in the
Arms of her Mother and Husband who attended her in every Stage of her lingering
Illness—Her Remains were brought over to
Ireland, and she was buried in Kilvernon the

337   z

Burial Place of her Husbands family in the
Co Waterford—Thus ended the lovely Fanny
Jephson, a Martyr to that gay Unthinkingness
that always characterized her Youth—Though
it added to her Charms, it proved a fatal Trait
in her Character—Poor Otway returnd from
the Funeral quite knock'd up by witnessing
the last Melancholy Scene of his old Playmate
and Companion—Indeed the Wit and Good
humour of those two, kept up entirely the
Spirits of both families—Mrs Lee left three
Daughters all of whom died Young and at her
Dying Request Mr Lee married a Second Wife,
Miss Gardiner Daughter to Lord Mountjoy—
To express the Grief of her family would be a
vain attempt—I draw a Veil over their Sufferings and return to the Year 1794.

The County Kilkenny Militia had been
station'd in Carrick for some time—Their
Officers were mostly all related to us—By their
coming Mrs Rothe got her husband, and Otway
a good Living—Lord Ormond was my Fathers
Patron—Otway gave him and his Regiment a
grand Dinner here from which the Ladies were
excluded—His Lordship took such a liking to
my Brother that he could do Nothing without
him and to testify his Regard he transferr'd the
Living of Knockgrafton from my Father to
Otway which as my Brother was very Young
appeard a most Advantageous Renewal—Mr
Rothe who was Lord Ormonds Bosom friend
whisperd good things of Otway who in Grati-

tude helpd forward his Courtship with Salisbury
Jephson—The Revulsions of my Thoughts on
this Occasion were many—I felt a melancholy
Conviction that I should never again renew the
blissful Hours that passd in that most interesting Spot, but as the Living did not go out of
the family I still remain'd in a quiet Security
and rejoiced at Otways Success.

When the Kilkenny Regiment went the South
Cork came in its Place and with them Lord and
Lady Barrymore—She was a beautiful little
Woman whom he had married for Love in
Youghal—Her Maiden Name was Coughlan
and she was distantly related to the Roes—
The Noble Pair spent most of their time at our
House—we often spent the Evening with them
at their Lodgings and they had always the Band
for us—It was reckond the finest in the King-
dom—There were besides great Amateurs,
and we had most capital singing by Lord Barry-
more Colonel Barry, and Mr Webb a Chorister
—Besides this set we had Mr Hutchinson a
recruiting Officer who was a universal Genius
a little Hairbraind indeed but the pleasantest
Creature possible—His chief forte was spouting
Plays with which he amused his Acquaintance—
We had also a Captain Forbes quarterd on us
a long time whilst the troops were learning the
New Hessian Exercise—He was no great
Lady's Man but we contrived to pick amusement out of him.

Altogether it was a very gay Jumble of Regi-

mental Scraps—We had nothing but Band playing Singing, leaping, and cutting Apples with the
sword's point on the Warriours Heads—In this
Manner we spent the latter End of the Year 1794

" *To please and be pleased* " was our motto.

CHAPTER 116

Lo the struck Deer in some sequesterd part
Lies down to die, the Arrow in his Heart
There hid in Shades, and wasting Day by Day
Inly he bleeds, and pants his Soul away

The Year 1795 led to many important Events,
but began with the triffling Circumstance of the
Devonshire Militia's coming in the place of the
South Cork—There was a Mrs Lucas and a
Miss Mitchel with them—Miss Mitchel was
a smart piece and set all the Gentlemen dying
for her—We had likewise their Colonels Lady
Mrs Urquhart who joind afterwards—We
gave them a Ball and they were here continually but for my part I did not like any of them—
however they kept our House in a constant
Bustle—How rejoiced was I when my Mother
declared she was so sick of it, that she would
go refresh herself for a time in the Solitude of
Knockgrafton—This was an unexpected Visit
there as it had been previously fixd not to visit
it this year—I was most agreeably surprized
and rejoiced to quit a Society I disliked for
Scenes I adored—Never shall I forget the first

beautiful Evening we spent there—quite sick
of our Carrick life—we sat at the Hall Door
to enjoy the fresh Evening Breeze—The whole
Horizon was illuminated by the Setting Sun—
The Sky rolled before us in purple red and
Gold fleeces being that Night remarkably
beautiful—The Cows and sheep playd up at
the very Door and everything looked at once
so peaceful and lively, that my Father Mother
and I enjoyd it beyond Measure—None else
of the family came up and our seclusion was
delightfully tranquil—But Alas this was the
only advantage we reaped by the Jaunt—all
intercourse with Rockwell was at an End.

Mr and Mrs Roe had given up their property
to their two Sons and went to live in Clonmell
where Miss Roe accompanied them—John
and Andrew no sooner got the House to themselves than they left it to the Care of the Servants
and went on a pleasurable Excursion to Lucan
where they staid the Whole Summer.

This was a Brain Blow to all my delusive
Dreams, however I felt a Melancholy Comfort
in treading the Stage of past Felicity, where
every trivial Object was dear to my Soul—
The Society of my friend Mrs Clarke was
another Source of Comfort to me—We often
met in Cashel or at the Parsonage—She had
changed her abode to another part of the town
where they had a beautiful Romantic Tenement
with the Rock of Cashel towering magnificently
over their Garden—This engross'd all our

thoughts and Conversation—Tom now paid
us a Visit on his first Circuit which was highly
interesting to us and where he made a few
Guineas — Nick had enterd College — and
Otway was reading for Priests Orders—Our
Young Counsellor remaind some time with us
and was succeeded by Mrs Bradshaw and Fanny
who came from Carrick after glutting with its
gaieties More to their tastes than Mine.
I shall conclude this account of our last pilgrimage to Knockgrafton with copying a fragment
of an Old Journal I burned—for as John Roe
was not there to fix my Memory I should find
difficulty in a New Detail.

Some Joy still lost as each vain Year runs oer
And All we gain some Sad Reflection More—

The Equinox now set in which was felt in its
fullest Force at Knockgrafton — This was
attended with Continual Rain so that we were
kept entirely within Doors—During this confinement I occupied myself in making Artificial
Flowers for two filigree Baskets with which
Mrs Clarke adorned her State Drawing Room
— One dry Day the family went out but I
staid at home to finish my Flowers—I was
seated at my work in the parlour when Mrs
Hare Wife to our Parish Clerk enterd—She
had brought us some present and I ask'd her

to sit down—Her husband was a Mason and
workd constantly at Rockwell or our Glebe so
that he and his Wife knew all that passd at
both Houses—and used frequently entertain
us with Anecdotes of the Rockwell family—
Mrs Hare this Day enter'd into a loquacious
Account of our Neighbours—She said the
place look'd shockingly lonesome without the
family—and much to that purport and clapping
her hands she suddenly Exclaimd, I wish to
God Miss that Mr John was married to some
good Young Lady that would keep the family
together and indeed all the Servants wish so
too for they dont like living in the lonesome way
they do—Every thing is so straggling and uncomfortable that they are always praying for a good
young Mistress to regulate the family—Mrs
Hare investigated my looks so Closely during
this Harangue that I felt myself Colour violently and being forced to say something to
turn it off I mutter'd out that Mr John Roe
seemd to have no thoughts of Marrying—
Indeed I dont know Miss said she but I know
Old Mr Roe is very anxious that he should and
I believe so is Mrs and Miss Roe—she again
clappd her Hands and exclaimd Oh then I wish
to God Miss you were married to him Oh how
happy it would make Purdon Hare and I and
all the Neighbourhood and indeed I m Certain
all the Servants at Rockwell would give their
Eyes to have you for their Mistress—This
sudden Good Wish of my friend Mrs Hare

threw me into the utmost Confusion, which I
turnd off by pretending to look for my needle
and with the utmost difficulty I suppressd the
Sighs and Tears that oppressd me whilst my loquacious Companion gave her Tongue full play.
The Day was at length fixd for our leaving
Knockgrafton and we went to Cashel to
take leave of the Hares and Clarkes—I presented my Offering of Artificial flowers for
their Baskets which they admired so much and
expressd themselves so grateful that I really
blushd that my Gift was not better worth their
thanks—We spent most of the Morning admiring their New House and Elegant Villa—I
never saw them appear so affectionate as that
Day—and both were much affected and grieved
when we took leave—We then drove to Mr
Hares where we heard that John Roe had
returnd to Rockwell the Night before—It was
now that I felt the full misery of leaving Knockgrafton perhaps for Ever and I thought myself
a most unlucky Creature to be forced away just
on his Arrival—The Girls as if they read my
Misery in my Countenance interceded that we
should stay another week but my Mother
having packed up every thing would not consent—As we pass'd Rockwell Gate our Servant
was sent down to know if the Young Gentlemen
had any commands to their father and Mother
—The Answer was that they were to be in
Clonmell themselves Next Day and would not
trouble us—On returning to Parsonage I gave

vent to the Tears that ever attended my Adieus
to the Paradise of my Heart.

CHAPTER 118TH

Heav'n first taught Letters for some Wretches Aid
Some banishd Lover or some Captive Maid

I had long anticipated the Horrors of my
Departure this farewell Year it being the last
of my fathers Incumbency as Otway was on
the point of being inducted and though he was
a most darling Brother I could not build on
spending three Months every Year there.
The thoughts of bidding a final Adieu to those
beloved Scenes set me absolutely distracted and
I continually Wanderd about the Glebe antici-
pating the dreadful Blow I was to receive in
being torn for ever from it and John Roe—My
Heart was convulsed with Sorrow and having
no other way of venting my internal Conflicts I
composed the following Poem in my Melancholy Saunters and felt some Relief in thus
giving loose to my Despair.

The Village Adieu a Farewell Poem

Verse 1st

A long and last Farewell I bid thee Now
Dear fatal Village! Nursery of my Woes!
In whose retired Scenes my lost repose
And all my Youthful Joys lie buried low.

2

Sweet Village in whose Haunts I first beheld
Him who has long all Happiness expelld
From my once tranquil Breast—
Where shall I now find Peace or Rest?
When banish'd from thy Interesting Scenes
To wander cheerless on far distant Plains
Where every Grove will seem a dreary Waste,
For little pleasure can the poor Wretch prove
Who writhes beneath the pangs of hopeless Love.

3

When first I visitted this humble Place
The flatt'ring World then smiled Around—
Youth, Health, Joy, pleasure, sparkled in my Face
I seem'd to Wander on enchanted Ground,
A thousand pleasures blessd the happy Hours
Ten thousand Hopes strewd all my paths with
flowers—

4th Verse

But now How chang'd!—How sadly changd the
Scene!
Youth, Health, Hope, Joy, are fled!
And hardly can I now sustain
The Sorrows heap'd on my unhappy Head—
Despis'd! forsaken! Cheerless, and forlorn!
Hopeless! depressd! forgotten now I roam
And quite heartbroken with Contempt and Scorn
I spy no Refuge but the peaceful Tomb:
For light unfeeling Mortals ever shun
The dim faint Glimmering of our setting Sun—

5th

Yet as *Ambition* ne'er possessd my *Heart*
How gladly could I part
With all the treacherous flatteries of this *Ball*
If one too cruel and unerring *Dart*
Had not conspired my fall—
But who can bear *Contempt, Neglect,* and *Scorn*
From those lov'd *Objects* whom our *Souls* adore?
Those are the pangs that never can be borne,
Those are the wounds which bleed at every *Pore*
Which no balsamic *Influence* can restore.

6th

Sweet *Village!* Once the *Cradle,* Now the tomb
Of all the dear *Illusions* of my *Heart!*
What powerful *Spell!*—What *Art*
Can dissipate the dismal *Gloom*
When from thy *Scenes* I must for ever part?
Oh! *Never, Never* shall I once more find
The long lost *Blessings* of a tranquil *Mind*—

7th

Dear peaceful plains! Where each lone rural spot
Some past *Delight,* some fond *Remembrance* bring
Can those bless'd *Moments* ever be forgot
Which flew so rapidly on feather'd *Wings?*
No! to those *Hours* the *Mind* still fondly *Clings*—

8

Here was I wont to wander and retrace
In every well known place

Each Spot graced by that presence so adored—
Whether I climbd the Hillock's Brow
Or loiter'd in the Plain below
Or gazed upon the Village Spire
Or brooded oer the Wood piled fire,
Or strove the heavy Hours to cheat
With saunters towr'ds his dear Retreat—
Still on his lov'd Idea I have pored—
But time no longer shall those Joys restore,
Those Haunts I never shall revisit more—

9th

Oh Rockwell! shall I never, Never More
Behold thy Verdant Lawns and smiling Meads?
Nor daily from Yon Eminence explore
Those happy peaceful shades
Where careless strays the Idol of my Soul?
There wrapp'd in blest Indifference, his Life
Glides calmly as a smooth unruffled Stream—
Whilst Grief, Love, Tenderness and Shame
In wild internal Strife
Subdue by turns my struggling Spirit to their fierce
    Controul.

10th

Ah why will lingring Memory still dwell
On the departed Scenes of happier Years
Why with relentless Industry thus Swell
The Bosom with Regret, The Eye with Tears
For scenes to which we now must bid a long a last
    Farewell?

348

11th

Why Memory thus unceasingly impart
Wild Sadness to the foolish, fluttering Heart
Too prone Alas! to Mourn
Moments which once fled to past Times dark Bourne
Must never more return!—

12

In vain doth Reasons Voice condemn
And seek the torrent of Regret to stem
The Sighing restless Mind
Pants for those Pleasures she has left behind
But fruitlessly she pants! The Splendid Rays
Of Happiness that gladdened former Days
Are vanishd like a Dream
For when Youths Rosy Hours are Sped
And all our Halcyon Hopes are fled
Pleasure withdraws her last enlivening Gleam
Tis then the World becomes a Vale of Tears
And Sorrow, Weariness, Disgust—gloom our
  declining Years!

13th Verse

Sweet lowly Village though about to fly
And quit for ever thy bewitching Scenes
For thee and thy too lovely Habitant
My woe worn Heart shall never cease to pant
Still must ye be the Objects of each Sigh
Whilst this poor Heart the Pulse of Life retains
But wild Despair involves me whilst I muse
Receive Dear Village then, My last Adieus!

349

We then quitted Knockgrafton after taking a
most melancholy Leave on account of my
Father resigning the Living—I shall finish this
Chapter with two Extracts of Letters I received
the following Year 1796 which shows the
oblique Manner of my friends on the Subject
I had Most at Heart—

Extract 1st

" Mr and Mrs Elliot spent some Days at Rock-
" well last week and I am told that Mrs Elliot
" is expected there for the Christmas, however
" they keep their Movements so Private that
" even Mr C. is not in the Cabinet—As for me,
" my Day is over—Whether the Wheel of
" Fortune will whirl me into Fortune again I
" know not—But do not be Saucy for it may
" Come About again, as You who are a great
" Moralizer know that the things of this Life
" are impenetrable—And as the Family are a
" little fickle that same fickleness may Seat me
" at Rockwell Fireside Again—especially as
" with all my Attractions there is no chance of
" my becoming Mistress of the Mansion
1796   Yrs &c

Extract 2d

" I saw Mr and Mrs Roe, Mrs Elliot, Miss Roe
" and Andrew—at the Race Course—They all
" looked Very Well—I have not seen John
" these three Months—He told me he had an
" Intention of going to England—However he

" has not yet put it in Execution—The Brothers
" lead the most retired Lives possible—The Old
" Man dined with us some time ago and Ex-
" pressd a Good deal of unhappiness at the Dis-
" inclination of his Sons to Marry—He said all
" his Arguments did not Avail and that it made
" him very Uneasy—He is really a sincere
" friendly Man as ever lived—

I am Yours Etcæta

1796

The unusually Grave Stile of this last Epistle
convinced me that my Friend in relating those
circumstances wished to destroy all remaining
Hopes from that Quarter, and though her Dis-
couragement wounded me deeply—I was much
obliged to her for her Sincerity.
Adieu then John Roe! Dear delightful Name!
at which my Heart so often bounded with
Extacy or sank in Unalterable Despondency—
Always heard with Emotions that None but
Lovers can know—and Not even Lovers can
Describe!

N.B. My Brother Otway was soon after Inducted and became Rector of Knockgrafton.

END OF BOOK THE SIXTH

CHAPTER 119TH

Tis not a Lip or Eye we Beauty call
But the joint force and full Result of All

Having settled my Brother Otway in the Living of Knockgrafton it is full time now to Introduce Miss Russel who was at that time just return'd from the Cork Nunnery—Her Father Captain Russel whom I have before mention'd made a large Fortune in the East Indies—He sent the little Nanno over when she was about two years old to be educated under the Auspices of Mrs English her Godmother—Her own Mother who was an East Indian died soon after Nanno was born—I remember seeing her when she first came over at Mrs Englishes and a sweet smart little Creature she was—dressd in a White Cloak and a little Gypsy Hat tied under her Chin with a pink Workbag hanging from her Arm—Whilst everyone hugg'd and kissd the little Stranger. When she was educated, her Father having returnd and settled in Carrick, he brought her home from the Nunnery—She was then about

fourteen or fifteen with a National Olive
Complection delicate features, a smart little
person elegantly turnd—beautiful Legs and
Arms—shining black Hair and the finest pair
of Black Eyes that could be immagined—
Nothing could be more graceful than her
Manners, and her General Disposition was
meek, soft, gentle, and insinuating, though
when rouzed I have often called her a little
Fury—She was very lively and animated with
very quick Sensibilities as those of her Nation
generally have—She sang and play'd touchingly
—danced exquisitely—and had a pretty taste
for Drawing and all sorts of Convent Needle
work—In her face and person she was so like
the bewitching Mrs Herbert of Muckrus that
Mr Herbert when here followd her up and
down the Street, struck with her Resemblance
to his beautiful but faithless Wife.

Miss Russel it may be supposed had many
Suitors when she came home thus accomplish'd
—Only Daughter and Sole Heiress (it was
supposed) to Captain Russel—Wherever she
went she attracted Notice, and gaind Admirers
—as my Brother Otway was her fathers chief
friend and confidant Captain Russel preferr'd him as her Cecisbeo to all others—Of
course Otway paid her every Attention and was
continually in waiting on her at home and
Abroad—Whenever Russel went out he threw
Otway the Keys and orderd him to regale himself and his protegee with a Miss Higgins

acting as Duenna—Otway got us to visit his
young favourite and he was so full of Captain
Russel and his Daughter that we could no
good of him whilst he escorted her about—He
often asked us Jestingly our Opinion of his
little Blackamoor—To see her and know her
was to like her and we did his protegee but
Justice in saying so—Miss Russel soon grew
as fond of Otway's Company as her Father
was and from liking his company began to
like his person too well for her own peace—
She had too much frankness of Character to
keep it long conceald from him and to the
World she openly avowed that she would never
marry any man but Otway Herbert—Otway
on his part though at first he regarded her only
as an amiable Child placed under, and claiming
his protection, soon grew attached to his heed-
less Charge and their mutual fondness being
known to each other and to every one Else,
they thought they had nothing to do but Marry,
as her father still took all Opportunities of
leaving them Alone together—After dangling
after each other a long time, they began to
wonder that Captain Russel did not speak more
explicitly on the Subject, and as Otway thought
that he had sacrificed enough to Delicacy—
he wrote to him a Proposal in form for his
Daughter—But what a shock did we all receive
when Russel in two different Letters commanded him to think no more of her—The
first Letter was merely a put off on account of

her Youth, and when Otway required a more
explicit answer he wrote a flat Refusal—They
now did every thing to soften him into terms
—and got all those who had any weight with
him to intercede for them, but Russel was
inflexible on the Subject though otherwise he
treated them with the greatest freedom and
good humour still leaving them alone together,
and by every Means cementing their friendship, whilst he forbad their Love.

CHAPTER 120TH

For it is hard to Wear their Bloom
In Unremitting Sighs away

Two of my Fathers Muckrus Nieces at this
period came to spend some time with us on their
Return from England—The Youngest was a
Beautiful Girl of seventeen Years of Age—
Otway escorted them every where, and whenever Miss Russel or we did any thing to dis-
please him he always threaten'd to propose for
Peggy Herbert—In fact his temper was quite
sour'd by the imperious behaviour of Russel and
his repeated Refusals—We continually preached
Patience and Perseverance to him—whilst poor
Nanno Russel used all her little Artifices to keep
him in temper.
The Arrival of the Muckrus Herberts afforded
us a pretext for giving a grand Ball which we
hoped would forward the Courtship of the Young

Lovers but they quarrel'd the Day before and
the Russels sent an Excuse—We began to despair of Matters ever coming to an Issue as both
possessd high spirits added to the natural impatience and petulance of Youth—Nanno could
not bear Otways threats of proposing for his
Cousin and he was mad at being triffled with by
Russel—in this situation we will leave them
awhile.

Every one was asked to the Ball and Every one
came except the Russels—The Dorsetshire
Militia were then quarterd here and we had
all the Officers of that Regiment—Lord John
Beresford and Mr Maude son to Lord de Montalt came from Curraghmore to it—Mr and Mrs
Rothe and Many other strangers besides the
people of the Neighbourhood and the Party in
the House at the time which consisted of Mr
and Mrs E Mandeville Mr Richard Butlar and
the Herberts—The Night before the Ball Mrs
Mandeville and we sat up to make spun Sugar
in the Parlour—They sent me up stairs for
something and I found the Lobby all illuminated by a Light from the Courtyard—on going
to the Window what was my Horror to perceive
Toms Room in the opposite Wing all in a Blaze
of fire—I ran to his Door and pounded but
received no answer—Distracted I ran down
screaming to the Parlour—and had just presence
of Mind to make them understand me—One
set ran up Stairs, and another to awake the Men
Servants who slept over the offices—When we

got up we found Tom at the Door in his Shirt
just Stiffled, unable to speak and very much
Scorched—He was faintly endeavouring to
buffet the flames with the Bed Curtain and his
Shirt was hanging in burning fragments round
him—We took the hint pull'd down the rest of
the flaming Curtains and brushed the Flames
from the wooden Tester and Cornice of the
Room which was at this time on fire in every
Part—Our Cloaths were burnd off our backs
in this service and some of us were much singed
but grown desperate we stood the fire and kept
it at Bay till the Men had procured Buckets of
Water which soon finishd our hazardous Undertaking—We were for some time enveloped in
smoak and knew not who was safe but on its
dispersion we received another alarm—Tom sat
stiffened with horror and Suffocation and neither
our Shaking or Remedies could bring him to his
Senses—Fanny was in fits by his Side, and my
Mother was taken down fainting to the parlour
with her fingers all burnd—we ran from one to
the other till we had restored them to animation
—And then quite exhausted and much scorchd
we sat down with them to howl out our panic—
The Men now enterd with the Lumber saved
which consisted of a Charged Gun that lay by
Toms Bed, a loaded Blunder Buss that lay on
the Table near it—where the Candle fell was
half a pound of Gun Powder in paper and near
it his powder horn—Miraculous to relate they
all escaped the fire though the four walls were

one sheet of flames—It seems Tom had fallen
asleep with a Book in his hand and the Book a
thick Classick was burnd through and through
—This was the first thing that awoke him—he
jumpd out of bed but had no power to stop the
flames till we rescued him—How to account for
so many Miracles of escape is impossible—Had
the Guns or Powder gone off we had been all
lost yet none of us suspected they were there till
the Danger was past—The whole House would
have probably been burned and blown up had I
not accidentally gone on the lucky Errand at the
critical Moment and alarm'd the family time
enough to save it—We spent the rest of the
Night in mutual Condolance and dressing our
scorched Limbs with various Nostrums—We
were all in queer order for the Ball next Day
but the Necessity of Entertaining our Guests
made us perform Wonders.

CHAPTER 121ST

A Grotto so compleat with such Design
What Hand Calypso could have form'd but thine

We next Day laid out in two Rooms united by
a double Door Case the most beautiful Supper
without Exaggeration that ever I beheld and I
have seen many that Exercised all the taste and
Genius of the Donors—The Tables reached the
length of the two Rooms and were Joind at the
Door Case by a small Central one, on which

stood an Artificial Temple adorned with Beads
flowers and purple and green Grapes hanging
in Festoons—The Door Case itself was formed
into an Artificial Bower over the Temple where
were entwined Ivy, Myrtle, Euonymus Berries
and various flowering Shrubs—Two ornamental
flower Baskets relieved the Temple and glasses
of Flowers were placed along the centre of the
Table alternately with pyramids of Jellies and
Creams—The Dishes were all done in various
fanciful Modes and every part of the Table was
hung or strewd with purple and green Grapes—
The Bower also was hung with the Delicious
Fruit—At each End of the House were two
large Mirrors and when the Doors of the four
large Rooms were thrown open, those Mirrors
reflected the whole Supper and its Multitude of
Lights in silver and glass Branches so that the
supper appear'd by the Deception Double the
length of the House—Nothing could be more
beautiful than its Effect and a general Murmur
of Admiration and astonishment burst forth
amongst our Guests, none of whom would sit
down till they had gone round and Round to
survey this perfect Image of Fairyland—The
Bower was the most Compleat Representation
of a natural one I ever saw and the Shining Green
Leaves and Scarlet Berries in the Midst of
Lights, gave a perfect Idea of a Garden Illuminated or rather it seemd a Magic Creation raised
by Supernatural Powers—The Person who
seemd most planet struck was Mr Maude—He

declared he had been at the first Supper Tables
on the Continent and had never seen any thing
so strikingly beautiful—When he went home
he Blazon'd us all about the Neighbourhood of
Cashel and said the Girls who had Genius to lay
out such a Supper must he was sure make
Superiour Wives.

I was very glad it spread through that Neighbourhood through such respectable Authority
—How I wish'd for John Roe's presence that
Night—but he alas! was far away—The great
hurry of our preparations gave me such a Bloom
that I never looked so killing—When I came
down dress'd Peggy Herbert utterd an Ex-
clamation at my beautiful Appearance which I
partly owed to my flurry in the fire the Night
before—I was in such demand in the Ball
Room that I was forced to refuse some of our
Head Beaux—I danced two sets with Mr
Maude who pleased me greatly as he had all
the natural easy politeness of John Roe without
any Affectation of the Courtly Breeding he was
accustom'd to—We chatted a good deal about
the Roes and he extolld his Neighbour John
Roe so that one would think he guessd the
Secret of my Heart—Indeed I could have
almost made him my Confidant, he lookd so
sedate and goodnatured—and besides there was
a striking Parity in the Manners of him and My
Adorable which ingratiated him not a little
with me.

In the middle of the Night Otway engaged a

partner but when he was calld for he was Non
est inventus as the Scholars say—The fact
was he had left Nanno Russel in Tears after
their quarrel which kept her at home, and his
heart give him no rest in the Merry throng
so he stole away from its Joys to comfort his
afflicted fair One—Our Supper and Entertainment were much spoken of even in Dublin
as our Correspondants declared in their
Epistles—John Roe only was wanting to compleat the Interesting Scene.

1796   CHAPTER 122D

" Created half to rise and half to fall
" Great Lord of all things Yet a prey to all

This Year died our Old Friend and Relation
Mr Daniel Cuffe Father to Mrs Wall of Coolnamuck—My Mother and he were reared
together and from the time of her Marriage
he spent some Months in each Year here—
We were so used to his agreeable Visits that his
death made a real Blank in our Existence—
Always friendly and pleasant he temper'd a
wise Old Age with the Juvenile pleasantry of
Youth and even at Seventy was agreeable to all
Ages—This Event brought Mrs Wall over
from England—she and family arrived some
time before his final Departure.

This Year died also the Reverend Jemmet
Browne whose Marriage with my Fathers

Niece Miss Blennerhasset I have before recited.

In March my Mother went to Tramore to attend her Niece Lucy Cuffe who had like to die of a Fever there but with proper care recoverd—When my Mother returned we all went to Bonmahon and spent a pleasant Season there—My Brothers visitted us whenever their different Avocations permitted but Otway was entirely engaged by Miss Russel—Tom was going on cleverly at the Bar but his Spirit of Knight Errantry always made him volunteer for poor wretches who had nothing to pay, many of whom he saved from the Gallows every Assizes.

We found the Neighbourhood of Carrick pretty gay on our return—The Dorsets were a pleasant sociable set of Men and had a fine Band—The Jephsons had for some years removed to Wilmar, and let the place next door to us to Captain Russel and Otway who were joint Tenants—This Summer passd without our visitting Knockgrafton as it was now Otways—Winter at length arrived to vapour us and continual toothachs kept me constantly Confined—One Day we observed that Otway appeared more disturbed and flurried than usual which we attributed to some fresh ill usage from Russel, but he was so dark and reserved that we questiond him in vain.

Next evening we were seated at Tea when Mr J O Donnels Servant came up to know if Miss Russel drank Tea with us—on being answerd in the Negative he swore by God then she was gone off—We ran to search for Otway but he too was Missing and we had soon enough to inform us of their Elopement together—We all ran about like people distracted—My Mother fainted away—the Girls and I were in hystericks and the Boys gallopd about without knowing where to pursue the fugitives— My Father was confined with a heavy lung Complaint which stuck to him a long time and greatly allarmed us—He was gone to Bed and we were afraid of disturbing him though we expected every Moment by an armed possé which Russel had collected—but they left us unmolested and took the Road to Waterford in pursuit of the fugitives by which they missd them entirely—Meanwhile Lory Jephson burst in on us reeling drunk and conjured so many horrible presages that he set us as mad as himself—We sat up all Night whilst the whole Neighbourhood was in an uproar and scouring the Country for the rash Pair, who, we at last heard, had taken the Road to Dublin—They got themselves married on the Road, and were remarried by License in Dublin.

CHAPTER 123D

Ne'er with your Children act a Tyrants part
Tis yours to guide Not violate the Heart

The Young Couple soon wrote an account of

their felicity with an Appology for the Rash
Step they had been forced to—Their pardon
here was easily obtain'd but Captain Russel
was frantic and swore never to receive either of
them—They staid sometime in Dublin where
our friends paid them every Attention—When
they came home Russel would not see them
and being a man of strong passions and dropsi-
cally inclined he fell ill—Their friends did all
they could to mediate in their favour but the
Young Couple had many ill wishers near him
who continually worked up his Mind against
them with too much Success—They were a
twelvemonth here in this Situation when Russel
one day met them at a Review and threatend
them in such a fury with his Horsewhip that
they were forced to leave the field to himself for
fear of breeding a public Riot.

Our sweet Nanno every Day improved more
and more on acquaintance and we look'd on
her as an invaluable Gift thrown in our Way
by Providence, supposing she never received a
penny of her fortune—Never sure was there
a more amiable and happy Couple than this
cherish'd pair—and their felicity was aug-
mented a Year after their Marriage by the
birth of a beautiful little girl who was christen'd
Anna Matilda after both their Mothers—I
must here go back to mention an Incident that
caused much Speculation on their future
prospects from Russel—a Circumstance as
extraordinary as it was unexpected.

Two Days after their Elopement—a Young
East Indian Boy arrived in Town and said he
was Son to Captain Russel—as no one ever
heard of his having this Son he was at first
discredited but was soon after taken in and
acknowledged by Russel to be his Son whom
he had placed at School in England and whom
he now intended to adopt as his Heir to the utter
Exclusion of his Daughter—Captain Russel
was universally known to have introduced
Nanno as his only Child and sole Heiress—
This new found Son was therefore produced
to the great wonder of all his friends—No two
could be more like than the Brother and sister,
but Russel said they were by different Mothers
—The Arrival of this Boy made him more
obstinately bent on disinheriting his Daughter
and no entreaties could disswade him from it.
Sometime after the Birth of their little girl
Russel took to his bed—and most unexpectedly
sent up for his Daughter and Otway—The joy
this produced amongst all their friends was
excessive—He strictly enjoined them not to
leave his House any more nor could he bear
that Nanno or Otway should quit his Bedside
for a moment—The little girl was every Day
dress'd and sent down to him and his whole
amusement was playing with her—But though
his returnd fondness seemd to have no bounds
not all the Entreaties of their friends could
prevail on him to make a Will—He kept each
party in the Dark as to his Intentions that Way

and each thought they had an Exclusive Right
to the fathers property—Henry Russel pleaded
Nanno's undutiful Marriage and she pleaded
his dubious Birth—Though they seemd on the
best footing together before Russel, they had
perpetual Squabbles and even Otways Influence
could hardly keep the peace as Nannos enemies
continually workd on young Russels Ambition,
and her temper could not bear his Affronts.

CHAPTER 124TH

Our time is fix'd, and all our Days are numberd
How long, How short we know not—

The joy of being reconciled to his Daughter
cured Russel for a short time but he soon got
a Relapse and grew daily worse and worse with
his Dropsical Complaint—One Evening Otway
and Nanno stole up to see us whilst he slept—
but shortly after a Messenger ran after them
to let them know that Russel had just expired
without making any kind of Will.
The Consternation this produced was terrible
and the poor young Couple went back in a
great fright—They found him stretchd to all
appearance quite lifeless—swelled up like a
Tun and as black as a Coal—Some one fancied
they saw him breathe and one Barthelemichi
a French Quack applied a Glass and found that
he had still life—He orderd a Cow to be killd
instantly and applied the Hot Entrails to his

stomach—In a few hours Russel shewd evident
Marks of Revivification to the astonishment
of all present—Dispatches were immediately
sent off for the most able physicians and he
grew so much better that they gave strong hopes
of his getting over it which produced a general
Joy—He now calld for paper and made his
Will which was legally signed and Witness'd—
He linger'd a long time after sometimes better
sometimes worse but at length expired to the
great grief of all his desinterested friends as he
was a harmless well meaning hospitable Man—
well principled and very goodnatured.

No sooner had he expired than Henry Russel
and his appointed Guardian Mr O Donnel
produced another Will—and we soon found
they would stop at nothing to establish it—
False Witnesses, forcible possessions every
thing that was terrible in Law had Otway and
Nanno to encounter—In the right will Henry
and his Sister were left Share and Share alike
with the reserve of Russels share in Jephson's
House which fell to Otway—Young Russel
would not be contented without the whole of
the property—To law they went and if hard
swearing would do the Adverse Will had prevaild, but after many Years Expense in various
Courts and all the variety of Quibbles of an
Unjust Cause the suit was decided in favour
of Otway and Nanno to our great Joy and
Relaxation.

We had this whole Summer the Examiner and

his Wife Mr and Mrs Knox—he was a very
pleasing little Man who Entertaind us every
Night with a Variety of Songs which he sang
with great Taste—Mrs Knox was a very handsome Woman—We had likewise Mr and Mrs
Rogers—he was Otways Proctor—They were a
good kind of Couple and had a fine little Boy here
—This Society kept us all on the alert the whole
Summer and they expressd great grief on quitting our hospitable Abode—We now added to
our place a Lawn that once belongd to Jephsons
place which vastly improved our Elysium.

Whilst the above Party were with us the Rebellion was at its height—They all put on Uni-
forms and even Otway though a Clergyman
volunteerd to fight—The Rebels advanced to
the Mountain of Slieveneman and the Army
went out against and had a smart Battle with
them six Miles from Carrick—As the Rebels
were in prodigious numbers we expected to see
them enter the Town that Night but our small
handful of Troops entirely defeated them and
took a number of prisoners—Nick who was
in the Curraghmore Rangers perform'd the
greatest Atchievements in this battle but came
home desperately batterd and wounded—his
powder horn was beat into his side by a stone
—whilst straggling he leap'd into an Inclosure
where were posted twenty of the Rebels—he
however by good horsemanship escaped and
drove two of them prisoners before him—They
were instantly condemnd to be shot though he

made every Interest to save them—We were
kept for some time in continual Alarm whilst
the most bloody Scenes took place all over the
Kingdom—The fifth of November we received
the Important News of the Battle of the Nile
where Lord Nelson beat the french Egypto
fleet and took or destroy'd almost the Whole
near Rosetto—Just as the Intelligence arrived
Nanno was brought to Bed of a Son and Heir
and we Christen'd the Child after Otways
Patron Lord Ormond and the fortunate Hero
of the Nile—The auspicious Babe was therefore
calld Walter Horatio Nelson Herbert and a
more lovely Creature never was born—He was
as he grew up every thing that was charming
and Sensible—As I have no dear Babe of my
own to share with him my equal Affections I
can never set my heart so much on any Child
again—His little Sister Anna Matilda died so
that he was now their Eldest Child.

1798   CHAPTER 125TH

Now drooping, woeful, wan like one forlorn
Or Crazed with Care, or crossd in hopeless Love

In the Spring of this Year I was attack'd with
one of the most frightful Nervous fevers that any
Mortal ever got over—brought on entirely by
Grief and Despondency of Mind—At the first
onset I was taken with a violent fit of Screeching
and continued that way delirious for some Hours,

from that I fell to singing Psalms and since heard
I sang so piteously as to draw tears from Doctor
Barker and all who heard me—But I soon sank
entirely and remember I felt as if Soul and Body
were sinking for ever and ever in some bottom-
less Abyss.

I knew nothing more of what pass'd for many
Weeks—The first Consciousness of Existence
I felt was in a Dream, I thought I was in the
Back Garden which was immediately filld with
singing Birds who assembled in Pairs chirping
the most ominous Melodies—I then thought I
was seated in Mrs Jephsons River cooling my
Legs which I then first felt burning with the
Blisters—From that I came more and more to
myself, but was kept constantly guarded as I
continually strove to escape from my Bed—On
first coming to my perception I was startled at
seeing a Stranger in full Regimentals by me—
This was Doctor Henning of the Dorset Regiment who attended me in my Illness and to
whose humane Care and Attention I mostly
owed my recover'd Existence—I was told that
the Fair Day of Carrick I was so bad that my
Horrible Screeches were heard all along the
Road by the Passengers—I was soon given over
and left for dead—Doctor Henning left me with
my Jaws fast lockd and told my Sister Matty she
might pour in as much Wine as she could which
was the Only Chance left—My Ingenious Sister
found a Hollow Tooth in my locked Jaw and in
this Cavity she pourd all Night with a Tea Spoon

till she had pourd down three Bottles of Strong
Port Wine—When she recounted her operation next Day to the Doctor he screeched with
Horror having no Notion she could dose me so,
but it had merely a Moderate Effect on me and
saved my Life.

When I grew sensible of any thing I perceived
that all my friends were worn to Skeletons with
watching and sitting up—My Mother too had
got a very dangerous hurt by falling over a Tub,
which Doctor Henning also had under Cure—
The Dorset Officers thought themselves all
pledged for my Recovery as their Doctor was
employed and they were out continually shooting
wildfowl or fishing Trout for me—They were
all now become domesticated with us and we had
them constantly with [us] but Especially the
little Doctor who became almost an Inmate here
—and was quite a spoild Pet amongst us—he
was a smart little Batchelor but on the point of
matrimony with an English Lady—One night
he took it into his head to leap with our Boys
but vaulting over a Deep Ditch with a Hedge
he was pitched Head foremost on a heap of
Stones—He was taken up senseless Bruised and
Bloody, but being bled and put to Bed he soon
recover'd—The Dorset were a very friendly set
of Men—Their Colonel Lord Dorchester took
Captain Russels House from Otway who refused
taking any Rent for it—Lord Dorchester then
made Nanno a present of two fine Horses but
these also being refused he said he must try and

do something for Mr O. Herbert in the Church
Line—However here the matter droppd.

His Lordship now gave a grand Ball at which
there was a great deal of fine Company and
amongst the Rest Sir Charles and Lady Asgil
came with the Curraghmore Set—the former
famous for his long Captivity in the American
War, when he was condemnd to be hang'd by
the Americans and had his Gallows erected in
view of his Prison for many Months—but he
was pardon'd at the Intercession of the Queen
of France and liberated—His Sister Miss Asgil
was at the Ball and we had many fine folks from
the County Kilkenny, Mr and Mrs Scott Miss
Bushe et cœtera—In our party was a Captain
and Mrs Bailie who were quarterd on us for a
long time—She was a great Dasher and much
admired at the Ball—We had a very fine Supper
and a most polite Welcome from Ld Dorchester
—The Officers were all a remarkably goodnatured unaffected Set of Men—Colonel Bing-
ham, Captain Hannam and the Doctor were our
chief favourites—besides them there was Colonel
and Major Pitt both Cousins to the great William
Pitt, two Calcrafts sons to the famous Mrs
Bellamy and many other genteel Men but only
one Lady Major Pitts wife a dashing fashionable
piece—They however took away two or three
wives out of Carrick—as they paraded in the
Green Morning and Evening we had every Day
a fine Military Spectacle with a charming Band
—a Circumstance very pleasing in such a Town

373

as Carrick, especially at this time when the frightful Battle of Vinegar Hill and the Bloody Masacre of the Wexford Loyalists threw a general Gloom on all Minds and renderd our Military friends doubly pleasing.

CHAPTER 126

What new accursd Attempt is now on foot?
What new Assassination?

We now went to Bonmahon to wash away the Fever compleatly from me but we spent our time in fear and trembling as the Rebels constantly assembled at a Neighbouring Chapel and often threaten'd us with a Visit—One Night about twelve or one Oclock the whole Village was alarmd by a dreadful sound of Hallooing and Gallopping through the place—Nanno crept up to the Garret where we lay and found us all shivring with terror—We all sat down en Chemise to Yell Out our Despair when we heard the Window of the Room under us burst open with a hideous Noise and the Clamour in the Street became every Moment more terrific —After a while however the uproar and Gallopping ceased—Next Morning presented a Woeful scene—Most of our Neighbours were found hid in the Ditches in a worse state than ourselves —But on investigating the Affair it appeard that our Assailants were a set of drunken half gentlemen and these Brutes after Carousing at the Inn

374

spent the rest of the Night in terrifying the peaceful Village.

Captain Hannam and Doctor Henning now came from Carrick to beat up our Quarters— We gave a Dance on the Occasion but it was thinly attended for no one had Spirits to come —A few Days after our Military Beaux left us we heard that the Dorset had got the Route which grieved us extremely as the Officers were become in a manner family Members and were with us Morning Noon and Night—They however got a Countermand and we found them still at Carrick on our return—The next Orders carried them off—we had great weeping and wailing and our poor little Doctor was so affected that he would not venture to come up and take leave till Hannam swore he would hoise him on his Shoulders up to make his civil Bow—He wept much at parting us and was really quite Childish about it—My Mother sent a Ham and many other Articles for their Voyage—They wrote several Letters to her after they got to England and in some months we heard of the Doctors Marriage with the English Lady he was contracted to—Lord Dorchester did not long survive his Irish Campaign, what became of the rest I know not—They were succeeded here by the Perthshire a Scotch Regiment.

CHAPTER 127

*Oh hideous Scene! My Soul within me Shrinks
Abhorrent from the view!*

Some time after this we received a most dreadful
Shock by an account one Morning that Richard
Shortis my Foster father and our Proctor at
Knockgrafton with his wife were both inhumanly
murderd by the Rebels at Parsonage—They
were found butcherd in a most savage Manner
—My poor Nurses Body was like a Riddle with
Shots—her neck and arm broke and other
marks of horrid Violence—Poor Shortis seem'd
to have been killd with a Hatchet—He was
dragg'd behind the Hall Door, and there
mangled all over—They both lay in the small
parlour—and the poor fellow as if he had a foresight of it, made his Wife rise and pray with
him, having for some weeks received threatening Messages—They had hardly lain down
again when the Villains enter'd, they butcherd
her in the Parlour and murderd Shortis in the
Hall outside—They then broke all the furniture
and as far as they could pulld down the House
leaving lighted Straw to set it on fire—An Old
Man who hid himself, and a little Boy son to
Shortis, extinguishd the fire when the Miscreants went off—The poor Child came home
to [tell] the horrid News to the rest of his family
who lived here—I cannot tell what a Shock I
got at such a transaction happening at a place

376

that had so often afforded me Delight—Otway
by the greatest good luck had returnd from it
the Day before but the Villains pierced his Bed
in a hundred places to shew what they would
have done had he been there—This Affair made
us all ill again and the sight of their wretched
Orphans especially their only Daughter a
beautiful Girl of Sixteen would have melted a
Heart of Stone.

1799   CHAPTER 128

What may the force of Care suspend?

After Christmas Matty and I went to Dublin
for Variety merely—We went by the Canal, the
first time I ever was on it—We had but one or
two Ladies in the packet but a number of
Gentlemen, and were from four Oclock in the
Morning till ten at Night coopd up in the
Cabbin as the Snow lay thick upon Deck—It
would have been pleasant enough if we had
known any of the Party, but they were all
Strangers—however in the Course of Conversation it appeard that some of them were of
Genteel Connextions—and they treated us very
politely and insisted on paying for our Wine.
We stole in on the Bradshaws and Fanny at ten
Oclock for they had no previous Notice of our
travelling Whim, and were all lost in agreeable
Surprize—They were now settled in one of the
handsomest Houses in Mountjoy Square, which

part of the town was then newly built—Lucy
did all she could to make it pleasant to us, but
my Spirits did not let me enjoy the Gaieties of
Dublin—The Girls however were out every
Night and were mostly escorted by Military
Beaux whom they had known in Carrick—The
Perthshire were suddenly removed to Dublin—
The Officers were polite agreeable men and
happy to meet their former Acquaintances—
There was also a Captain Thomas an English
Officer who had spent some weeks at our House
and now thought he could never shew us enough
of Attention—They all did every thing to shew
their Gratitude for the Reception they got at
our House in Carrick—Lucy gave a grand
Supper Party to which they all came from Castle
Island and were very grateful for being asked—
Such a Shew of plaid petticoats made the Scene
appear Grotesque enough—Their Colonels
name was Porter a plain good kind of man, and
goodnaturedly Attentive to us.

The Union Business took up every ones Attention, and the Town was one Scene of Military
Preparation for fear of a Rising of the Rebels at
that Critical Juncture—The Union Question
was carried after a great deal of Tumult, and the
House of Commons was forced to be surrounded by Army—No Member that voted for
the Union could stir out without a guard, Many
were assaulted by the Mob and the whole City
was one scene of Confusion and fearful Apprehension.

A Melancholy Accident happend in our Square at this time—Counsellor Powel a friend of William Bradshaws was shot in a Duel with his own Cousin German Counsellor George Powel —Mr Bradshaw attended him to the last Moment and for two Days his Funeral Preparation sadden'd the whole square.

We now thought of returning to Carrick towards the End of Lent—As I did not spend abroad I hoarded my little stock of Money for presents to my Carrick Friends, but in the Midst of my Shopping I lost my Purse and its Contents which gave me more vexation than losing double the sum at another time—Just as we prepared to set out a letter from my Mother informd us that they were all coming up to get the Carriage new painted and carry us home—which News afforded the Bradshaws and Fanny infinite pleasure—We staid a good while in Dublin after they came, and had all our Friends and Cousins about us, but nothing very remarkable happen'd and we all return'd to enjoy the Spring in Carrick.

CHAPTER 129TH

Where Smiling Spring its earliest Visits paid
And Parting Summers lingring Blooms delayd

Soon after our Return Nanno lay in of another son calld Nicholas after my Father but he died some time after in the Small Pox so that out

of three they had but one remaining Child—
However he was worth A Million and our
whole Affections centred in the dear little
Walter—We found a New Regiment in
Carrick on our Return—These were the North
Mayo—As all the Officers were Men of Property and genteel families they were Next to
the Dorset one of the pleasantest Regiments
we ever had—We gave them a grand Dinner
at first setting out, And I had the pleasure of
seeing our dear Nanno look better than ever
she did after her Lying in, dressd in a very
becoming pink puckerd Cap with a pink
Hyacinth to Match which I brought her
down—She was greatly admired in it and I felt
more pleasure in this little Article that set her
off than in any thing I bought for Myself—
Indeed from the first there was a something
in her that excited Pity and Affection and she
improved more and more every Day—Nothing
could exceed her attention and Affection whilst
I was ill, and her unbounded Attachment to
Otway endear'd her to us—She could not bear
to let him go to one Room from another without
her, and her Love for him was equally returnd
—Never did Heaven unite a sweeter Pair.
We had now our House full of Company—
Lady D. Blunden Mrs Baker Miss Shearman,
and William Blunden came, and we had the
South Mayo constantly to Dinner whilst they
staid—Our chief acquaintances were Captains
Burke and Ormsby and a Mr Palmer related

to the Hares—also Colonel Jackson who had
lately escaped from the French and Rebels when
the french landed at Killala—which Town they
sacked and for some time Tyranized over the
Bishop and Inhabitants, but were at length
driven back to the Ocean with great Slaughter.

In the midst of our Gaities Dinners Parades and
Band Playing a New Star appear'd amongst
us who made dreadful Havoc in the Hearts
of our Beaux—This was Bessy Herbert of
Muckrus Daughter to the beautiful but undone
Mrs Herbert—She was the very Image of her
Mother but larger and not quite so handsome—
however in almost any other Company she was
a Nonpareil of Beauty.

Mr Blake a Young North Mayo Officer soon
fell in Love with our beautiful Guest—She
flirted away with him and my Brother Tom felt
himself bound to hint to him that she was a girl
of large fortune and Expectations—He spoke
to both Parties but without Effect, and her
governess a Mrs Lavender thought it best to
carry her home, Mr Blake followd her as far
as Clonmell and had a Letter convey'd privately to her—On hearing he was gone there
Tom follow'd them post haste—and made her
Governess convey her away privately—and
Tom escorted them half way to Killarney—He
then wrote to her Father to put him on his
guard and received a grateful Answer, but
when Blake found out how Matters were he
sent a Brother Officer with a Challenge to Tom

—They met at the Coffee House and had a
great Boxing Bout—but the Officers interfered
and perswaded Mr Blake to make an appology
and so the Affair dropp'd.

We were very pleasant whilst the N. Mayo
staid—They had a most delightful Band
always at our Service and which play'd at
Parade every evening where we generally
attended—They gave us a Grand Ball and
Supper whilst Bessy Herbert staid, at which the
Band playd all Night—They dined and suppd
with us every Second Day and we had very
pleasant Singing from Mr Palmer and the
famous Counsellor Lysaght who often came—
His Poetical Talent and Versatile Genius were
universally admired—He sang his own Compositions delightfully especially a Song calld
the Green Island and other[s] always encor'd
with Applause in both Kingdoms which were
long entertaind with his Wit and Publications—
Palmer also had a good poetical Genius and
sang very witty Songs of his own Especially
one calld Flirt Away for Ever Oh—As I was
the most demure Person in Company—the
brunt of his Wit was general[ly] turned on me
by the whole party—and one Night he so cut
up the poor prudes and applied his Songs with
such Wicked Looks that I sat in the Utmost
Confusion under the Sarcasms of my Relentless
Tormentor—The Ladies all sat enjoying my
Distress—Mrs Wall indeed sometimes exclaimd Alas poor Dolly! which encreased the

laughter at my Expence—However Captains
Burke and Ormsby goodnaturedly supported
my drooping Spirits by plying me with Wine—
and I sat out the Entertainment—We were
altogether very pleasant but this Acquaintance
Ended like all other Military ones in their
getting the Route for Other Quarters.

CHAPTER 130TH

*Now thou canst see me wretched, pierced with
    Anguish
With studied Anguish of thy own Creating
Nor wet thy harden'd Eye*

Otway and Nanno now went to Knockgrafton
to prepare for their future Residence there—
Fanny and I went with them—The dear pair
would I believe have served me if they could—
but Otway and John Roe had long had a Coolness though they were now partly Reconciled
—Mr John Roe however was generally from
home whilst we staid on Parties of Amusement—Unmindful and Careless of the Woes
he inflicted—

*" On the giddy Brink
Of Fate you stand—One Step, and All is lost!*

One Evening he dropp'd in to pay a short
Visit, he declined sitting down thinking it no
doubt more prudent to stand chatting and
laughing at Cashel Fun with Fanny in the

Window than to enter into Conversation else-
where—Poor Nanno did all she could to get
him to sit down and Otway with friendly
Warmth press'd him to join in a Bottle of
Wine but he ungraciously declined their repeated Solicitations till he put them out of
All Patience at his Coxcomical Visit—He at
length Condescended to approach the Fire and
placed himself with his Back to the Chimney
Piece opposite my Chair—There he stood
uttering his Bon Mots, lolling carelessly, and
displaying his pretty person to the best Advantage—with his Eyes fixd on my face whilst he
address'd his Discourse to Otway and Nanno—
He affected great gaiety and Indifference—
How vain did he look? How conscious of his
power over me?—In quitting Fanny, he seemd
to say You see I can flirt with others as well
as you—Beware of my Charms and look on all
that pass'd as merely meant for my own Amusement—I felt much stung by his Confident
Behaviour and behaved with all the Non-
chalance I could Muster—Though he seemd
to be in a great hurry to depart he staid till
pretty late triffling away the Hours with all
the Brilliancy of Badinage—Repartee—and so
forth but did not repeat his Visit.
We had terrible Work at Knockgrafton repair-
ing the Damages done by the Rebels—It was
not without the greatest horror we enter'd
it and beheld the Scene of their Cruelty—
Poor Shortisses Blood still dyed the Hall and

could not be washed out—The floor was all broke with their feet where they dragged him out of the Parlour, and the Staircase and Bedchambers all black and burnt.

We spent but a dismal time there amid these Vestiges of Horror—Besides being under Martial Law, for Troops were quarter'd in the Village ever since Shortises Murder—They made us put out our Candles every Night at Eight Oclock and one Night that I sat up till ten they broke open the House and searched it all over to our great terror as we were as much afraid of the Soldiers as of the Rebels—Some appearances of Dissaffection caused the Village to be proclaimd during our Stay—but Otway prevail'd on the Colonel to take off the Proclamation, otherwise the Inhabitants would have been all ruind—The Horrors of the Times had such an Effect on me, that One Night I dreamt as follows——

I thought I saw a Cashel Gentleman nicknamed Humpy Kearney drive up in a Chaize—that he prevaild on Otway to enter it and they drove off with incredible Fury, whilst I pursued and overtook them—I thought the Chaize Driver a wicked looking Wretch gave a sudden whisk round and overset the Carriage—Poor Otway I thought was taken out quite dead, stiff and black and that Kearney and the Driver gave me a most Malicious Grin and ran off laughing—The whole Scene was dressd in such Horrors that I awoke all in a Cold Sweat and could

not perswade myself but that something had
happen'd Otway—I ran to their Bedchamber
expecting to see both him and Nanno piked by
the Rebels and hardly could Nanno convince
me they were safe—Dreadful foreboding of
our Future Catastrophe!

We soon after returnd to Carrick as the Kingdom was in such a State that all the Country
Gentlemen fled to the Towns for protection—
The grim Horrors of War now took place
almost universally, but Carrick escaped the Car-
nage that ensued.

In this Manner ended the Year 1799 and the
Century closed with Blood and Slaughter.

END OF BOOK THE SEVENTH

CHAPTER 131ST

—Still still she thinks
She sees him, and indulging the fond thought
Clings yet more Closely to the Senseless Turf—

The Beginning of the present Century was as
fatal to our Domestic Happiness as the End of the
Last was to Public Felicity—How indeed shall
I get through the Relation—for my Head gets
confused whenever I think of the Melancholy
Events that blasted all Our Domestic Happiness.
In the Commencement of the Year we spent our
Time between Carrick and Bonmahon—At the
latter place we washed away our Cares and as
the Rebels were every where defeated we hoped
for a happy Termination of Intestine War consequently of private Calamity—Our Dear Otway
came constantly out to us and out of tricks used
to bring Company out at twelve Oclock at Night
to rout us up and Torment us with providing
Beds and Supper for them—Everyone re-
mark'd that he was more wild with spirits than
ever they had seen him, and we dreaded his
coming to Bonmahon on Account of the many
tricks he play'd us.

387

When we had finish'd our Time there, we return'd to Carrick all in perfect Health, and sat
down to plan out our future Happiness—The
Country began to be more settled after the Rebellion—Otway was almost clear'd of his Law
Expences and he was to go to his Rectory and
reside comfortably there, with his darling Nanno
and her beautiful Child—They laid me down as
a Standing Dish at Knockgrafton and all these
happy prospects raised all our Hopes and I could
not help thinking I had still some Chance of
John Roe—Otway and Nanno indeed seemd
bent on setting us Girls off at their Rectory—
Tom was also a source of Comfort to us as he
was going on Swimmingly with his Law Business—Nick was just out of College through
which he had passd with credit—And our three
Young Men were the Pride, the Boast, and
Comfort of us all.

Mr Briscoe of Garrnarhea and his Wife now
came to spend some time with [us]—He was an
honest Country Gentleman and a great friend
of Otway's—She was a dashing Country Gentleman's Wife very dressy, very fashionable, very
huffish and passionate but very good natured
and droll with all her Eccentricities—My Father
out of Fun christen'd her Lady Pelter and Mrs
Briscoe was in a continual Huff at it—The
gloomy Month of November and the Hunting
Season now approachd but were to set in Clouds
that could never be dissipated.

One Morning at Breakfast we observed our dear

Otway lookd very dark, ill, and lowspirited—
Mrs Briscoe strove to rattle him out of it—but
he complain'd of a Heaviness and said he believed it was his Saturdays Journey that lay
heavy on him (for he was just setting off to do
Duty the Next Day at Parsonage—However as
Mr Clarke was there, the Gentlemen perswaded
him to stay for a great Hunt they were to have
that Morning—He accordingly set off with
them to the Hunt though very Lazy and Stupid
—Just before he went he complain'd of a heavy
Cold, and pain in his side—but we laughd him
out of it—Surely I foreboded ill Consequences
for I cast a wistful Look after him—and my
Heart died away when he left the Room.

At One Oclock an Express arrived to inform us
he had got a fall from his horse but not [to] be
frighten'd—on further Enquiry we found he
was more hurt than they cared to Own—To
paint the Horrors of this dreadful Day would be
impossible—Express after Express went out—
but no good Tidings did we receive, and at ten
oclock at Night our Darling was brought home
on a Door, bruised, mangled, bloody, and
almost a lifeless Corpse—Here let me draw a
Veil over his and our Sufferings! In a few Weeks
our Dearest Otway was No More!—My God!
—How did we ever get over it?—How interesting! How dreadfully Interesting were the last
Moments of our departed Saint!—His poor
Body broken, and dislocated all over!—His
Disorderd Brain!—His beseeching Looks—We

389

were all distracted but had no power to save him
—How dolefully did he supplicate for Mercy to
the poor helpless Wretches round him—How
many Times did his Easy Moments cheat us!—
How often did he cheat himself whilst he plann'd
out future Happiness with his dear Nanno, his
Child, and us at Knockgrafton! Vain Hopes!—
Unrelenting Death met him in all its Terrors!
His last Agonies were indescribable!

Oh!—What a Meal was our Dinner when the
Darling who had so often render'd it chearful
and sociable was now a lifeless Body in the large
Parlour of his own House at next Door! Who
can paint our Distraction!—Our unutterable
Woe!—The poor little Orphan hung round
his Mothers Neck crying—Poor Nanno! What
a doleful Object were you whilst hugging your
Infant to your Widow'd Heart!—Our poor
Father and Mother—what Spectacles were
they!—Oh Otway! Dear beloved Otway!—
Your Loss blasted Every Hope—All Happiness fled with You sweet Saint!—To look at
him was to love!—To know him created Adoration! What Darkness fell on us when he was
hid from our Eyes for Ever!—Our Darling
was not 29 years old when he died!—He left a
Widow of Eighteen and an Orphan two years
old—What a Catastrophe!—I stood over the
sweet fellow fifteen Minutes before he died
still hoping—The two Servants cajoled me out
of the Room and a Scream soon after informd
me his Soul was fled!—I am told the Dear

Creature's Looks were Mild, Placid and Serene
even in Death and that he had all the Appearance of a beautiful Angel—His little Boy
though only two years old said he was sure his
Papa was gone up that way pointing to the Cieling—Poor Nanno never shed a Tear, she was
all stupid Grief—Cold and Senseless as Marble!
No groan—no sigh escaped, to relieve her unutterable Woe.

CHAPTER 132

Oh slip'pry state of things!—What sudden Turns?
What strange Vicissitudes in the first Leaf
Of Mans sad History? To Day most happy
And ere tomorrow Sun has set most abject—
How scant the Space between these vast Extremes

My Grief took a different turn and broke out
in loud Shrieks of Despair—In losing this beloved Brother I felt as if the Tie was broke that
bound me to Heaven—His poor Brothers and
Sisters too! What a House was Ours!—Our
friends crouded round us from every Quarter
but without doing us good they did themselves
a great deal of Mischief—If my pen could describe our Dear Boy in interesting tender relationship the most unfeeling wretch must
shudder at our Loss—In Happiness so enlivening! In Adversity so consoling—In the
last sad scene so moving, pathetic and affectionate—How often did he catch our Hands

and beseech us to stay by him!—How easy
was he when he had any of his friends near him
to rub the sweat from his pallid Brow—and
moisten his parchd Lips!—Oh he used to cry
I feel a Love for my Nanno—a something more
than human tongue can Express!—If I get
over this he would exclaim—I will do so and
so and we will all be so happy together at
Knockgrafton!—Poor Nanno what a loss was
yours!—His affection for his child too seemd
to encrease tenfold if possible according as the
fatal Hour drew nigh that was to sever him from
all human ties—Eagerly he grasp'd the Unfortunate Babe who with difficulty was severd
from his last parental Embraces.

Thus bereft of my Darling Brother all the
Pangs of Hell seem'd to lay hold on me—The
Bitterness of Despair continually rent me with
such insupportable feelings that none but those
who have writhed beneath them can form any
Idea of their black Horror—The Dear Creature
was always planning some scene of Happiness—
Whenever I was gloomy he used to seize my
Arm and force me to walk over every little
improvement in hopes of amusing my Mind—
If he took a farm or had any new scheme in his
Head he was never Easy till he shewd it to me
—He had an Affectionate warmth and friendli-
ness Peculiar to him in every thing he said or
did—God only knows how he was adored in
the Family!—Poor Nanno used to follow him

about like a Dog and often miss'd her Prayers,
as she could not bear to let him go even to the
Stable without her.

What became of us for some time after his
Death I know not—I shall close this Chapter
with two remarkable Dreams—One I had Two
Days before his Death—the Other some Weeks
after it.

Before his Death I dreamt that he came to me
with a grave Sedate look—his face pale and sad
—he was dress'd in a plain suit of brown Cloth
like a Quaker—I thought he remarkd that I
was a head taller than he and immediately his
whole Person sunk to a Size much smaller than
when I knew him—He gazed earnestly and
ruefully for some time at me—and uttering a
heavy sigh he waved his hand as if to say We
part to meet no more—And then suddenly
Vanishd.

After his Death I thought I was in the Outlets
of Dublin, when he flew over me with Angels
Wings and a light Phantom like Appearance—
I thought he hoverd over one Street, then another—Beckoning and laughing as he flew
with sportive Mockery, till I was quite Weary
and Sinking in vainly pursuing him—He at
length enterd a Necessary cover'd with Roses
and Jessamine with one Glass Door facing a
Wood and another opening on a beautiful
Garden hung all over with Garlands of flowers
and Grapes hanging in festoons—I thought he

sunk fainting on one of the Seats and I heard a
Voice saying he must be purged before he
enterd the Garden—two Angels I thought
upheld him and applied hartshorn and Drops
to recover him from his Swoon—He then I
thought was borne by his Angelic Attendants
through the Glass Casement into the Garden—
I made a Strong Effort to follow him but the
Door was clapt in my Face and a great Black
Boar out of the Wood behind me leap'd on my
Back and tore it from head to foot to Atoms.

1801   CHAPTER 133D

Tell us Ye dead! Will none of you in Pity
To those you left behind, disclose the secret
Oh that Some courteous Ghost would blab it out!
What tis you are, and we must shortly be!—

A long and dreary Winter of Woe succeeded—
Barren of anything but our Supreme Misery—
We were indeed like the fallen Angels tumbled
from our happy Heigth into an Abyss of the
most dreadful Wretchedness—We moped about
the House indeed—but like Stupid Creatures
entirely bereft of Rationality—Those Objects
which appeard most fascinating whilst he
brightend the Scene, now excited the greatest
Horror and Regret—Torpor inactitude and
Silence reignd gloomy as in the Vault that
entombd our lost Delight.
The first thing that rouzed us was Nanno's

being forced to go to Knockgrafton to get our
sweet fellows Corn Merchandized for he was a
remarkable fine farmer and had that Year a very
valuable stock of Corn—Ah my God! What a
heartpiercing Work was this to us—Knowing
how active he would himself have been about
it had he lived—Every thing dolefully reminded
us of our loss—The Workmen pitied the poor
little Widow and the work was soon done—
We then returnd to spend another dreary Interval at home—To make things more dismal
Mrs Weldon my Mothers Niece came to us
after just burying her husband—We pass'd
a sad time of it.

Poor Nanno was very ill with something of her
fathers complaint and she was orderd to Castle
Connel to drink the Waters.

CHAPTER 134TH

Explores the lost—the wandring Sheep directs
By Day oersees them and by Night protects

Nanno—Walter—and I set out accordingly on
our Journey towards the healthful Springs of
Castleconnel and on our way slept at Mr
Clarkes who with his family and Scholars was
now settled in Tipperary—He and his Wife
were rejoiced to see us and did all they could
to detain us—but we could not stay more than
a Night—They were delightfully settled had
an Elegant place call'd the Abbey and seemd

very happy and Comfortable—We took leave
of our Affectionate Hosts next day after Breakfast and towards Evening arrived at Castle
Connel.

Nanno had been often there with her father
whilst a Spinster and was well known to most
of the good people that frequented the Spa—
We took a small House in a retired part of it
and with the assistance of our Neighbours were
soon comfortably settled—The variety of the
Scene and the many strange faces we saw helpd
to banish thought—but all pleasure settled in
our little Walter who improved every hour, and
kept us quite alive as he was continually playing
some Queer Prank—Indeed he soon became
the Merry Andrew of the whole Village—They
were constantly stealing him from us—Poor
Nanno was amused at every little thing they
told her of him for now her whole Soul was wrapt
up in that one precious Darling, and God knows
I was not much better about him—The lovely
Creature seemd designd by Heaven for her
Comfort for he was the Perfect Model of his
sweet Father with a strong Resemblance to
Nanno herself.

He was indeed the most Charming Child that
ever blessd fond Mother—We drank Tea
mostly amongst the Neighbours up and down
and Nanno had their Jaunting Cars constantly
at her Service for they hardly used any other
Vehicle there—Towards the end of our Stay
we gave them a General Party which was

much praised for its Elegance in so small a House.

We met with many Curious Adventures which sometimes forced us to laugh, but it was the laughter of People who had lost the dearest Treasure of their Souls—Our Landlady was a very poor Woman but a droll Woman in her own way and she would have us Merry in Spite of us—Walter made us all Merry by discovering to the whole Village a flirtation that was not at all to the Credit of the Ladies Reputation who was a Grocers Wife, and Walter being asked to Dine with her Gallant discoverd their whole amour.

I here had a violent attack one Night something in the Manner of my former fever but not of so long Duration—however I frightend Nanno out of her Wits—We had a great many fine people at Castle Connel it being so near Limerick and a Central Place—At last we quitted it half pleased half sick of this really beautiful Village which is about a mile long, and consists of a Number of Charming Villas along the Banks of the Shannon Six Miles from the City of Limerick.

CHAPTER 135TH

Man like the generous Vine supported lives

We now returned to our melancholy home but I had then another long Journey before me of

somewhat a similar nature—My Father had
long been complaining of a Cough and was
orderd to Mallow—His Nephew Mr Herbert
wrote to insist we would visit Muckrus as
Mallow was so many Miles in our Way—My
Father, Mother, Matty and I therefore set out
on these Expeditions—We staid a good while
at Mallow—My Father was sometimes quite
well, sometimes alarmingly ill.

We there met the Nottingham Fencibles whom
we well knew—Their Surgeon Doctor Stanley
had attended my Father once before in a
Dangerous fall he got—so that we felt very
happy in having a skilful man and an old
Acquaintance about him—We had Races there
that Year and went to the Course every Day—
Matty attended the Assemblies but I did not—
Our chief Acquaintance was a Mr Kehls
Family and the Nottinghams—Young Kehl
and his Sisters were ever with [us] and extremely
serviceable on every Occasion especially in
Nursetending my Father—Nothing indeed
could be more friendly than they were—The
Brother we had known a long time but the Miss
Kehls acted from Spontaneous goodnature—We
had the Band playing up and down the street
every Night which greatly enlivend the Scene—
We had also a famous Review of all the Troops
within many Miles and witnessd their Skir-
mishes, Sham Battles Sieges, etcœtera.

From Mallow we proceeded to Killarney and
spent some time there but met nothing remark-

able in social Life—Miss Herbert was at Lord
Glandores—Lady Glandore being Sister to her
Mother—Mrs Lavender her Governess did
the female Honours of Muckrus—We had a
fine English Gentleman there some Honourable whose name I forget — He boated us
about the Lake whenever Mr Herbert was
engaged as he often was at a beautiful Cottage
under Mangerton built for a Chere Amie
of the female Sex — Matty gave Madame
Lavender and I a terrible fright in one of our
Walks—She climbd to the Top of Turk Mountain by a Path no living Creature except the
Wild Goats had ever gone before—Though we
expected Company to Dinner we waited till it
grew dark and then hurried home to tell our
Story of her going up and not returning—The
whole family were in Consternation, and various
Scouts were sent out but she agreeably surprized
us before the Messengers returnd.

We spent a delightful time at Killarney having
the whole Place to ourselves and full leisure
to contemplate its wonderful Perfections—
The Boats waited on us continually—The
Nut Groves were in their highest bearing
and when we grew Tired of viewing the
Wonders round us we returnd to taste the
sweets of Money Beg where Eyes and Palate
were equally feasted.

Mr Herbert never appeard more affectionate
and seemd quite delighted to have his Uncle
all to himself—The Herberts of Cahernane

Killarney and Mrs Delaney did all they could
to make the place agreeable—and Madame
Lavender and her Daughter laid themselves
out to be obliging.
We returned to Mallow quite pleased with our
Excursion and after spending some Days there
set off for Carrick where we arrived amidst the
Joyful Acclamations of our friends, for my
Father was so ill leaving Carrick that every
One was alarmed about him and seeing him
now so much recoverd told us their former
fears—Even poor Nanno herself shook off her
Sorrows to share our Joy—" Oh Blindness
to the Future "!

1802   CHAPTER 136TH

Return sweet Peace and cheer the weeping Swain
Return with Ease and Plenty in thy Train

The year 1802 began Auspiciously—A General
Peace was concluded after a long frightful and
universal War—Such an Event produced
great Rejoicings—A Time there was when we
would have been foremost in them but our
Deplorable Loss deaden'd all our Energies—
Nanno and Walter now went to Tramore and
took a small House there for the bathing
Season—When she was settled she wrote to
Fanny and I to go there and mention'd that
she had left one Side of the House consisting
of two Bedchambers and a back parlour

entirely for us—I was in a most wretched
state of health and had like to die the Night
before I set out—However the Journey did
wonders for me and sea bathing I thought had
perfected my Cure as my spirits grew better
than for a long time before—We spent our
time very pleasantly—were most comfortably
accomodated and settled quite to our liking in
the Domestic Way, as we could be either in
Company or out of it as our present Temper
dictated—Nanno's and Fanny's Dispositions
inclined them to Society—Walter and I kept
House at home for them whenever they went
to an Evening Party—Nanno was always a Pet
wherever she went.

Fanny also was a Girl much liked, so they
soon made a general Acquaintance—As for
Walter he was a Universal Sprite the Delight
of all Ranks—The Nicholsons of Wilmar had
long been Residents at Tramore—They had a
nice Place on an Eminence that overhung our
Lodging house and for old Acquaintance Sake
did every thing to make it pleasant to us—
Nanno was the nicest pleasantest Housekeeper
possible so that we were perfectly comfortable
and at our Ease.

My Father and Mother now wrote to have
Lodgings taken for them and as the Bradshaws
were just arrived from Dublin the whole family
resolved to come out so that we were to be a
formidable party there—We took the finest
House in the Place with Stabling and Coach

House and prepared all things for their Reception—As ill luck would have it I was just then
taken most desperately ill—and lay for some
Days insensible to any thing but my Various
Agonies—Fanny and Nanno had again the
disagreeable Task of Nursetending me—Night
after night they sat up with me and my Disorder took so alarming a Turn that they sent
off for my Mother to come out immediately—
The whole family came and I remaind so ill for
a long time that they had great fears about me
—However the usual Remedies of blistering
Etcœtera restored me and when I was able
I was removed to their Lodgings.

Tramore was now as full as it could hold—
Amongst others the Blundens all came out there
—We spent the rest of our Time very pleas-
antly—had Nanno's House and our own, and
were in the foreground every where—We gave
a very fine Supper and had Millions at it—
Nanno did the same at her little Dwelling—
When the place was empty we left it.

Nanno went to Cork to renew her Acquaintance with her old friends in the Nunnery, and
to introduce her little Walter to the Sober
Suited Sisters—We spent the Winter at home
dull enough as my Fathers Cough return'd
with double Violence—However by dint [of]
Care, Blisters and Syrrups we got him pretty
well over the hard Season—My wretched
Mother seem'd to have suffer'd more than he in
the End——

Heaven from all Creatures hides the Book of Fate
All but the page prescribed their present state.

CHAPTER 137TH

This, less than this, might gorge thee to the full
But Ah! rapacious still, Thou gap'st for more—

In the Spring of fatal 1803 we all assembled
once more at the paternal home—Nanno
return'd from Cork and brought our little
Boy safe and much improved—Mr Kehl of
Mallow, and Mrs Lyons of Tramore came to
renew their Acquaintance with us—Mrs Weldon and her family were also here and we sat
down to enjoy this large Society little expecting
the Thunderbolt that was ready to Strike us.
I was wholly taken up in Nursetending my poor
Father who must have me every Night about
his Bed to give him his Hoarhound and Phthi-
zan—No one pleased him so well in settling
his Pillows and Bed Cloaths and he every night
bade me goodby saying God bless you Miss
Herbert!—God bless you my Dear—I know
not what I should do without you—In the Day
time I amused him at Backgammon, and if
he was able to ride I accompanied him.
We began to flatter ourselves that he was
perfectly cured—One night (April 30th) I
was playing Backgammon with him when I
observed a sudden fall of his Countenance
which grew pale as Death from a Ruddiness

403

always remarkable even in Sickness—The
family were all in high Mirth with Mr Kehl
and Mrs Lyons—My Father complain'd of a
Weariness, and we stole out of the Room that
he might go to Bed—but when he lay down
I found him so ill that I call'd my Mother to
him—The next Morning he was up at Breakfast—I was anxiously watching his looks for
we always breakfasted together at a small
Table apart from the rest—Suddenly I perceived his looks again change to a deadly
Paleness and he was seized with such a fit
of Shivering that he was forced to go to Bed—
We sent Nick off for Doctor Ryan of Kilkenny—
but when he came he at once pronounced that
there was little hopes of this second Treasure
of our Souls—God knows what then became
of us all—For my part I have hardly any
recollection of the Event that deprived me of
one of the best of Fathers.

As the fatal Crisis grew more evident, he had
all his miserable Family about him, but did not
seem to like to have me near him—I therefore
moped up and down the Hall outside his
Room, and there waited for every Intelligence
—Indeed my desponding Countenance was not
fit to be seen by one in his Situation, which
deterrd me from going near him—Thus
pass'd the last woefull Morning of his illness—
the Servants only could stand the dreadful
Scene—At night they put me to Bed with my
unfortunate Mother—The Girls all sat up

to watch—My frantic Horrors were such that
I had not even the Humanity or Self Command
to let my wretched Mother dose—and she
held me in Bed in spite of me—However at
four Oclock I stole down to his Room—They
were all still watching and beckon'd me out—
I advanced only to the Middle of the Room
for a groan from his Bed made me run out of
it in a fit of distraction—A Terror seized me
whenever I attempted to go near him, and he
expired without my seeing him (*May 4th*) At
Eight Oclock the universal Cry announced
the Departure of this Dearest of Parents.

I know not what fiend possessd me to leave my
Dear Father and Brother before they Expired
—I can never forgive myself for my want of
Resolution—and it is one of my greatest present
Miseries that I was not near them in their last
Moments—Not to take one parting Adieu!
How dreadful! The wretched Family met on
the Landing Place and sunk down in each
others Arms—Our Friends did all they could
for us, but how Vain their Efforts!

Never shall I forget the Horrors I underwent
the Succeeding Night—My Mind was indeed
the black Abode of Despair and Terrors of
every kind—My poor Mother affected the
Heroine, but her Head was quite deranged
and wandering—We were all in the same Pre-
dicament, our Misfortunes had compleatly
turnd our Brains.

We spent our time afterwards mostly in Bed—

Our Friends conducted the Interment of all that was precious to us!—He was laid by his darling Son in the family Burying Place Carrickonsuir.

In the Confusion that ensued it is impossible to relate our Movements—Really I know not how we got out of the black Chaos that surrounded us.

At his Decease the three Livings went back to the Patron Lord Ormond, and were purchased by Mr Grady and Mr Lloyd of the County Limerick—Thus upward of eighteen hundred a Year went out of the Family after an Incumbency of forty Years—The whole time he lived Adored and Respected in his parishes and hardly ever quitted them for a Moment—Indeed I believe the Parishioners felt all due Gratitude and Regret for him and his Son.

CHAPTER 138TH

For them no more the blazing Hearth shall burn
Or Busy Huswife ply her Evening Care
No Children run to lisp their Sires return
Or climb his knees the envied kiss to share

We had now but one small Stake left in the beloved Church and that was my Brother Nick who as soon as he was able after the severe Stroke set off to get himself ordain'd—Poor fellow a

406

hard Task had he now to support in Conjunction with his only Surviving Brother—It was indeed a gigantic Business to conduct, sustain, and console our lost Family and our poor Boys were ill prepared for so arduous a Task feeling as they did at every Nerve theirs and our irretrievable Loss—It was a sad thing to us to see others in possession of the Livings—and officiating in the Room of our dear departed Saints— Mr Grady however behaved in the genteelest Manner possible and immediately gave Nick the Curacy of Carrick though he had previously promised to it a Relation of his Own—His Son now came to take possession of the Livings here —Knockgrafton was given to a Mr Lloyd— Custom and Necessity alone reconciled us to the Unavoidable Change but Happiness was fled for Ever!

Our little Abode being a Lay Possession, luckily afforded us a Refuge—My Mother has it during Life—My Father left us a thousand Pound each with two hundred over to me and some landed property to Tom and Nick.

Here ended what was once call'd the Herbert family at Carrickonsuir—We are all now a Set of poor Melancholy Wanderers without a head, and hardly knowing what to do with ourselves.

We had to enter on a new State of Life—but Oh Heavens! Under what Circumstances!— Deprived of my Father's and Brother Otway's sweet Society, and Solid Advice we were indeed

Scatter'd like Sheep, having no Shepherd—
Every Spot that once afforded Delight now only
served to remind us of our deplorable Misfortunes—But to describe the vacant Scene would
be impossible—The family were soon obliged
to disperse on different business—Nanno went
to Cork—Tom and Fanny in June to Dublin—
Nick was forced to be continually from home—
Matty, Sophy and I were the three that remain'd
mostly at home with my Mother—What a sad
Autumn, and Winter did we spend! It was indeed a frightful Blank—No longer our rural
Paradise, or chearful fireside afford us Pleasure
—Their brightest Ornaments were lost to us
for Ever—All Joy went with them.

1804　　CHAPTER 139TH

Is there in Nature no kind Power
To sooth Affliction's lonely Hour

The Spring of 1804 brought us a renewal of
Grief on the Bradshaw's coming down from
Dublin, and the general Assemblage of the
family so unlike former Meetings—Lucy was
always very delicate, and her Head like mine was
always unsettled after Misfortune—However
the joy of seeing her Mother somewhat calmed,
sustained her in this first sad Interview.
I now relapsed into all my former Complaints
—My Mother unknown to me sent for Doctor
Stanley to Cashel—He pocketted the fee and

gave me some learnd Advice but I thought it a folly to fee Doctors for Disorders of mind and brain——however I was passive under his Investigation.

My Mother had a long fit of sickness somewhat about this time——During her Confinement Mrs Mandeville of Ballyna often visitted and they fix'd a Match between Young Mandeville and my Sister Sophia which took place on my Mothers Recovery.

Mr John Mandeville was a very pretty Young Man having a good landed Property in expectation as he was an only Son and had but one Sister——The Mandevilles were a very ancient family in this Neighbourhood, but had of late Years dwindled to decay in every branch by Extravagance and Eccentricities——This important Match rouzed the whole family here to new Energy but I can't say I felt it much——His family were a good deal here before it——And as his Mother was a very droll Woman she drove New Life into all but myself who mostly kept my Room——A new Brother in law was a poor Substitute for my Double Loss.

Sophy before her Marriage went to Knockgrafton to settle what tythe Money was due before she commenced Bride for she had always assisted in settling the Parish affairs——The important Day arrived——We had a large Party to Dinner and a much larger one in the Evening—— The Bride looked very handsome and her settlement caused universal joy.

The Young Couple remaind here till all matters
were arranged for their Reception at Ballyna—
But his Mother dying soon after both Father and
Son fell into a strange, straggling kind of Life—
They quarrel'd with this family about Money
Matters—and his Young Wife seldom saw him
—She had however the joy of bringing him an
Heir christen'd Ambrose after old Mandeville
—Her fondness for the Child made her more
quietly bear the injurious conduct of her Hus-
band—She went to settle at Ballina but his
Brutality soon obliged her to return—He often
came to beg pardon, but as often Offended again
and all her friends advised her to keep safe under
the paternal Roof.

CHAPTER 140TH

" *That was indeed a Sight—*
" *To Poison Love—To turn it into Rage*
" *And keen Contempt*

I scarce know how this Summer roll'd on—
I remember Lord Desart then Lord Castlecuffe
paid us a Visit with Mr Rolleston who had
just married my Mothers grand Niece Miss
Weymes—They went to see Curraghmore
when a curious Mistake excited great laughter
—Commissioner Beresford offer'd Lord Castlecuffe the Key to the Shell house which he not
hearing, Nick calld out My Lord the Commissioner is offering you the key of the Cellar—

this faux pas afforded great Merriment whilst they Staid—I must now Mention an affair I long dreaded would happen and which at length left me benighted for ever—but had not at the Moment the Strong Effect I anticipated or the terrible Influence it afterwards had on my Mind.

I was one Evening Sitting with the family at the fireside when Nanno blabd out something of Young Mrs Roe—I listend attentively and the rest of the Conversation convinced Me that John Roe was married—Married! Good Heavens what a Thunderbolt!—I soon after heard in pernicious Detail that he had married a Miss Sankey Daughter to Counsellor Sankey of Dublin—I was inexpressibly Shocked at this News and a Tear of bitter Regret stole down my Cheek, but his contemptible Nuptials had an almost instantaneous Effect in eradicating the unfortunate Predilection I once felt for him—Not indeed till some Months after did the stagnating Contempt I felt for him suffer one Tear or sigh to fall to his Memory— But it was my Doom to love him however unworthy of my Affections—And Passion at length return'd on me with a fuller Tide.

Here then was a final End to all my long fosterd Hopes but not to the flame that consumed me which seems essential to my very Being and Coeval with my Existence.

I shall always regard him as My Husband though his renegade Amour has placed a Barrier of Vicious Obstacles to my Claims—

Virtue led Me early to him—I met him as a
Bride adornd for her Husband—No surrepti-
tious Wedlock can invalidate the just Claims
of the Miserably unfortunate Dorothea Roe.

1805   CHAPTER 141ST

" *That awful Gulph no Mortal eer Repassd*
" *To tell whats doing on the other Side*

My Mother had now a new subject of Grief in
the Death of her favourite Brother Otway Lord
Desart—but her Mind could hardly feel any
addition to the Blows it had sustain'd.
In June she went to Dublin on business and
spent her time with Tom who had some time
past possessd a very nice Tenement at Phibs-
borough in the Suburbs of Dublin—it consisted of a large Garden a field and the House—
The Garden open'd on the Canal by a Wicket
and the packet boats sailed by the windows—
Here my Mother and Matty who accompanied
her could in a Moment be in Dublin or out of
it as convenience Suited.
I spent a disagreeable time in their Absence—
Nanno and Sophy were at home but we scarce
saw any one but one Count Dalton an Officer
who was here every Moment—and as he seemd
a desperate fellow I knew not what frolic might
enter his head—however I thought it more
prudent to stay at Work in my Room than
alarm the Lion by watching him though his

Assiduity about our sweet young Widow often
made me uneasy—Mr Grady was also often
here—he was then on the point of being married
to his Cousin Miss Grady of the County
Limerick.

My Mothers return from Dublin October 29th
eased me of my Fears for the tender Lambs—
Both she and Matty reaped great Benefit from
their Journey as to health and Spirits and were
greatly restored in their Looks—My Brother
Tom from being a Philosopher had commenced
Lover—he was then very assiduous about a
Miss Gayer a great Beauty but her friends
thought her too young to marry—and triffled
so much that Tom was soon off—Shortly after
her Father cut his Throat and this Misfortune
left them pennyless this is all we heard of the
family—Fanny now went to Birchfield to her
Aunt Blunden, Matty to Lowesgreen Mr
Butlars—thus ended the year 1805—of John
Roe I heard Nothing having no opportunity
of getting Intelligence.

1806   CHAPTER 142D

But sometimes Virtue starves whilst Vice is fed

In the Commencement of this Year my Brother
Tom went to England to try if he could get
Lord Dorchesters good word with the Duke
of Bedford then coming over to Ireland as Lord
Lieutenant—hoping to get some little Employ-

ment to carry him better through Life as the
Bar affords but a fluctuating profit to a Young
Lawyer—Lord Dorchester however was not
in Confidence and Tom returnd as he went but
much lighter in Pocket—Besides his own Cares
he was greatly embarrass'd about William
Bradshaws Affairs who was every Year involving
himself more and more in Debt and drinking
away his health and Substance—His Creditors
this Year threw him into Prison—Poor Lucy
followd there and would not leave him—Her
situation was truly dreadful with three Children
and her House shut up for fear of Seizures—
Tom help'd them as long as he could without
totally ruining himself—but he found it a Vain
Idea to hope to extricate Mr Bradshaw from
his numerous Debts—At length a Compromise
was made with the Creditors for ten Shillings
in the Pound and William Bradshaw got more
Liberty for his Law Business.

Fanny was all this year occupied about a great
wedding between two of her Cousins—Young
Mr Baker of Bally Tobin and Miss Cherry
Chaloner of the County Meath—the former
was Grandson to my Aunt Blunden and the
latter Granddaughter to my Aunt Herbert—
Fanny figured away as Chief Matchmaker and
Bridesmaid but the Wedding was long omin-
ously delayd by the Death of Mr Bakers Aunt
Mrs Shaw, and our Cousin Mr John Weymes
who was killd by a fall from his horse in London
—Mrs Weldon spent most of this Year be-

tween this Place and Tramore where she went
for the bathing Season—Young Lord Desart
was often with us and generally brought some
Gentleman with him.

This Year died Mrs Anastatia Dobbyn a very
good old Carrick Lady and an old friend of
ours for forty Years.

Married the Revd Thomas Maunsel of Whitechurch our Cousin to Miss Blackmore of Craig
—A sorry Match enough.

In the list of our deceased friends I forgot to
mention three people very much esteemd and
lamented by us, who all died since the Year
1800—These were my Aunt Cuffe Sister to
my Father—Mr Carshore his old Friend and
fellow Townsman and Mrs Waring Araminta
Blunden that was—She was Niece to my
Mother & on Otways Death came here and
shewd that sincere Sympathy that None but
the true in Heart can feel—she died in Childbed
the other two sank under the infirmities of Age
and Sickness—This Year died Mr Curtis Mr
Carshores son in law.

Mr Grady now brought his Young Wife to
Carrick—they took the next house so that we
had them as close Neighbours—She was a great
Beauty and he a handsome Man both young
rich and fashionable.

The Blundens, Boltons, Weymes, and Math-
ewses spent some time here this Year and
afterwards the whole Kilkenny Hunt beat up
our Quarters for some Days.

But the following was the Visit that most surprized me and caused me emotions too Painful
to be described——One Morning a Dashing
Carriage and Equipage drove in about the last
week in July——out of which stepd Mr John
Roe and his Doughty Spouse——As we were
quite unacquainted with his good piece I can
account for this unexpected Visit no other way
than that he meant it as an Insulting Triumph
——The Event was so sudden and unlook'd for
that I could not assume Composure to go down
or I would have been tempted to steal in and
make my humble Observations——They staid
but half an hour——but their kind Visit did me
a twelvemonths Damage——How Wanton——How
barbarous was this affront——

——Hence unworthy Tears
Disgrace my Cheeks No More——No More my Heart
For one so cooly false.

Here I must mention that I had Other Woes
and Insults to Combat besides the Cruelty of
my Unworthy Husband.
Within these two Years I had more reason than
Ever to lament the Death of my Father and
Brother Otway——My family rose in Cabal
against me and treated me in the most savage
Manner——I can no more Account for their
Brutality than for the illtreatment I received
from John Roe, unless that they really wanted
to get rid of me and divide my wretched fortune
amongst them.

CHAPTER 143D

" Th' Avenging Sisters trace my footsteps still
" The hunters still pursue the trembling Doe
" Where am I?—Gods!—Black heavy drops of
  Blood
" Run down the Guilty Walls—

No words can describe the ill usage I now
experienced from my Guilty Family—Continually was I haled up by my Brothers with
brutal Violence and almost Masacred in my
Bedchamber—Continually did my barbarous
Mother and still more Cruel Sisters stand insulting over me to see the work Compleated—
or aiding and Assisting in the Diabolical
Tragedy and all this without once deigning to
assign a Reason for their Cruelty—Sometimes
I was locked up—sometimes half famish'd with
only an Allowance of poor Veal or some such
unwholesome food—Sometimes I was debarrd
of my usual Beverage and left to languish with
Thirst and Fever—inshort every insulting
Cruelty that the black Malice of Man or Woman
could invent was put in Practise against me
whilst my Mangled Body often testified to the
Violence they offerd—Nanno and Walter were
in Dublin, Fanny at Birchfield, Tom only came
down at Vacation time—My Mother her son
Nick, and her Daughters Martha and Sophy
were the chief Perpetrators of the horrid bar-
barities inflicted on me—Mr Nick and the

Ladies entirely managed their Mother and all
her Affairs, and seemd bent on becoming entire
Masters and Mistresses of this once free and
happy Abode—They were out continually
feasting and Carousing about the Neighbourhood—This House only exhibitted a melancholy Contrast—It was now Converted to a
Solitary Prison where I alone remaind a
prisoner—It became a Penitentiary but I was
the only famish'd wretch in it —Servants—all
—were accessory to the horrid plunder—All
conspired to my imprisonment and Murder and
were well pamper'd as a Bribe for their Treachery
—But I must for a while wave any account of
my Private Calamities to give an account of
other Matters more remote from what personally concernd the Wretched Victim of unnatural
Malice.

CHAPTER 142D

On whose wild Wave by stormy passions tost
So many hapless Wretches have been lost

I have in the foregoing Chapter mentioned that
Nanno and Walter were in Dublin—they spent
the Summer Months at the Black Rock and
were shortly to proceed to England where
Walter was to be put to School, thus I was soon
to lose another chief Solace of my Life—without taking leave of this cherish'd Pair.
Tom came down at Vacation and meeting

Young Mandeville here they had very high
Words about his Neglect of his Wife and his
frequent calls for Money—The Lie was given—
The words Rascal Scoundrel were interchanged
and to Blows they fell during Breakfast time—
We had much difficulty in parting them—
Mandeville went down to town to look out for
a Second to bring Tom a Challenge but being
Disappointed here he powderd off to Clonmell
and at ten Oclock at Night a Carriage drove up
to the Door with the Mandevilles, Father, and
Son, and three other great fellows all Armed—
They carried Tom off but we got the Carriage
stopp'd on the road and rescued him—My
Mother and Matty now got the whole set
hawled into a public house opposite—where
they shut the Door whilst Young Mandeville
loudly exclaim'd that the Mob was gatherd by
our Family to assassinate them—No Arguments could disswade them from their purpose
of fighting—Tom went down to town to find
a Second and we sat up all Night expecting the
most dreadful Consequences—At length the
joyful News came up that all Matters were
amicably settled by the interference of the Town
Gentlemen—And soon after our Young Men
enterd and confirmd the Intelligence—The
Mandevilles however drove by uttering a
Volley of threats and Execrations—Some time
after Mr John Mandeville paid a more amicable
Visit here and harmony was again restored
though not of a lasting kind.

Thus I have brought the history of our Family down to the End of the Year 1806—The Period that has since elapsed I have pass'd in a bitter imprisonment and a total seclusion from Life and all its Cheerful Joys—continually Maltreated by a family in whom I once implicitly trusted—Of whom I was always a most Affectionate Member—I in vain try to Account for their Ruffian like Conduct.

Fortuitously my Life is as Yet spared though the Bowls and bruises I continually receive has often endangerd it—It seems indeed that I am preserved rather as a Whetstone for their Malice than out of any Pity or Remorse they feel— Amongst my other grievances the Old Lady keeps back a great Part of my Yearly Interest so that if I escaped from those barbarous Tyrants my small Pittance would Scarce afford me Subsistence but indeed they have enveloped me in so many Chains of Darkness that I have scarce a chance of ever Escaping their Snares.

Here I conclude my History a long and Arduous Task Plann'd and Accomplish'd in my Melancholy Confinement—Some Years of my Life remain undetailed but I finish at the Year 1806 anxious to finish my Work though my Chief Solace in Solitude—I may perhaps at a future Period if I live give the Events of the remaining Years of my Life, but it shall be in an Appendix partly unconnected with this Work—I have Accomplishd four large Volume[s] with Plates

in my Prison viz Poems, Plays, Novels and
these Retrospections—They were the only
Amusements I had and I flatter myself are not
uninteresting—As I have a good Voice I sometimes enliven my Solitude with Vocal Music
or Plays all plants of my own rearing—Oh that
I had wings to fly wherever Taste, and the
Muses led me; but Poverty Chains me to my
prison—Oh that I could fly where love and the
Muses lead me—then should I hover over the
dwelling of my Dear John Roe—Perhaps he
would relent if he knew his Unfortunate Wife
Dorothea Roe.
At Christmas this year Mrs Mandeville had a
Second Son calld Nicholas.

END OF BOOK THE EIGTH

A DIRGE

To the Memory of my Dearly beloved Brother the
Rev'd J:O:Herbert, Rector of Knockgrafton who died
of a fall from his horse in the Year 1800 Set to the
flowers of Edinburg an air he was passionately fond of

1st

Ah me! what Scenes those sounds recall
   This was my lov'd Brother's favrite Air
Oft did his Sweet Angelic Soul
    With Tenderness melt when they reach'd his
      Ear
In Vain, In Vain, fond Memory recalls
   In vain do I grasp at his fleeting Shade
      My Beloved now lies
        In his Grave, Nor hears my Cries
In his Chill dark Tomb is our Darling laid—

2d

Sweet was his Soul, Affectionate, Sincere
   Affable, and gracious, and loving to All
Softening each Sorrow, and soothing each Care
    Without Guilt, without Guile, without Ran-
      cour or Gall
Pleasant his Wit, and Attractive his Mien
    Lovely his Smiles without Malice or Art
Often did his Sallies enliven each Scene
    Often did his presence rejoice ev'ry Heart

No More shall we see his Angel Face!
  No more shall we hear his animating Voice!
No More shall he come—And cheer our happy
    Home!
No More make the Hearts of his friends
    rejoice!—
He's lost! He's lost! for Ever he is lost!—
Lost! lost for ever is our Darling Boy—
      But though on Earth he's lost
      Oh let us humbly trust
That his happy Soul now floats in Eternal Joy—

Sweet is that thought; and precious is that
  Hope
  What thanks do we owe to the blessed God
    of Love
No longer in Darkness and Misery we Grope
Whilst we look for the bright lasting Raptures
    Above
Once More we may meet him, a blest happy
    Saint
  Triumphant once More—May we meet
    after Death
      Then to the Prince of Peace
      Let us high our Voices raise
And Sing Jehovah's Mercies with our latest
    Breath

Oh then let us dry up those salt bitter Tears,
And humbly resign'd, let us wait the Great Day
May his Widow, his Orphan, his Parents bent
    with Years,
His Brothers, and Sisters, and Friends never
    Stray—
Great Shepherd of Israel! May He that is gone
And we who remain all rejoin thy blest Fold;
      And Oh! May all the Earth
       Tell the Blessings of thy Birth
And for ever in the Heavens their Redeemer
    behold.

A DIRGE

To the Memory of the Reverend Nicholas Herbert
Vicar of the United Parishes of Carrick, Kilmurry,
and Kilsheelan who died May 4th 1803

1st

Tis done! My Fathers sainted Soul
   To other worlds is fled!
Oh God! I heard his dying Groan!
I witness'd his last piteous Moan!
   My Cries extorted the last Tears he shed
      And do I live?
        Wretch that I was who did not grieve
My stubborn Heart to stone
   The Effort struggling Nature Made
   To part me from his Reverend Shade
Was Impious—Is he gone! and gone alone!

2d

Oh Most ungrateful Child! who couldst survive
That dear, that mild, that soft, benignant Sire
   Unfit to Live!—But with the heavenly Choir
That sang the Requiem to his parting Soul
And bore it from this Earth to Heavens wide
    Pole
   Thou wast not fit to join
   Or in those pure unsullied Regions Shine
Polluted Wretch!—Then grovel still below
Whilst Wreaths of Glory circle his dear Brow

425

3

How often did I pierce his honest Heart
Alas!—Some Wen or Wart
  Like me is left behind
  To teach Repentance to the guilty Mind
Whilst Saints are taken from this wretched Mart

4*th*

What Parents Arm shall now enfold my Frame?
  As if to shade it from an Angry God
  Whose just Afflicting Rod
And Awful Thunder bolt with righteous Aim
Seemd lifted to destroy and quite Explode
  A Wretch oerwhelm'd with Guilt and Shame

5

Nor shall I more find Means to quell Remorse
  By my sincere, tho Vain Attentions paid
Beside his Couch—The Dear—The Reverend
    Shade
  No longer heeds my Tears, my Groans, my
    Sighs
      Not e'en his Corse
Remains to satisfy my eager wand'ring Eyes

6

Oh Wretch Tis now indeed thou art undone
Quite lost indeed, to ev'ry Hope quite lost
Long hast thou harass'd been and tost
  On wild Misfortunes Stormy Seas
  Knowing No Peace

But now thy fate seems fix'd as the Cold Stone
  That lies on thy poor Fathers Mournful
    Grave
  Thou now canst only weep and rave
And wander through the World Alone
  To seek Despairs Sad Cave
There lay thee Down—forgotten die
  And end thy Misery——

7

Yes my Dear Father—I will follow thee
  The self same Grave at least shall hold us
    twain
Flashes of Madness—Phrenzies wild Arise—
  Unhappy lucid Intervals between,
Sick Sorrows—Passions—Broken hearted Sighs
And the relentless Worm that cure defies
  Shew that both Life and Sense are in their
    Wane—
      My Brother Lost
      My Father's Ghost
Beckon me hence and chide my long Delay
  ——Cruel it were behind to stay
Then burst poor Heart! and hasten hence
  Away.

FINIS   RETROSPECTIONS

INDEX

429

INDEX

430

INDEX

INDEX

433

INDEX

INDEX

435

INDEX